ROUMELI
Travels in Northern Greece

In *Mani* Patrick Leigh Fermor revealed an ancient world living alongside the twentieth century, high in the Peloponnese. 'Roumeli' is the Greeks' ancient name for the north, and for Leigh Fermor it is also the world that he encountered while wandering through this exotic region.

Wherever he goes he joins in the local way of life, his accounts of which spring from the page. The marriage ceremony of the Sarakatsan with all its fascinating ritual and Uncle Elias's story of subtle begging methods have equal place with a sifting through of history, searching for explanations and binding past to present.

'This traveller understands Greece and the Greeks, their language, dialects, their humour, and self-laughter, their generosity and their vitality' *Daily Express*

'Paddy draws the reader, like his huge acquaintance, into instant intimacy. He is always keen to share experience, pleasure, wine, and above all laughter'
Max Hastings

'Roumeli is the man himself. He lives in Greece, speaks Greek, knows the Greeks themselves as well as any man can, and loves what he knows'
Sunday Telegraph

Patrick Leigh Fermor, 1915–2011, was born of English and Irish descent. After his stormy schooldays, followed by the walk across Europe to Constantinople that features in *A Time of Gifts* (1977) and *Between the Woods and the Water* (1986), he lived and travelled in the Balkans and the Greek Archipelago. His books *Mani* (1958) and *Roumeli* (1966) attest to his deep interest in languages and remote places.

In the Second World War he joined the Irish Guards, became a liaison officer in Albania, and fought in Greece and Crete. He was awarded the DSO and OBE.

He lived partly in Greece in the house he designed with his wife Joan in an olive grove in the Mani, and partly in Worcestershire. He was knighted in 2004 for his services to literature and to British–Greek relations.

Also by Patrick Leigh Fermor

The Traveller's Tree (1950)
The Violins of St-Jacques (1953)
A Time to Keep Silence (1957)
Mani (1958)
A Time of Gifts (1977)
Between the Woods and the Water (1986)
Three Letters from the Andes (1991)
Words of Mercury (2003) *edited by Artemis Cooper*
In Tearing Haste: Letters between Deborah Devonshire and
Patrick Leigh Fermor (2008)
The Broken Road (2013)
Abducting a General (2014)
Dashing for the Post (2016)

Translated and edited
The Cretan Runner *by George Psychoundakis*

ROUMELI

Travels in Northern Greece

PATRICK LEIGH FERMOR

JOHN MURRAY

For
AMY and WALTER SMART

First published in Great Britain in 1966 by John Murray (Publishers)
An Hachette UK Company

This paperback edition 2004

18

Title page drawing and map by John Craxton

A CIP catalogue record for this title is available from the British Library

ISBN 978-0-7195-6692-9
Ebook ISBN 978-1-84854-544-1

Printed and bound by Clays Ltd, St Ives plc

John Murray policy is to use papers that are natural, renewable and recyclable
products and made from wood grown in sustainable forests. The logging and
manufacturing processes are expected to conform to the environmental
regulations of the country of origin.

John Murray (Publishers)
338 Euston Road
London NW1 3BH

www.johnmurray.co.uk

Contents

Introduction

Roumeli is not to be found on maps of present-day Greece. It is not a political or an administrative delimitation but a regional, almost a colloquial, name; rather like, in England, the West or the North Country, the Fens or the Border. Its extent has varied and its position has wandered rather imprecisely. A few centuries ago it meant roughly the north of the country (as opposed to the Morea, the archipelago and the Greek-inhabited provinces of Asia Minor) from the Bosphorus to the Adriatic Sea and from Macedonia to the Gulf of Corinth. After the War of Independence, the name shrank to designate the southern part of this great area; the mountainous strip of territory lying between the Gulf and the northern frontier that separated the new Greek Kingdom from the unredeemed lands that still remained, politically, part of the Ottoman Empire. The line stretched from the Ambracian Gulf to the Gulf of Volo. The Balkan Wars and then the Great War advanced Greece's frontiers in two great northward leaps and doubled the extent of the country; but, on modern Greek lips, Roumeli is still limited to that part of it between the Gulf and the superannuated line. Rather arbitrarily, rather high-handedly and with some misgiving, perhaps seduced by the strangeness and the beauty of the name—the stress falls on the first syllable, turning Roumeli into a dactyl—I have reverted, as cover for these wanderings, to the earlier and looser application of the name. This obsolete and elastic use simultaneously provides an alibi from the strict modern sense and an illusory semblance of unity to these random journeys. Better still, the trisyllable itself is full of echoes and hints and buried meanings which are deeply relevant to the book's main theme.

Greece is changing fast and the most up-to-the-minute account of it is, in some measure, out of date by the time it appears. The record of these journeys, then, undertaken a few years ago and all of them prompted by abstruse private motives, would be a deluding guide. Commodious charabancs have now replaced the ramshackle country buses, great roads cleave their way through the heart of remote villages and quantities of hotels have sprung up. Monasteries and temples which, almost yesterday, were only to be reached by solitary and exacting climbs are now the brief staging points of highly organized and painless tourism in multitudes. For the first time since Julian the Apostate, fumes drift through the columns, and a traveller must retire deep into the hinterland for the wireless to be out of earshot. All this is a source of direly-needed revenue and a joy to many; the occasional Greek or foreign dissenter can always stalk off petulantly into the wilderness and out of range. Indeed, it is into this contracting wilderness that these pages for the most part lead.

A list of all the Greek friends who have helped with advice, guidance, hospitality, criticism and every conceivable support would be impressively large; but not nearly as large as the debt I owe them for many years of kindness, stimulus, and delight. I would also like to thank other allies for their patience and forbearing during a long gestation. The only sad aspect of the task of rendering thanks is the thought that this book will only reach one of the two friends to whom it was dedicated at the outset.

P. M. L. F.

St Fermin—Passerano nel Lazio—Forio
—Locronan—Lismore—Dumbleton—
Branscombe—Sevenhampton—Kalomitsi.

CHAPTER I

The Black Departers

Alexandroupolis is a large town, but there is nothing over-poweringly urban about the Alexandroupolitans; rather the reverse. Athenian civil servants groan when they are nominated here and young officers, faced by this Thracian exile, look at each other askance. (It was not always so. In the tales of my friend Yanni Peltekis, who lived here in Turkish times as a child, it sounds as full of adventure and mystery as a city in the *Arabian Nights*.) I had taken a strong liking to it, perhaps because it was my first Greek town after a few years' absence. But I could see that too long a sojourn might wither its delights.*
Many of the limitations of a new provincial town pervade it, and the evening hours of the officers and civil servants are spanned by familiar anecdotes and yawns and yet another coffee and the click of amber beads falling through fingers that refrain from raising a cuff to reveal the time; they know full well that it is still too early for bed. The tedium of unchosen and un-changing company lurks there. If a joke is worth making, it is worth making often, think some; other more fastidious ones suffer acutely from the Inbite of Agenwit.

All at once, however, the yawns of the evening boulevard were halted by the passing of a wild, solitary and alien figure that no streets or houses should ever have confined: a man as

---

* Decades or centuries ago the only notable thing here was a hermit living under a tree. Both have vanished but the old Turkish name, Dedea-gatch, which commemorates the hermit-tree, is still sometimes heard. Its new name celebrates Tsar Alexander II, the victor over the Turks in the Balkans, not King Philip's great son.

3

inappropriate in these tame surroundings as a wolf in the heart of
Athens. A rough black pill-box was tilted askew on his matted
and whiskered head. His black double-breasted waistcoat of
homespun goats' hair was tucked into a black sash below which
a hairy and broad-pleated black kilt jutted stiffly to his knees.
Black tights of the same stifling stuff covered his long legs and
he was shod in those Greek mountain shoes that turn up at the
tip and curl back in a broad canoe-like prow and end in a wide
black pom-pom covering the front of the foot. The thick soles
were clouted and the nails grated underfoot. He loped along the
middle of the road, gazing ahead as though to avoid the con-
taminating houses. A long shepherd's staff, whose crook was a
carved wooden snake, lay across his shoulders. He had looped
his arms over it in the flying and cruciform position in
which many mountaineers carry their crooks and their guns.
He was, in fact, a Sarakatsán. Heads turned under the dusty
acacias as he passed and the smack of cards and the clatter of
backgammon counters died down for a few moments. I got up
and dogged his steps at a discreet distance.

Sarakatsáns have always filled me with awe. I first saw them
years ago when I was walking across Bulgaria to Constantinople. A gathering of beehive huts was scattered over the
wintry hills slanting to the Black Sea; brushwood folds ascended
the green slopes and thousands of shaggy black goats and sheep
grazed over the rainy landscape, their heavy bronze bells filling
the air with a many-toned and harmonious jangle. Here and
there like dark monoliths under the wheeling crows herdsmen
leaned on their lance-long crooks, their faces almost lost in the
deep hoods of high-shouldered goats' hair capes reaching to the
ground; capes of so coarse a weave and so stiff with rain that
their incumbents could almost step forth and leave them standing like sentry-boxes. Riding across Greek Macedonia the next
year, I saw them again and even stayed a night in one of their
smoky wigwams. Later I met them often, all over northern
Greece: in the plains in winter and in the mountains in summer;

always on the skyline or in the middle distance. True nomads, these self-appointed Ishmaels hover on the outskirts of ordinary Greek life as fleetingly as a mirage; they manifest themselves to mortals in faraway glimpses. Suddenly, in the high midsummer Pindus and Rhodope and in the Roumeli sierras, a ravine's twist lays bare their impermanent hamlets of cones. In winter, from the snows that have banished them, one can discern their clustering huts in the plains, the ascending smoke and the grazing flocks. In spring their beasts and their long caravans of horses, laden with all they possess, wind into the thawed mountains, halting at night in a brief village of sombre tents; autumn sends them streaming downhill to the withered plains which the rains will soon turn green. One discovers them binding lopped branches and osier twigs into the hemispherical huts which will house them for the season; shelters whose blackened and moulting thatch will later mark where they settled for a few months and then vanished. Sometimes a far-off barking and the murmur of bells hints at their presence deep in the ilex woods or along a dazzling canyon where nothing stirs but a pair of floating eagles. They are nearly always out of sight. Except for these rare apparitions, this fugitive community—about eighty thousand souls with flocks amounting to several million heads—has the gift of invisibility.

Unlike the semi-nomads of Greece—the Koutzovlachs and the Karagounis, who all have mountain villages from which to migrate and to which they return after their half-yearly journeys in search of pasture—the Sarakatsáns have nothing more solid than their abodes of wicker and rush. All of them, however, look to some range of mountains as their home, some fold or cordillera where they have grazed their flocks for centuries of summers. Their lowland pastures are more variable; these uncertain sojourns have few claims on their allegiance. The Sarakatsáns of the north had the widest range. The sudden cage of frontiers which sprang up after the Balkan Wars failed to confine them and they fanned out in autumn all over

southern Albania and across the lower marches of Serbia as far
as Montenegro and Herzegovina and Bosnia and into Bulgaria
to the foothills of the Great Balkan. Those who thought of the
Rhodope mountains as their home—the very ones, indeed, in
the highlands that loom above the Thracian plains—were
particularly bold in the extent of their winter wanderings. Not
only did they strike northwards, like those I saw by the Black
Sea, but, before the Hebrus river became an inviolable barrier,
their caravans reached Constantinople and up went their wigwams under the walls of Theodosius. Others settled along the
shores of the Sea of Marmara and spread over the rich green
hills of the Dardanelles. Many crossed the Hellespont to pitch
camp on the plain of Troy. Bold nomads would continue to
the meadows of Bithynia and winter among the poplar trees
or push on into Cappadocia and scatter their flocks across the
volcanic wildernesses round the rock monasteries of Ürgüb.
The boldest even reached Iconium, the home of Jellalludin and
the metropolis of the whirling dervishes. They never looked
on these enormous journeys as expatriation: until the deracina-
tion of the 1920's, much of Asia Minor was part of the Greek
world; and even beyond its confines there were ancient Greek
colonies. Established for thousands of years but reduced by the
later tide of the Seldjuk Turks to scattered islets of Hellenism,
they still survived and prospered. The invisible frontiers of
nomadism overlapped and dovetailed with those other pastoral
wanderers, the Yürüks. These Anatolian shepherds, nominally
moslems, grazed their flocks in the hinterland of Asia Minor
for centuries before the Seldjuks came; they even paid return
migrations, now and then, as far as Macedonia. No wonder,
then, that some of the aura of a fable hangs about the
Sarakatsáns.

A quarter of an hour after sighting him I was sitting at a table
next to this isolated nomad. Round us were the smithies and
harness-makers of the outskirts; old artisans had settled down to
quiet narghilés after knocking off work. I watched him order

and drink a coffee, pondering how I could get into conversation. Soon, with a clap of horny palms, he was summoning the *kafedzi* and preparing to depart. The *kafedzi* came with an armload of elaborate gear and a boy leading a horse. The Sarakatsán mounted and laid his crook across his lap, the *kafedzi* handed him two six-foot candles adorned with white satin bows and ribbons; then followed the snowy baubles which, as I know to my cost, a *koumbáros*—the groomsman, sponsor or best man—contributes to the crowning of the groom and his bride at an Orthodox wedding. There were smaller candles, lengths of satin in brown paper, parcels of sweets and finally the box containing the tinsel wedding-crowns themselves. My luck changed: as he gave his horse a kick and moved off, a muslin bag of sugared almonds slipped and fell into the dust. I dived for it, ran after him, and, my luck still holding, remembered as I handed it over, to utter the ritual phrase of a wedding guest to a *koumbaros*; it is adapted either from the tenth chapter of St Luke or the First Epistle to Timothy: '*Axioi tou misthou soul*', 'May they be worthy of your hire!' He reined in, placed his right hand over his heart and bowed his head in a ceremonious gesture of thanks. Then, after a glance up and down and a pause, he asked in a thick rustic accent where I was from. I told him and asked him where the wedding was to be. 'Tomorrow at Sikaráyia,' he said, 'two hours from here.' After another pause, he said, 'Honour us by coming.' He repeated his graceful bow and, bristling with his crook and his candles and fluttering with satin ribbons, clattered off.

*　　*　　*　　*

Next day the rail ran parallel to the Aemilian Way, the legions' road from the Adriatic to Constantinople: a thread on which Alexandroupolis and a dozen more ancient cities are strung.

The carriage that bore us along a narrow-gauge track seemed obsolete as an equipage in a museum. High and narrow, the coachwork was painted to mimic the graining of yellow wood and upholstered in threadbare tasselled velvet. This delightful carriage, fit for two travellers out of Jules Verne, carried us swaying through the Thracian sky and over the gorges and forests of plane trees, the rocky river beds and the scrub-mantled mountainsides at an abnormal height. The ancient Thracians used to hold their mares with their heads downwind in order that the wind might put them in foal. Over which of the Rhodope passes did this invisible stallion come snorting? Every so often we passed solitary police posts and lookout platforms on stilts, each one a pedestal for an armed and hel-meted soldier; reminders of the nearness and the danger of the Bulgarian frontier. Asprawl among trees and bracken, blown there by guerrilla mines, the rusty remains of carriages were gloomy mementoes of the civil war. The country shook in the noonday.

As though its owner were flying alongside, a jovial, un-shaven face appeared in the tall frame of the window. It was the ticket collector. When he had climbed in and pocketed our tickets, we watched him work his perilous way along the duckboard of the corridorless train like a cat-burglar. An open cattle-truck was hitched to the rear: raucous singing was wafted to us and a blue flag whirled overhead on a pole. The conductor, now settled in our carriage for a chat on his return journey, confirmed what we had surmised. 'Yes, it's a Sarakatsán bride-groom on his way to a wedding at Sikaráyia. They've been drinking for days. . . .' When we pulled up at the next wayside halt, the whole party, with the banner aswirl, leapt shouting and singing to the platform and bore down on a small group under an acacia tree. The groom and his cronies returned a few moments later carrying the bride. This figure, dressed in a stiff black and white costume of angular and Aztec strangeness and borne aloft in her captors' arms, sailed the length of the train with the immobility and the silence of a sacred image translated from shrine to shrine. As it careered past, I saw that the shaft

of the standard-bearer's banner was topped by a pomegranate.
Another carried a ribboned wooden cross with another pomegranate affixed to the top and two more to either end of the
crossbeam. When they were aboard, several of the groom's
party fired their guns into the sky: singing and intermittent
firing accompanied the rest of the journey. '*Paráxenoi anthropoi*'
vouchsafed the conductor, after clicking his tongue censoriously
a dozen times. 'Odd people. . . .' They did seem a contrast to
the lofty Victorian stateliness of our carriage. The groom, we
learnt, was the son of a great *tsellingas*—the head of a clan, as
it were, of Sarakatsán shepherds—an *architsellingas*, in fact—
called Kosta Zogas, who wintered at Sikarayia and pastured
his sheep in the Rhodope mountains in summer; the bride's
father, another *architsellingas* called Vrysas, grazed his flocks on
the same summer grass, wintering near Souphlí by the banks
of the Hebrus. 'You'd think,' he went on, 'when you see them
in their rush hovels and their old capes, that they were poor.
Not a bit of it! They've got pots of money. Literally pots: they
fill pitchers with gold sovereigns and bury them, no one knows
how many. Whole fortunes hidden in the ground. . . .'

We came to a standstill in Sikarayia. It was an entire village
of beautifully thatched Sarakatsán huts, giant beehives swelling and tapering in tiers of cropped reed which overlapped
with the precision of the plating on a seven-banded armadillo.
They were topped with wooden crosses near holes in the thatch
through which thin blue smoke curled. Black-clad Sarakatsáns
crowded below the nuptial truck, the bride was hoisted to
earth, and, in a chorus of shouts and greetings and a rattle of
musketry, the whole mob headed for the little white church.
The train, expelling a whistle and an answering obligato of
steam, dwindled swaying down the valley.

Inside, two rows of columns sustained the white barrel-vault
of the basilica. A gilt iconostasis blazed; overhead hung a
great candelabrum formed by double-headed Byzantine eagles
joining their brass wing-tips in a ring and from the centre an

ostrich's egg was suspended.* The noise and the heat were considerable and thonged wooden flasks full of warm red wine circulated freely among the congregation. The loose blue-black hair of the celebrant—a commanding and raven-bearded man in a white dalmatic crossed by a broad blue and silver stole —cataracted to his waist with the ampleness of Rapunzel. His chanting soared heroically and effortlessly above the hubbub. All the faces were scorched, many were aquiline and blue-eyed and the hair of several shepherds was bleached by the sun to a flaxen fairness. Apart from the priest's, the only grave faces there were those of the bridal couple. The bride's withdrawn expression, her downcast eyes under her flowered headdress and the small blue cross which was strangely pencilled or painted on her brow, never changed. The groom was dressed in a gold-embroidered red velvet waistcoat, a silk sash with the blue and white Greek colours, jutting white fustanella and tights and, disappointingly, pointed black townee shoes. His face, rather a commonplace one for a Sarakatsán, was a mask of confused virile earnestness. In only one thing did his outfit differ from the full-dress Greek mountain costume: black woollen armlets, embroidered with specifically Sarakatsán geometric zigzags, encased his forearms below ample white sleeves which ended at his elbow. In spite of the chaos the service evolved unperturbed. On either side of a portable altar erected in the nave, two little shepherd boys held the tall ribanded candles like the lances of heraldic supporters. The *koumbaros* switched the flimsy white flower-crowns from head to head and arranged and rearranged their hands and bound them with ribbon and performed yet more complex manipulations with the ring; he followed them in kissing the bossy silver binding of the proffered missal. Hand in hand, led by the priest under a fusillade of flung rice and sweets, he accompanied them thrice round the altar in a slow and dignified dance. More than

* This addition is frequent, especially in monasteries. I have never succeeded in discovering why.

any other stage in the solemnization—for the offered wine is merely a commemoration of the wedding at Cana of Galilee—this hieratic pavane hallows and confirms the sacrament.*

Out in the sunlight, all was levity, flourished banners and gunfire again. We made our way through the wigwams to the house which the groom's father, striking up-to-date roots in his winter-pastures, had recently built. As the newly-wed couple reached the threshold, someone handed the groom a sieve, which he threw over his shoulder: a measure which is said to forfend marital discord. They both kissed the hand of the groom's father, laid it reverently to their foreheads for a second and vanished under the lintel. My friend of yesterday, Barba Petro, introduced us to this pastoral dynast. He welcomed us with the same graceful inclination of his hand laid on his breast and led us indoors.

Guests were seated on the low divan all round the room and crowded cross-legged on the mats which padded the floor. As each new guest arrived they intoned a welcoming song while black-swathed aunts and grandmothers offered the newcomers saucers with a spoonful of jam, a glass of water and a thimbleful of raki: 'Mother, our friends have come,' they sang, 'our bidden guests. Bid them welcome with honey and sugar and with golden words.' The room was filling with dark figures, sitting with their thick-shod legs crossed beneath them or with one, wide outflung, rearing a clouted shoe at an odd angle and here and there a tufted brogue, the other leg grasped round the shank. Some sat with hands linked round their doubled-up knees, others leant back against the wall or the divan with a knee cocked up to support an outstretched arm whose fingers released the amber beads of a *komboloi* at intervals of a few

* I write with feeling of the complications involved in the office of *koumbaros*, for I performed it a short time ago at the marriage of Antony, the son of an old Cretan brother-in-arms, Grigori Chnarakis of Thrapsano. This bond, both a compliment and a responsibility, is held more binding than kinship.

seconds. All were luxuriously asprawl and akimbo. The company bristled with crooks; they lay across their laps or tilted at a slope over their shoulders; some were held bolt upright in gnarled fists with their butts on the floor. Others leaned against the wall, the tip of the shaft of each well-worn staff slotting into a different twirling summit carved in the shape of a dolphin, a dragon, a ram's head or a snake. Two of them, as though they were the property of two hedge-prelates, had crosier-like hooks of steel. Only a few of the guests were dressed in black kilts. The others were hosed in rough, hairy, black jodhpurs. One or two of the wildest and shaggiest were shod in rawhide moccasins tilting up in canoe tips and worn over swathes of white wool and bound and cross gartered over padded ankles with wide thongs. All of them wore their soft and rakish black kalpaks askew. Except for the white and pleated bridegroom standing by the door to receive horny handshakes and whiskery embraces as the guest ambled in, nearly all the people in the room were of advanced or middle age. Some were deeply stricken in years but all were hale and weatherbeaten: tall, beetling, white moustached, venerable and indestructible patriarchs, *tsellingas* and *architsellingas* and substantial shepherds from all over Thrace. A couple looked inappropriately scholarly in steel-rimmed and wire-mended spectacles. The old men endowed the room with the aura of an august and exclusive club.

I could scarcely believe that at last I was sitting with several score of these evanescent and almost mythical men. They conversed in a roar. Used to shouting against the wind to each other from hill-top to hill-top, they find it hard to modulate their voices at close quarters; the smallest talk is stentorian. (The only alternative is a collusive and almost inaudible whisper, to which they suddenly resort if they detect a look of suffering on their interlocutor.) The aroma of the folds hung thick and the smell of raw tobacco. Every so often, a savoury whiff of roasting drifted in from outside. Now and then, too, there was that faint reek of singeing cloth produced by the dried fungus which they use as tinder. They hold a pinch of it against a piece of steel shaped like a magnet, which they strike with a flint until the fungus catches fire; then they light their rolled cigarettes or lay it on the rubbed leaves in the bowls of their home-made pipes. When the elaborate business is over, they wrap up all this gear in a goat-skin wallet and stow it in the folds of their sashes.

I am not very accurate in picking out regional Greek accents, but their thick rural tones did not sound the same as those which I had so far noticed in Thrace. They resembled, rather, the dialect of Roumeli and of parts of Epirus, much farther west; an accent which suppresses the final vowels and most of those in the middle of words as well. It makes speech sound oddly chopped and consonantal. Their talk was even harder to understand, as the Sarakatsáns have a vast and arcane vocabulary for the minutiæ of their calling: for different kinds of springs and qualities of grass, for ways of hut-building and bell-tuning and for breeds of sheep and goats and horses and watch-dogs. They have their own expressions for all the tupping, lambing, weaning, shearing, carding, spinning, milking, seething, scalding, straining, basket-weaving, path-finding, tent-pitching, camp-striking, trough-scooping and weather-divining round which their whole life turns. How should a layman know that a reddish or dark-faced sheep is called a *katsnoúla* or that belling them is called 'ironing' or 'arming' them? *Óti siderónoun i armatónoun tes katsnoúles*, in fact? Or how many *okas* of bronze, and of what pitch, should be slung round the neck of a bell-wether? Or that the best time to arm the flocks is at the Feast of the Annunciation, 'when the first cuckoo is heard'? Such were the topics that boomed about the room.

This squatting on low divans or on the mat-strewn floor gave a new angle to life. It was strange to stand up all at once and look across the empty upper part of the room through two shafts of sunlight (split up by the window-bars into three-dimensional

smoke-blue parallelograms slanting down into the throng) to
the flickering ikons at the other end: and then down at the black
kalpaks and the bristling crooks of the hundred nomads below.

Barba Petro pointed out the celebrities: 'Uncle George over
there, with only one eye—he's one of the biggest *tsellingas* in the
Rhodope: over ten thousand sheep and goats he's got and I
expect this is the first time he's been inside a house. The one
talking to him is ninety-three; he used to pasture his flocks near
Saranta Ekklesies or Forty Churches—Kirk Kilisse, the Turks
call it—away, away, beyond Adrianople. Then after the Balkan
Wars the Turks closed the frontier, so now he has his winter
huts along the coast, west of here, below Xanthi. The other
one, with a scar on his forehead, used to winter between
Haskovo and Stara Zagora—wonderful grass!—but now, what
with the Bulgars, the hornwearers, he's had to look elsewhere.
. . . I had a few, but good ones. I used to graze them not far
from Kios, in Bithynia, near Nicaea on the Asian coast. That
was years, years ago. . . . Caïques sailing past in the Sea of
Marmara could hear my bells. . . . But the Rhodope is where
we all belong. . . .' I asked him what the name Sarakatsán
meant, saying that I had heard it was really *Karakatchani*, a
Turkish word meaning 'the black ones who depart' or 'the
black departers'. He shut his eyes and flung back his head,
clicking his tongue in the negative, 'Tk, tk! That's not right.
We don't know, but some people say we get our name from
the village of Syrako, in Epirus. They say Ali Pasha burnt the
place down and drove us away and left us wandering ever
since.' I said Syrako was a Koutzovlach village.*

* It is, in fact, the birthplace of Kolettis, the War of Independence hero,
one of the early Prime Ministers of Greece, and at one time the Greek
Minister in Paris, mentioned in the Goncourt diaries; also of the poets
Krystallis and Zalacosta. It is a large Vlach village on the Acheloös—Aspro-
pótamo, or 'white river' in demotic. The inhabitants are known as *tzintzari*,
which resembles the Rumanian word for mosquitoes. In winter their huts
are scattered inland from Preveza by the hundred.

Uncle Petro testily stabbed the butt of his crook into the mat several times. 'I don't know anything about that! *We are Greeks.* Nothing to do with the Koutzovlachs. Who knows where they come from? You can't understand what they say when they are talking among themselves.* People are always getting us mixed up, because we both wear black and graze flocks. We keep clear of them. You'll never get a Sarakatsán marrying a Koutzovlach. Let alone a Karagouni! *Po, po, po!'* At the mention of these Black-Capes, who are alternatively called Arvanitóvlachi (i.e. Albanovlachs, from the north-western Pindus and the southern provinces of Albania, who speak a mixture of Koutzovlach and Albanian),† he caught the hem of his jacket between finger and thumb in a pan-hellenic gesture of squeamish disdain, and shook it lightly to and fro as though to rid it of dust and vermin. I noticed that, apart from us, the priest squatting not far away with his tall cylinder hat poking above the archipelago of kalpaks was the only non-Sarakatsán in the room, or indeed, as far as I could make out, in the village outside.

The reiterated song of welcome, after gradually swelling in volume while the room filled up, had stopped long ago. Low circular tables, all ready laid with glasses and with com-munal dishes of roast and steaming lamb skilfully hacked from the carcases turning outside and sprinkled with rock salt, were being moved in and wedged among the company as tightly as jig-saw pieces. Glass jugs of wine were beginning to travel from hand to hand overhead. Glasses clashed convivially together, miraculously half-filling again as soon as they were drained; plates were returning again and again for second or third help-ings. Outside the window a swarm of guests feasted under

* Both these derivations of the word Sarakatsán are wrong. More of this later, and also, later still, about the Koutzovlachs.

† To embroil matters further, the word 'Karagouni' is also used for the inhabitants of several Greek villages near Karditza on the Thessalian plain, and, loosely and chaffingly, as a derogatory knickname for any Thessalian.

the trees. Whole lambs were being flourished sizzling and smoking on their spits and we could hear the crash of cleaver on block and the crunch of hewn bones as a sinewy nomad toiled like a headsman to keep pace with two hundred magnificent appetites. Nothing accompanied this delicious roast except for cross-sections of dark and excellent bread sliced from loaves like minor millstones hot from the domed ovens outside. It was, in a way, a Stone Age banquet. Strangers, on occasions like these, are the objects of eager solicitude: special titbits, forkfuls of liver and kidney, and yet more recondite morsels are constantly being proffered and helpings of brain are delved from heads which have been bisected lengthwise and opened like a casket, each half, sometimes, still equipped with a singed and twisting horn. Avoidance of the sheep's eyes is a recurrent problem for outsiders. They are highly prized by mountaineers but for all but the most assimilated travellers the message they flash from the prongs is one of harrowing reproach.

After an hour or so the hum of talk sank to a single deep bourdon note which resolved itself into the opening phrases of a klephtic song. The first stanza was sung by a group of two or three and then repeated, in a slow and long-drawn roar starting with the vehemence of a lurch, by the rest of the shepherds. Rather surprisingly, so far from the Morea, it was about the great War of Independence leader, Kolokotrones. (I would have expected some more northern Klepht, and above all, Katsandónis from the wild Agrapha mountains, a great paladin in the time of Ali of Yanina, and himself a Sarakatsán; or Karaïskakis, perhaps.) 'Kolokotrones shouted,' sang the nomads, 'and all the world trembled: "Where are you, poor Nikitará, you whose feet have wings?"—*pou choun to pódia sou phterá*? Go, go and seize the Turks, drive them like hares into a trap, slay some and capture some, and lock some in the castle. ... At Antikorpha and Trikorpha the blood is flowing like a brook. ...' This gave rise to another deep melopee from the south: 'They have blockaded all the roads of the Morea, they have sealed up all the passes. . . .' When the massed voices died down, the steady and unchanging note of the smaller group continued half in a wail and half in a roar, setting up its own curious vibration. This comparative lull was always followed by the long deep cry of conjuration—*Oré!*—'O, you!' or 'Hark!'—which ushers in most klephtic stanzas; and another act from the warlike past began, heckled and abetted by sudden ejaculations from the others and goaded on by ear-splitting pastoral whistles.*

These songs unfold with a slow metrical elaboration of semi-tones and recapitulated half-lines and with a force of delivery which seems to strain the singers to the brink of syncope. Their heads are flung backwards with eyes half closed or faraway and the veins of their foreheads and necks project like thongs. The stories, usually heroic narratives, frequently veiled in a parable, are as fierce and melancholy as the music. The slow cumulative incantatory power fills the smoky air overhead with toppling minarets, blazing fortresses, volleys from long-barrelled guns, the smell of powder and the clash of yataghans as the Klephts and the janissaries close with each other on semicircular bridges over fabulous ravines. . . . Across the Valley of Tempe, Klepht-sheltering Olympus thunders reproach at Turk-trampled Ossa. Flame-eyed pallikars gallop into churches to receive communion from the saddle; hoary in years and slaughter and scimitar in hand, they lie bleeding to death under

* Another ritual conjuration that is often inserted at a break in the line is *Amán!*, the Turkish for 'mercy!' Though its role is often that of a stopgap, I think it is basically a railing at fate, an unspecific act of compassion, as it were, for intolerable sorrows and disasters in the past; half 'willow willow waly', half '*aï de mi*'. At the end of each fifteen-syllable line of the rhyming couplets which are the most common metre for these mountain epics—spun out and embroidered, however, into many more than fifteen when they are being sung—several *amáns*, strung together as a single word, boom in a deep bass from the whole company: *amánamánamánamánán!* There was no dearth of this today.

plane trees by a stream. . . . We are transported to the fastnesses of Roumeli, Tzoumerka, Pindus, Hasia, Kakosouli: names to make the hair stand on end. The power and fierceness and lyrical beauty of these words unite in creating all round the singers and listeners the free world of mountaintops far from the spawning Turks of the lowlands. It is the eagle-haunted realm of Klephtouriá! *Oré amán!*

The Sarakatsáns were not great virtuosi but their singing had the merit of vigour and conviction. I was struck by one of their songs, in which the last word—*makaronádes*, a derogatory epithet for the Italians—had obviously, judging by the style of the words and the tune, replaced the name of some much older foe in order to fit the winter campaign of 1940: 'Would that I had wings to soar on high, up to the topmost peaks of the mountains, to alight there and gaze down, down over Epirus and over poor Chimarra; to look down on the war, where the Greeks are fighting the *Makaronádes*.' The modern ending was a bit of an anticlimax, especially after the mention of Chimarra, a warlike Greek stronghold in the Acroceraunian mountains over the Albanian border which is almost as celebrated for its martial stubbornness, in Turkish times, as Souli and the Sphakian mountains of Crete. There was a distinct trace of anticlimax too, but also of oddity, about another of their songs: 'Any one who wants to go to America, let him sit down and ponder. Forty days at sea, days of sorrow and sighing. They get into a boat and go ashore in New York. They know nobody there so back they fly like birds.'* A sad little tale, but most peculiar here because, although in most Greek gatherings of this size, at least half a dozen would have spent a few years in Brooklyn or Chicago or Nebraska, Uncle Petro assured me

* I must apologize here for a bad mistake in *Mani*. I stated there that sixteen-syllable verses (as opposed to the almost universal fifteen) only exist in Maniot dirges. It is not true: there are several other very small pockets of this verse form dotted about and this very song, I see from my notes, is one of them. I wish I knew where it came from.

that nobody in the room had been to America, nor, as far
as he knew, any Sarakatsán, ever. Ideas of its whereabouts and
character, for those who had heard its name, would be as hazy
as a layman's notions of life on Mars.

During the banquet and the long procession of refilled
glasses and the concatenation of songs the two falling shafts of
sunlight from the windows had slanted up to the horizontal and
veered askew down the room: the long sunlit parallelograms
on the opposite wall were turning to an apricot evening hue.
During these cheerful hours there had been no glimpse of the
bride. 'She's upstairs', Uncle Petro said. 'We must go and look
at her', and grasping the shaft of his upright crook like a punt
pole, with joints momentarily acreak after long session, he
levered himself to his feet. '*Ta Gerámata!*' he said with a smile,
'old age. . . .' He led the way up the ladder-staircase and the
clamour dwindled.

Dead silence reigned in the upper chamber. The dowry was
arranged down the two side walls: rolled bales of dark homespun for capes and for the bivouacs which are pitched on the
march; a few of them white, some grey or a dark russet but
most of them black; the colours, indeed, of the flocks from
which they had been shorn and many of them of a matted and
shaggy texture like rolled-up smoke. Scratchy blankets with
angular patterns were piled in tall heaps and pillows that looked
hard as granite and the bride's black and white trousseau. In the
centre of the end wall, with bowed head and lowered eyelids
and her brown hands crossed over her midriff, the bride stood
motionless. On either side of her on the floor sat her retinue
of wild but subdued-looking girls. At our conventional
wishes—'*Kaloriziki!*', 'may the marriage be well rooted'—
she inclined her head a few inches, but uttered never a
syllable. Nor, beyond a stiff bow, did she or her lips move
a fraction when other late-comers arrived and hobnobbed
with Uncle Petro and us as indifferently as if the figures at
the other end of the room were effigies in an ethnological

museum. Their extraordinary outfits were nearly identical, except for the flowers and the gold coins which adorned the bride.

In those Greek villages where the women still wear their regional costumes on feast days and ceremonies—and there are still a large though diminishing number—and in some out-of-the-way spots where a simpler working version of this gala rig is worn on week-days too—one is astonished by their richness and variety and grace; by voluminous skirts, expanding from tight waists, of Damascus brocade or Broussa velvet; by their soft and tilted mulberry-coloured fezzes with long satin tassels, or gold embroidered velvet pill-boxes or intricately arranged silk kerchiefs; even, in one part of Macedonia, by headdresses topped by a semi-circular plume like the helmet of Pallas Athene. There are satin-covered buttons, chased silver clasps and oriental filigree from Yanina: and, over their velvet boleros and their tight sleeves—or sleeves which may hang slashed and loose from the elbow like the petals of tulips—a riot of gold braid uncoils and ramifies in flowing oriental, baroque and rococo flourishes as richly and elaborately as over a post-Tridentine cope. In the wilder mountains they are stiffer and rougher but the basic canon is a dazzling variety of colour and material and a style that is fluid, feminine and deeply romantic. The visions summoned up by Byron's Haidee and the Maid of Athens are, in fact, pretty near the mark.

All was different here. Not only was there no silk or satin or velvet or gold braid from the West and the Levant but hardly a stitch which came from anywhere but the backs of their flocks and their prehistoric-looking looms; and, complex though the costume was, not a single foliating curve or circle or ellipse, nothing swaying or branching or interweaving or flowering. The only rounded things were the chains and necklaces, the gold Napoleons, Turkish sequins and gold thalers that hung round the bride's neck. Another latter-day curvilinear after-thought to the angular whole, and one which was common to both the bride and her retinue, was a wide white goffered or crocheted circular collar like a flattened hidalgo's ruff ending at the shoulder in scallops. The complex headdress of flowers and stiff muslin and the veil which hung down the bride's back had the extraneous and charming air of votive adornments attached to a processional statue on a Calabrian or Andalusian feast day. From a rosette over each of her ears a long cluster of ribbons hung; they framed her face in the manner of the pendants on the diadem of the Empress Theodora at Ravenna.

But apart from these festival trimmings, all was made up of stern black and white lines and angles and so broad and solid-seeming were the black white-banded pleats that if any of the girls made a movement, their heavy and unwieldy clothes moved with the stiffness of armour. Aprons hung to knee-length as stiffly as stoles or heralds' tabards; their tunics were as rigid as dalmatics and nothing bore any relationship to con-ventional ideas of the human shape. They were related to the curvature and the jointing of anatomy as arbitrarily as are the plates of a metal fish or the sections of a toy wooden snake to their prototypes, or the layers of a Samurai's armour. Each garment looked as though, removed, it would be able to stand like cardboard. Their forearms and legs were encased in geometrically patterned armlets and greaves and the bride's wrists were a-clank with heavy bracelets. All, strangely and touchingly, were shod in stout, flat-heeled walking shoes. (Their mothers would have worn pom-pommed *tsarouchia*.) It was hard to determine, therefore, why these clothes appeared so beautiful. They exerted, it finally dawned on us, the peculiar captivation of ancient Greek vases of the geometric period; every design was made up of straight lines and triangles with here and there an inchoate beginning of those patterns of white crosses on a black ground, and black on white, that cover the vestments of frescoed prelates on the wall of a narthex. All was angular: triangles mounting in pyramids or shooting diagonally in zigzags and saw's teeth and staircases with, very seldom a small triangle or chevron subtly placed among the dominating black and white, of pale ochre or terracotta or a deadened blue. 'Geometric' and 'neolithic' were the epithets which began to float to the surface of the mind, to hover there ever since, bringing with them the excitement of the thought that these clothes and these designs might not have changed for three thousand years or more. One knows that these thoughts must be banished, till confirmation should be forthcoming, to the limbo of improbability. But such dalliance is always stimulating. It was backed, in this case, by the certainty that nothing like these clothes exists in Greece or in the Balkan peninsula or in Europe or the Near East.

The bride's forehead, with the blue cross, was surmounted by black hair as coarse and lustrous as a mare's tail under a stiff linen coif and a load of baubles and flowers. Her face was burnt a deep bronze. It had the metallic, wide-browed, heavy-lidded beauty, the slightly sad mouth, the clear line of jaw from chin to ear, and, springing from the flattened ruff and a stomacher of coins, the strong columnar neck which I admired so much, a few years ago, among the Mayas of the Honduranean and Guatemaltecan jungles. Obsidian, chalcedony or basalt would have been the stone in which to carve those features and the posture of melancholy stillness of which the twilight was fast abolishing the details. She had an arresting distinction, a Gauguin-limbed strength at variance with the Tanagra sinuosity which seems to have left an indelible stamp on Western ideas of grace and style.

There was no time for more of these cogitations. The reedy blast of a clarinet sounded under the fading window; then, after a few twiddles, a violin and the twanging of a lute and a tentative flutter of hammers over the wires of a zither. 'Ah, the instruments', Uncle Petro said. '*Ta órgana!*—at last!' I asked if they were Sarakatsáns. He looked at me in surprise. 'Sarakatsáns? We only play the flute. They are gypsies.' And so they were, very dark ones, lined up under a tree in blue suits and

pointed black shoes and all wearing ties, the only ones for miles.
They looked sleek and urban among these other nomads, and
rather bad hats. There was a crunch of hobnails up the stairs and
the groom, flanked by his comrades, came to claim the bride
and lead the first dance. She was reft from her shadows, conducted downstairs and under the trees. The sun was setting at
the end of the valley. The groom then accompanied her
through an extremely formal *syrtos*, and then a *kalamatiano*; each
took alternate places at the head of a dozen guests with their
hands loosely linked in a crescent. Neither looked at the other;
there was a distinct hint of constraint in the air. No wonder;
they came from neighbouring summer pastures but it was
quite likely they had never met. Their marriage was as free
of choice as a dynastic alliance between a Wittelsbach and a
Hohenstaufen in the Middle Ages. It is hard not to wonder
about the early phases of primitive marriages all over Greece;
the shuddering apprehension which must prevail on the one
hand and the unmanning strangeness on the other. Till recently
in the Mani, the shyness of newly-wed strangers was so inhibit-
ing that a sword was placed under their pillow in the hopes that
it might symbolically sunder this knot of constraint in one
Gordian slash. . . . These handicaps must have been made all
the more debilitating by gloomy preoccupation with the inviolacy of the bride: by the vigil of the guests outside the
nuptial dwelling till the groom's mother could blazon the
all-clear in red on white with a flourished sheet or a shift.
Salvos and rustic epithalamia saluted the tidings. In these strict
societies, such proofs were surely redundant; but I have heard
of Cretan bridegrooms, convinced, and probably baselessly,
that others have been beforehand with them, repudiating
their brides, and unloosing, as though in compensation, unstaunchable bloodshed between families. And what about the
poor bridegroom? Would the floodtide of wine swirl him
triumphantly through all obstacles or unmast him amidships?
No wonder they looked shy. Young Sarakatsáns now do their

military service like the rest of Greeks and no doubt head for
the lanes on the outskirts of garrison towns on mating-forays
with their fellow-recruits. But formerly, living in a ferociously
chaste society, they approached wedlock unarmed by all but
theory, hearsay and rule of thumb. Perhaps, as their detractors
jovially hint, unconventional young shepherds, like pastoral
folk everywhere, may have cast a thoughtful eye among their
ewes for the quenching of early flames. This, again, would only
be of relative help now.

Her two dances over, the bride withdrew to her upper
chamber and general dancing began. It was uncomplicated,
formal and correct. Plenty of the younger Sarakatsáns were
well on in wine; they had been so for days; but their dash and
high spirits deserted them the moment they joined the long
chain of the dancers. Their pace subsided to a ritual shuffle.
There is nothing unusual in this; with a few exceptions, Greek
dances, however many people may be joined hand in hand, are,
in effect, solos; everything devolves on the leader, and each
dancer, when his turn comes, fulfils the temporary role of cory-
phaeus. The job of the others, and especially of his immediate
neighbour to whom he is linked by a handkerchief, is to
support him in his convolutions. These are astonishing when a
real mountain dasher is in the lead. But today, even after the
first bridal saraband, the dionysiac zest seemed to abandon the
others the moment they linked hands. The dominance of form
in the life of these nomads began to dawn on us.

Outside this semicircle, however, all was rejoicing. Staidness
evaporated on release and scores of young nomads were carousing under the branches in uninhibited and growing festivity.
Squatting or standing among the wigwams, rings of geometrical women confabulated or sang together and there was
even an exclusive little ellipse of dancing women. Some of the
younger of these squaws had wooden cradles slung papoose-
like on their backs, each containing a miniature swaddled
nomad. Their songs had the same epic themes, laced with

lament, as those of the men. The murmur of their talk was broken, again and again, with peals of laughter.

The Sarakatsánissas, usually so silent in the presence of men, look forward to weddings as their only chances of fun. The talk, as though preordained, takes on a bawdy turn of hair-raising frankness. None of the exciting, comic or absurd aspects of sex are left unexploited. Rhymes, anecdotes and reminiscences are eagerly repeated and capped, crone mumbles toothlessly to crone, wives gesturing like anglers make boastful and teasing claims about their married life, girls listen agog. Fits of laughter punctuate this scandalous chat, hands are flung in the air in hilarity, faces are covered in mock shame. All this goes on beyond male earshot, while, at a distance, their husbands and fathers and descendants smile indulgently at the seasonable ribaldry.

Nightfall had transformed the scene indoors. Late arrivals and one or two indefatigable ones were still at meat; the rest, lit now by scattered oil-dips, had lapsed into a semi-trance of wine and song. Our return with Uncle Petro evoked hospitable cries of greeting and invitation, repeated many times and driven home by the clashing of wine-tumblers, to stay the night, as it was so late; or for a week, a month or a year or forever, to forget London and take to the huts. Alas, some tiresome fixture in Alexandroupolis next morning compelled us to leave; so, after manifold farewells, we climbed the stairs to pay our respects to the bride in her hushed upper chamber.

The rushlight on a stool cast so dim a light that the group at the end was hard to discern. One of the seated bridesmaids, mown down by her vigil, was fast asleep where she sat; a nudge from her neighbour shook her blinking into line. None of the other tiring-women had moved and the bride had re-mained frozen for the hours since we had last seen her in the same posture of submission. The faint radiance robbed them all of a dimension. Darkly haloed by their interlocking shadows, they melted into the wall and their black and white figures assumed the aspect of a fresco, half-lit; here and there an ear-ring, a coin, a bracelet, a ring or a necklace gleamed for a moment and dimmed again with the rise and fall of the wick like fragments of gilt or isolated gold tesserae in a mosaic. The bride silently bowed in answer to our farewells, the only one to move in this still and hagiographic troop of virgins and martyrs. We tiptoed out.

'Doesn't she ever speak?' I asked Uncle Petro when we were out of doors.

'Not now,' he said.

'It's rather sad, during her own wedding.'

'Ah! That's the way it is. . . . That's as it should be.'

By the firelight, the scene out of doors assumed a Breugelish look. Dancers were still sedately moving in silhouette, a last spitted lamb was turning over a bed of glowing charcoal and groups of nomads reeled arm in arm and filled the night with loud voices and laughter. Overcome by wine or exhaustion, a few slept under the branches in disjointed attitudes as though snipers had laid them low in mid-career. A heroic, unsteady figure, egged on by his companions, was draining, with head and trunk flung back, the last dregs from an immense wicker-cradled demijohn. Empty, it fell with a thud and rolled away amid cheers. A flaxen-haired boy, bent double against a tree-trunk, vomited the day's intake in a sombre gush. Chewing and snarling sheepdogs wrangled over bones. The huts, now softly lit from within by the glimmer of oil-dips and hearths, had become vague dark globes looming out of the night, and deeper still in the shadows we divined the presence of tethered horses. The singing grew fainter as we reached the railway line.

'You should have seen the weddings when I was a boy,' Barba Petro was saying, as the serpent of lighted train windows grew larger down the valley. 'We used to set out on horseback a hundred strong to carry off the bride, firing off our guns as fast as we could load them. *Dang! Dang! Boom! Boom! Dang!*

... Horses used to be lamed, people wounded, sometimes people actually got killed. Whereas now ...'

The train had clanked to a standstill in the little halt. We were aloft once more among the anachronistic fringes and tassels of our Victorian carriage.

'Come to see us up in the mountains, up in the Rhodope!', he shouted as the train began to move. 'The plains are no good.' He pointed with his crook into the night. 'In the Rhodope——'

The wheels drowned the rest. The light from the carriages flashed across his dwindling figure at faster intervals, and the glimmering huts and the fires and the tiny moving silhouettes behind him looked as strange now, and as alien to Europe, as a nomadic encampment in the steppes of Central Asia.

* * * *

Who are these extraordinary people, and where do they come from? As in the case of the Greeks themselves, no one knows. All is problematical, starting with their name.* The first faint mention of them, in the pages of Eugenius the Aetolian, occurs in 1650, and everything before or since is folklore and surmise. Every symptom and every particle of evidence is circumstantial.

Western travellers, when confronted by nomads and hut-dwellers, have almost invariably set them down as 'Walla-chians', or 'Vlachs'; rightly, quite often. There are many thousands of these semi-nomadic Arroman people, migrating twice yearly between their villages and the plains, speaking a Latin language of their own which is closely akin to Rumanian, and as different from Greek as the Welsh language is from English. Theories about their origins abound, all of them hotly debated. To an uninitiated eye and ear, there are points of surface resemblance between the Vlachs and the Sarakatsáns. Both are nomads, hut-and-tent-dwellers, and shepherds; and

* The rich conflict of derivations for the word Sarakatsán is developed in Appendix I.

the garb of the men, but not of the women, has something in common. The confusion among foreign travellers was probably furthered by the word 'vlachos', written with a small 'v'. This word designates not only the Latin-dialect speaking Arromans, the 'Koutsovlachs' proper, but it is losely applied to shepherds generically all over Greece. In fact Greeks, if they want to make it clear that they are speaking of Vlachs, not merely of herdsmen in general, nearly always use the word 'Koutzovlachs' (or 'limping Vlachs')—another promising subject of linguistic speculation—or, in the case of those whose Latin language is more mixed with Albanian than (as among the Koutzovlachs) with Greek, 'Arvanitóvlachi', or, more colloquially still, 'Karagounides', or 'Black-Cloak Men'.* The Vlachs are much more numerous than the Sarakatsáns but less widespread; they played a prominent if minor part in Byzantine and Balkan history; they inhabit remarkable villages in the mountains and form the bulk of the population of several Macedonian and Thessalian towns; all this, with their difference of language and, some say, of race, from the rest of the Greeks, has been a fascinating anthill for linguists and ethnographers. For the last hundred and fifty years, unfortunately, they have been a theme of bitter political discord in the Balkans. These considerations, with the muddle over the word 'vlach', and the fact that the habitats of the Vlachs and the Sarakatsáns largely overlap, has edged the more reticent and fleeting Sarakatsáns ever deeper into a cloudy and unchronicled hinterland. Till almost yesterday they lived in a forgotten historical dell to which the paths were few and overgrown and finally, not there at all. It is only in recent decades that lone scholars have begun to ply their billhooks. The confusion between the two groups has never existed among the Greeks themselves; it is a foreign reserve. Indeed, under scrutiny, their dissimilarity pierces any surface resemblance more and more sharply. Everything—manners, customs, clothes, folklore, beliefs, appear-

* All Greek nomads wear hooded goats' hair capes in winter.

ance, feeling and, above all, language—thrusts them further apart.

Semi-nomadism exists all over Greece; shepherds leave their mountain villages in winter in search of lowland pastures free of snow; lowlanders do the reverse in summer. Among the true semi-nomads, the Vlachs, however, where village economy depends entirely on livestock, autumn brings about an exodus to the plains of the whole male population with all their flocks. They leave a skeleton population of women, children and old men behind to keep the home fires burning till their return to the mountains in spring. In winter, they live in huts in the plain, or, more and more, nowadays, in villages which have sprung up on the sites of their invariable winter sojourn. Alone among the pastoral people of Greece the Sarakatsáns have no fixed abode. They are, unlike the Vlachs, with the substantial villages and towns they have inhabited for centuries, entire nomads.

Apart from their wandering, they regard their summer pastures as their true home. The details of their life are formalized and codified; custom, ritual, tradition and taboo beset them thickly. Nothing is improvised or haphazard. No trace of the slovenliness which makes gypsy life, after unknown ages, seem half-learnt. Each detail in choice of ground and orientation and hut-building and hearth-laying, almost every sentence uttered and every gesture made, is hallowed by usage; it is the accumulation of hundreds, and perhaps thousands, of years; hereditary, patriarchal, established, immutable, conservative, and self-sufficient, everything emerges from a vast expanse of time as smooth with long handling as the shuttle of a loom, the blurred carving on a distaff or the patina on the shaft of a crook.

Ancient literature ignores them and there is not much in modern times. Linguistic evidence proves a wandering life since the fourteenth or fifteenth century; the probabilities point to a much earlier period. All are agreed on the north and north-western tincture of their speech. No surprise here:

these are the regions where they are most plentiful. But it is surprising that the Sarakatsáns who, save for the southern Peloponnese and, with three exceptions,* the archipelago, are scattered all over mainland Greece, should all speak identically. Similarly, centuries of winter migration deep into Slav and Albanian and Turkish lands have left no trace on the hoary Greekness of their idiom. Costumes in Greece, especially those of the women (and, most notably those of the Vlach women), change, even more frequently than accents, from village to village; yet the garb of the Sarakatsánissas, with the barest minimum of variation, is the same all over Greece. So are their customs, down to the last detail. Everything, especially their feeling of solidarity and of aloofness from everyone else, underlines their common origin. It is very noticeable in their attitude to the Vlachs: 'If you hear a shepherd use the word *lapte*'—the Vlach and Rumanian word for 'milk'†—'hit him over the head.'

Ordinary Greek villagers approve of their Greekness, envy their freedom, admire the primeval sternness of their regimen, and despise their primitive ways—'they never wash', they say 'from the day they are born till the day of their death'. Their aloofness promotes distrust. Plainsmen speculate about their buried and suppositious wealth. They regard them as sly opponents and the two are often at loggerheads when nomad flocks encroach on their grazing grounds. They were always looked on with suspicion by the authorities. Wild habitat, mobility and evanescence placed them beyond the range of the Ottoman tax-collector and sheltered the boys from the press-gangs and the girls from the harems. Their eyries were a sanctuary for robbers and guerrillas and they engaged in both pursuits. Two of the greatest Klephts were almost certainly Sarakatsáns from the Agrapha mountains: Katsandónis and Karaiskákis. When

* Aegina, Poros and Euboea.
† Deriving from the Latin *lac, lactis*, as opposed to the ancient and modern Greek word *gala, galaktos*.

the nomads came under the Greek law, their reputation for poaching pastures and for acts of banditry and ambushes for ransom, stuck. (For long decades, as in the old days, they were out of the range of taxation and military service.) Watchful and independent—unlike the Albanovlachs, who would flatter the pashas and graze their flocks—they had a fierce feeling for freedom. 'We and the monasteries were the backbone of all the revolutions against the Turks', they say, perhaps a shade boast-fully; there were others. Shepherds and monks were vital to resistance in Crete and elsewhere during the German occu-pation. They alone knew all the passes, springs, woods, caves, short-cuts and look-out points. *Klephtouria* was theirs.

They, in their turn, thought the plainspeople tame and slavish hinds, but hinds with an unfair advantage; they know how to read and write.* The villages and plains are a threat to free-dom: if nomads pass through a village, they do it at dead of night, and pitch camp far away. Boojums to a man, they have perfected the art of snark-like vanishing at the approach of trouble. *Adespotoi*, 'masterless', is their key epithet.

There were many more than eighty thousand of them twenty-five years ago, and, two hundred years ago, many, many more. So vast a population could not all come from one village; let alone (though his campaigns did promote shifts of populations among the regions under him, and, no doubt, among some of the Sarakatsáns as well) as recently as Ali Pasha's day, a century and a half ago. Apart from the contrary evidence, we would have known. The invariable tendency for nomads is to slow down and settle, not the opposite. When war or trouble drives villagers away they settle elsewhere. The nomad Sarakatsán life is a tissue of customs and usage from origins unreckonably remote.

How remote? The reader will have guessed how the wind is blowing . . . let us pause for a moment. There are few facts to build on but possibilities begin to assemble on which an edifice

* Not all, by any means.

of further surmise may provisionally and diffidently be raised, and here it is: no one challenges the Greekness of the Saraksatsáns; all of them share common origins, customs, language and way of life; they have been total nomads for several centuries, probably much longer; they have always dodged official molestation and contact or marriage with strangers. They originally lived in the north-eastern mountains beyond the margin of history in regions hard of access and impervious to change; it is hard to say whether the duration of their way of life must be reckoned in hundreds of years or in thousands. Its origins are lost, as they say, in the mists of time.

But one aspect of their life may dispel these mists for a moment, and enable us, with utmost caution, to attribute a possible origin to these strange people: the identity of their textiles with the earliest Greek ceramics. Could those black and white rectangles, those woven dog-tooth staircases and saw-edges and triangles, that primitive interplay of angles and figures, spring from the same source as the geometrical designs on early Greek pottery? Are these the missing clue to the beginnings of the Sarakatsáns? Were it so, the fragments cohere in a will o' the wisp hypothesis. No less than this: when the earliest Greeks wandered through the northern passes into the peninsula, some may have turned longing eyes on the pastures of the Pindus which lay all about them; on the Acarnanian mountains further south and the green winter grazing-grounds at their feet. They may have detached themselves and their flocks from the shining destinies of their ambitious brethren; while these expanded to the south over the Thessalian plain, founding villages and towns, and later, city states, perhaps the slow-moving drovers lagged behind in a pastoral splinter-group. Living primordially, grazing their beasts from their winter to their summer pastures, they may have remained in those regions until, at some intermediate date, they put forth shoots into the Macedonian and Thracian mountains, which in turn penetrated the more northern Balkans and Asia Minor in their seasonal search for fresh pastures. Given the mutual distrust which severed them from the plains, their horror of marriage with strangers and their skill at the vanishing trick, they would have escaped all contact with the Slavs and the other invaders in Byzantine times. Their aloofness would have exempted them from the foreign deposits which later comers left; leaving them, for better or for worse, the most Greek of all the Greeks. Far from commerce and the routes of civilization and the greed of the city states, their haunts made a late entry into recorded history. No wonder, then, that they went unchronicled.

Were all this true, they must have grazed their flocks in mid-air for aeons, vaguely aware, perhaps, of the War of Troy, the clash of the Greek cities, the elephants of Pyrrhus assembling in the valleys and Alexander's departure to conquer the world. News of the Roman onslaught, the landing of St Paul on the Macedonian coast and the fall of the West would have reached them late and garbled; the barbarian influx and the long afternoon and evening of Byzantium would have been slow to impinge. How soon would they have grasped the import of the passage of the Fourth Crusade just below them, and of the drums and tramplings of Amurath and of Bajazet the Thunderbolt and of the entry of Mohammed II into Constantinople? Perhaps they participated, in some peripheral way, in all these events. They are more likely to have remained aloof until the waterline of events, in the shape of guerrilla warriors in search of sanctuary, rose to their wigmans and sucked the nomads into history for a century or two. Now it has sunk, leaving them high and dry once more, their reclusion only broken by a change of pastures now and then, or a frontier closing, by grazing-disputes with the villagers, outbreaks of disease among their flocks and the shadowy siege of demons and ghosts and by the recurrence of red-letter-days and feasts and weddings.

* * * *

Lone scholars sniping from the walls
Of learned periodicals
  Our fact defend;

Our intellectual marines
Landing in little magazines
  Capture a trend.*

Axel Hoeg, a Danish scholar flourishing earlier this century,
was the original trail-blazer. I already knew his books, articles
and pamphlets on the Sarakatsáns and their dialect, and his
collection of their songs. I had an inkling, too, of his ideas
about their origins. But what I had *not* read, for they only
appeared recently, were Angelika Hadjimichalis' two quarto
volumes, *I Sarakatsáni*: wonderful books, based on a great
knowledge of Greek art-history, ethnology, folklore and craftsmanship and many decades of research and fieldwork among
the Sarakatsáns themselves. This lone scholar captured my
trend at once. A third volume is in preparation—the great task,
alas, has been delayed by ill-health—which promises to be
the most interesting of the three. A lifetime of devotion and
study has been lavished on these labours. It is impossible to
speak of a definitive work; all here is surmise and the verdict
must remain open: but *I Sarakatsáni* is the nearest thing to it;
a rare and distinguished achievement in its incomplete state,
the finished work will remain as a monument.†

The only drawback to these volumes, is, for my purposes, an
advantage: the author is advanced in years and the bulk of her
exploration, perforce, was undertaken some time ago, and
many of the nomads among whom her researches began, were
chosen for their age and their long memories. The agents of
detribalization, of which the author herself writes so sadly,

---

* W. H. Auden: *Nones*.

† Unfortunately they are only in Greek. Infinitely worse, just as these
pages go to press, death has halted these labours.

have been hard at work. The tendency to settle has been accelerated by the closure of frontiers, the limitation of wandering,
compulsory military service, and the denial of old grazing by
civil authority and the settlement of two million refugees in old
and undisputed pastures; and friction with villagers has helped
to change the way of life of many of them. Some, though they
still live in huts, became static a few generations back. Numbers
of these live not far from Athens. 'Yes, we're Sarakatsáns,'
they ruefully say, 'we think we come from Roumeli. Our
grandfathers or our great-grandfathers settled here. . . . *Allá
eimaste bastardeméni*: we're bastardized. . . .' The last quarter of
a century has probably done more than the last three thousand
years to change the traditional life; it is amazing that so many
have remained intact. Yet even among these, who are fortunately still the majority by far, the last few decades have
taken toll of many ancient ways. The life described, then, in
I Sarakatsáni belongs less to today than to forty years ago. It
presents a fascinating and curious picture.*

The pre-Christian legacy is never far from the surface in
Greece.† In a society like the Sarakatsáns, pagan magic survives
in a yet more pronounced shape and the superstructure of
Christian form is correspondingly more shaky. Traditionally,
there is no awareness of the existence of the Trinity. God the
Father and Jesus are the same Person and He (or They) is
known as *Aï*, a dialect abbreviation of *ayios* (*hagios*)—'saint' or
'holy one'. Sometimes He is known as *Proto Aï*, or the First
among the Saints, sometimes as *Aphenti*, the Lord, from the

---

* I have visited a number of nomad camps in the last month or two in
the Epirus area, and many of the customs described in *I Sarakatsáni* are still
in full force; some have recently died out, some are only recalled by old
men and toothless crones; a few have vanished from living memory. As this
is not a scientific work, I will not elaborate these distinctions. To avoid
a barnacle growth of caveats and provisos, I will put all in the present tense.
But much of it, especially the religious part, should be dated half a century
ago.

† See Chap. 10, *Mani*, by Patrick Leigh Fermor.

ancient Greek word *authentes* (from which the Turkish title, '*effendi*', also derives). All over Greece, the army of saints has taken the place of the ancient pantheon. This is especially true among the nomads; *Aï* is little more than the first among His peers. As one would expect in a masculine and patriarchal society, male saints have cornered the high places in this celestial company. Numbers have been drastically reduced. Only a handful, from the thousands which overlap and crowd each other in the villagers' calendars and the Synaxary, have found their way into the huts. The greatest, as horseman, protector of flocks and folds and slayer of dragons and other predators, is St George; his feast day, on April 23rd in the Gregorian calendar, corresponds perhaps to the great Roman shepherd festival of the Parilia on the 27th. The prominence of horses in the life of the nomads also hoists St Demetrius and St Theodore, equestrians both, to a height which only St George overtops. St George's day is more important even than Easter, the crux of the Orthodox year. Red eggs similar to the Easter-symbols are distributed and the finest black lamb of the flock—black animals are more highly prized than white—is ritually sacrificed. (Easter is only marked by a white.) Oaths taken in the name of St George are the most binding. St George and St Demetrius have another claim to fame: their feasts—May 6th and November 9th in the New Calendar—mark the start of the pastoral summer and winter when the leases for grazing begin and end and the *tsellingas* makes a new pact with his clan. They are days of decision. His mountain-top shrines make the prophet Elijah especially revered. (*Elias* in Greek; the nomads call him 'St Lios'. When the Greek world went Christian he took over the hilltop fanes to Helios-Apollo, on the strength of his name and partly because both their careers ended in the sky in fiery chariots.)* 'He's a mountain man like us,' they say, 'he lives in the wilderness and wanders from peak to peak. He helps us and we hallow him.' The Blessed

* See Chap. 13, *Mani*.

Virgin is addressed under one of her many epithets; they call
her *Parigorítissa*, the Consolatrix; as an alien and a woman who
has somehow insinuated herself into their midst, her honours
are fairly cursory. St Paraskeví is another female saint with
some status. Each *stani*—each 'fold', clan or gathering of families and huts—has its own feast day, fortuitously depending
on chapels that lie in their favourite pastures. Some have won
general acceptance: the Assumption—like Elijah's, the epony-
mous churches often perch on mountains; St Constantine, the
champion of Hellenism; the Deposition and the Purification;
and in the Agrapha mountains, the Nativity of the Virgin,
thanks to her great monastery there, hard of access in the
Proussos gorge. Our Lady of Vella, between Yanina and
Konitza, is honoured for a like reason. St Athanasius is not cul-
tivated as a Doctor of the Church, but, unexpectedly, as a war-
den of flocks. They neglect his January name-day because it
falls in lambing-time and celebrate it later in the year. The
fondness of Macedonian Sarakatsáns for St John the Baptist is
probably due to his shaggy iconographic outfit: it looks far
more like their own goatskin homespun than camel-hair; he
lived in the wilderness too. They boil beans on his feast day
and distribute and eat them in church. The bean-feast is linked
with pagan magic ceremonial at harvest time and commemorates, almost certainly, the Pyanepsia when the ancients boiled
and ate broad beans to bring fertility and a year of plenty.

The usual pan-hellenic spirits—Pagans, Airy or Shadowy
Ones, Exotics, vampires, werewolves, dragons, ghosts and
Kallikantzaro-centaurs—people their cosmogony and infest the
folds. They can be exorcized by counter-spells and baffled by
phylacteries of dog's droppings; a dried snake's head, hidden
in a church for forty days and then retrieved, is sovereign
against many baleful manifestations. To the Nereids, a danger
for all lonely shepherds near pools and streams, young Sarakatsáns are particularly exposed. They are struck dumb and
robbed of their wits by blundering on their revels by mistake,

as mortals were sometimes turned into trees if they had the bad luck to interrupt the dances of the nymphs. There are mixed nomad-Nereid marriages and these water-girls steal healthy Sarakatsán babies from their hanging cradles, leaving sickly changelings in their stead. Demons of every kind and gender dog shepherds' footsteps uphill and down dale and 'chase them into woods', as the saying goes. The nomads are a special target for female supernaturals called the *Kalotyches*—('the good fortunes': like the name *Eumenides* ('the kindly ones') for the Furies, this is a wry placating misnomer)—who are half women, half she-asses and snake-locked like Medusa. They plague the flocks and bring bad luck at lambing time and childbed and they are especially dangerous during the forty days following a birth. Other Shadowy Ones lurk round the pallets of the ailing and the dying. But the darkest villain in Sarakatsán demonology is a male spirit known as the *Daouti*. *Daoutis*, sometimes called Pans, are the wildest, strongest and wickedest of them all. Shaped like satyrs, with a body half-goat, half-human and long legs with cleft hoofs, they have the heads of rams and long twirling horns. Like other demons—the Shadowy Ones and the *Kalotyches*, in particular—*Daoutis* are doubly threatening to flocks at three seasons: in Advent (just before lambing, that is); in late April or early May, as the shepherds prepare to leave their winter quarters for the mountains; and from the feast of the Transfiguration until the end of August. They swoop shrieking like birds of prey and the flocks cower in caves and sheepfolds. After two or three of these onslaughts, the beasts begin to perish by the dozen. They swell up and die. Sliced tortoise meat is brought into play as a counter-spell and the shepherds shift camp at once. If a priest can be found, he sprinkles the new site with holy water and the bells are removed and blessed. Unlike most wicked spirits, these *Daoutis* attack without shame in broad daylight, and, having the knack of making friends with the dogs, they pad along after the flocks unmolested; so, when an emergency fold is

built, the shepherds leave their dogs behind and kindle fires to
form a magic circle of smoke. *Daoutis* learn the Christian names
of mortals, so if they hear strangers calling the shepherds hold
their tongues: answering might strike them dumb for ever.
These terrible spirits spread sudden panics and when they are
not busy doing evil they settle out of sight but within earshot
and play their flutes.

Trees are the dwelling-places of spirits. They are the haunt of
the *Kalotyches* and unless countercharms are murmured while
felling and lopping, these wretches are loosed on the woods.
Many bushes, all thorn trees and especially the wild pear, have
powerful spirit-repelling properties. Box is a powerful apotro-
paic; the osier which is woven into all their huts is the strongest
and most hallowed of all. Flowers are plaited into phylacteries;
their sweet smell, and even the memory of it when the flowers
have faded, drives evil away. They have odd and hazy notions
about the past: they believe that the Hellenes, the ancient
Greeks, were taller than oaks and as strong: they spanned wide
rivers at a single pace and strode from peak to peak. They
never fell ill; they died suddenly and often broke their necks by
falling down cliffs in their bold mountain pacings, turning at
once into benevolent ghosts. The nomads speak of a heroic and
mythical Macedonian character called Roublouki, whose attributes sound rather like those of Alexander the Great, the
hero and darling of Greek folk tales and the only one of the
ancients to gatecrash the Karayiozi shadow-play.

Running, wrestling and racing each other on horseback are
favourite pastimes and they vie with each other in tossing
heavy stones, sometimes weighing as much as five okas. They
also compete in stealing-matches; jokes and tales about theft
abound. When a gypsy smith forged the nails for *Aï*'s cruci-
fixion, one of them is said to have been stolen by a Sarakatsán
—perhaps he meant to save *Aï*'s life by stealing all three. It
was rammed up his behind 'by the wicked Jews' in retaliation.
(A good deed seldom goes unpunished.)

As of old, good and evil omens are discerned in the flight of birds. They abhor eagles and vultures and all birds of prey that hover on high: they are minions of the Devil in league with all evil spirits; when these harbingers of peril hover above a caravan they are spying out the destination. Abomination for these birds also springs from occasional raids when new-born kids are carried piteously bleating into the sky. The nomads haruspicate from entrails; like most ancient and modern Greeks, they read the future in the markings on sheep's shoulder blades. Their sacrifices—*kourbania** as they are called—are frequent. A *pitta*—a kind of cake which is baked in a wide metal pan— is the rather gloomy fare at most of their feasts; they consider it wrong to kill and eat an animal without some ritual pretext. They only get meat when a beast is slaughtered for a sacrificial occasion, so they pine for these pretexts, even when the cause is a distressing one: their eyes kindle as the great festivals draw near. A wedding or the christening of a *tzellingas*'s son, the illness of one of their community, an epidemic among the flocks, the birth of a seven-month child, the arrival of an honoured guest, or the end of shearing—all these are an excuse for meat. They lay the sacrificial beast on a flattened branch with its eyes looking into the sun, then cut its throat and roast it whole on a spit. The act is surrounded by much mystery and they peer at the insides for mantic significance; at Easter, a bloody cross from the Paschal lamb is dabbed on the shoulders of children.†

* I have just read, in a Hakluyt Society account of a sixteenth-century Portuguese embassy to the Prester John, that *Qerbān* is the Ethiopian or Amharic word for the Host in the Monophysite Mass. Both must have been stolen from the Turkish word for the Moslem sacrifice of a lamb at the kourbān-Bairam, commemorating the sacrifice of Abraham and the ransom of Ishmael by the slaughter of a lamb.

† Badly wounded nomads are wrapped in the skins of newly killed rams. This suggests an analogy with the Aesculapian formula at the Amphiareion in Attica, and at Epidaurus, of making invalids incubate in ram-skins as a preliminary to their cure.

Fire is sacred and the hearth especially so: '*Aï* was born close to a fire.' Extinction is a particularly bad omen if it happens in the winter sojourn or in a wayside camp. They keep up a blaze during the twelve days of Christmas to fend off the Pagan Ones; a troublesome breed of the *Kallikantzaros* is abroad then; it is known as the *lykokantzaros*, the 'wolf-centaur', or, rather oddly, the *astróvoli*, 'starstroke'. A vast log burns slowly all through Advent to proof the settlement against the supernatural pests of the season; buried at the door of the fold on Christmas day, it keeps illness, Shadows and the Eye at bay. Women always give birth next to the hearth for the same defensive reason and the powers of darkness are driven off with foul-smelling smoke for the following twelve days. Miscarried babies, also the caul when a live baby is born, are buried under a flat stone beside the hearth; not in the middle, as people entering the hut must tread across a burning log, which, were this precaution not observed, would breed vampirism in the mother's blood.* Burial by the hearth 'charms the child back to life'; that is, it reincarnates it quickly in its mother's womb. They used to stow stillborn babies in a goatskin full of salt and hang it on a branch by the hut for forty days, then burn it lest it should take its mother with it. A cross is inscribed on a newborn child with burning wood, then quenched in water. The Fates visit the suckling's cradle three nights running; the usual offerings are left for them, and people with good souls can eavesdrop and expound their prophecies.

Sarakatsáns think Christmas is a private feast of their own, a reminder that *Aï* was born in a fold, laid in a manger and watched over by shepherds and their flocks. A host of pagan customs surrounds the Christmas octave. Some of them are very ancient observances connected with the winter solstice; others,

* Children are often born in the autumn and spring migrations. Alerted by the start of travail, the mother drops behind the caravan with a companion and the baby is born. Then they hurry to catch up.

more recent, derive from Mithras and the Unconquered Sun. (Mithraism in the Levant was only stamped out by St Basil in the fourth century.) A twig of mock-privet and another of ilex, heavy with acorns, are thrown into the fire on Christmas Eve to induce fertility among the flocks; the way they burn indicates how the lambing will go. A ewe is then sacrificed to Aï and the shepherds gather to eat and drink and carouse from hut to hut: rejoicings that put the swarming fairies, demons, infidels and monsters to flight and Antichrist himself. At dawn they cut and spread new grass for the newborn kids and lambs 'to sleep on fresh beds for the first three days of Aï', and the children all go down to the springs and drink in dead silence. They throw butter and cheese into the water and return with twigs of ilex, mock-privet and terebinth, which they cast into the flames. The sizzling of the green wood is called 'talking' and 'singing', and 'many kids, happy lambing!' is its burden.

At New Year, the *tsellingas* gives every shepherd a pomegranate which he breaks and scatters about the fold. Dried maize is ritually devoured on the vigil of Epiphany and the old women sprinkle the animals from oak and olive branches dipped in holy water. At this feast, too, the girls wash the year's smoke and rust off the ikons beside a spring with hanks of red wool and then hang them on branches.

The approach to Lent is the signal for further doings, especially the Saturday night and the early hours of Cheese Sunday which immediately precede it. The season gives rise to singular conduct not found elsewhere, and now, alas, largely extinct: transvestitism, the wearing of masks, the painting of faces, the donning of whiskers and beards of goats' hair—all this, with copious drinking and horseplay and cheerful frisking about among the wigwams, is still pretty current practice, a token of rustic carnival zest; but it can take a more stylized form. A heavily painted young man in a scarlet dress and long goat-skin locks is chosen as a bride and a whiskered and skin-clad comrade as the groom; others are rigged out as the priest, the *koumbaros* and the wedding guests. Then a cod Christian marriage is irreverently solemnized, followed by dances far less inhibited than are those at a real marriage. The bridal pair retire to a hut and, to the hilarity of all, comic simulacra of considerable indecency are enacted within. The groom is found wanting and thrown out; candidate after candidate enters with visible promise and each one is ejected in disgrace. At last a fitting champion is elected and, during a final mime of triumphant bawdiness, the entire company dance round the hut singing 'the Pepper Song', the dancers alternately banging their noses and their rumps on the ground with a see-saw motion I would give much to see.* Mock baptism follows a mock birth and mummers dressed as gypsies bang each other about with sacks full of ashes. Then a grave is dug and a shrouded nomad is buried with pseudo-pomp and covered with pebbles and twigs; candles are lit and dirges sung. But, with the approach of dawn and the first cawing of the crows, the dirges, the wails, the gnashing of teeth and the rending of garments take a more lifelike turn until at last the company seizes the corpse by the feet and, amidst general clamour, he bounds from the grave; and then, as day breaks at last, the whole clan dances a universal *syrtos* round the fire. These goings on are said to drive away drought and guarantee an abundance of leaves and grass for the flocks. Another resurrection play commemorates the feast of St Lazarus. A boy dressed as the corpse of the Saint lies in each hut in silence for half an hour. Next day, on Palm Sunday, a huge Lazarus-doll made of anemones and the other flowers, which at this season cover the mountains and the plains, is borne processionally by boys, who also carry huge baskets of flowers, to the tune of special songs and the clanging of goat bells. (These resurrection pageants might

* I tried to do so this year, in a *stani* near Nea Philippiada, not far from Preveza. There was lots of merrymaking and some mild transvestitism, but no more.

be the cue for specialists to seek analogies with the feasts of Adonis; they might be on the right track.)

The Lenten fast is observed with rigorous ferocity. In some folds, on Good Friday, the old women used to tie two sticks together to form a primitive doll with a ball of cloth for a head, on which eyes, a nose and a mouth were drawn in charcoal. Wrapping it in a shroud of rag and laying it on a table or a heap of stones, the women would sing, all day long and over and over again, the seventy couplets of the Song of the Consoler. This was to help the Blessed Virgin to forget the death of her Son, and, in so doing, bring consolation to everyone else for any bereavement they may have suffered. As night fell, they smashed the doll and threw the bits into a wood or a gully. We have seen that Easter, the crown of the Orthodox year, is a lesser feast among these shepherds; but they light a large fire to burn a stuffed effigy of Judas.* They arm their animals with their heavy bronze bells on the feast of the Annunciation—the 25th of March—'about the time when the first cuckoo sings'. They drive the flocks along to try out the harmony of their chime, and disarm them again in the evening; then children make the round of the huts ringing the bells and singing an Annunciation song in their honour; they carry a basket of flowers which their elders fill with money and eggs. Transient as mushrooms, each little gathering of huts has a calendar as strictly appointed and as scrupulously observed as the cycle of an ancient metropolis.

The feast of St George is most propitious for christenings. Babies born immediately afterwards often have to wait a year, but they are always named at once and, if they fall ill, they are given a lay baptism on the spot, lest, dying, they should turn into little vampires. The average family varies between five and fifteen children. Random fornication, adultery, divorce, rape and bastardy are unknown and, should a

---

* In Crete he is hanged and burned. In Hydra he used to be stood up before a firing squad and shot down amid execration.

case of bastardy ever crop up, death to all concerned is the only remedy. This is not only for reasons of morality; these ill-starred children are thought to be personifications of Satan; they bring a curse on the tents and the huts, and, should they grow up and die a natural death, a ghost rises from the grave and haunts the folds and blights the pastures.* Marriages are never love matches; apart from other disadvantages, they are thought to be unlucky, and often the couple are total strangers. Under the Ottoman Empire, girls were frequently married at twelve lest the Turks should carry them off to their harems. Between eighteen and twenty-five is now the usual age; it gives the bride plenty of time to prepare her dowry. Till recently, eight days was the regular period given over to a wedding: it involved eight days of statuesque immobility, silence and fasting for the bride and eight days of blinding carousel for the groom and his troop: an open season for every kind of prank and excess. In one famous case in the Agrapha mountains, the groom and his gang raided the bride's dowry and dressed up in her clothes. (It is interesting how often transvestitism crops up in these rustic saturnalia.) A recent and as yet unpublished source casts new light on the obscure drama of nomad marriages. A dozen pages back, I mentioned the sword in the Mani which, by sympathetic magic, is said to cleave asunder the bonds of fear and shyness between the two married strangers when they are finally alone together. In Sarakatsán embraces a blade plays a much more direct part. Alone in the hut, lying on cut branches padded with blankets—for there is never a bridal bed or a sheet and only the strictest minimum of undressing—the groom, with a sudden masterful swoop, leaps

* It is all the more remarkable, then, that Karaïskakis should have been such a one. Not only did he grow up and prosper, but he became *protopallí-karo*—a second in command of guerrillas—to the great Sarakatsán hero Katsandóni, and, when he died, inherited his band in the Agrapha. In the War of Independence, he was one of the great glories of Greece. This example might have softened their harsh prejudices.

athwart the bride, seizes her by the scruff of her neck and with
bared teeth and burning eyes, lays the edge of a dagger at her
throat; and, most strangely, this time-honoured stratagem
works: timidity boils up into hot blood on either side, confusion is ripped to shreds, the dagger is flung away, and the
union is driven home and fiercely clinched in a lightning tussle.
Apparently, too, the bride's days and nights of silent and standing vigil, with nothing to eat or drink and a veto on her leaving the hut, twist her insides into appalling knots and can bring
on permanent damage, and, on rare occasions, death. The
nomad approach to all feminine physiological troubles is dark
and primitive. They never undress, all exposure is anathema
and there is some truth in the village rumour that they never
wash. Oddly, they scarcely smell at all, perhaps because of the
time-stiffened carapace of clothing which encases them. The
source I have quoted was present at the death of an old Sara-
katsánissa. There was no undoing the thick geometric livery
in which she was cocooned, so it was torn open with a knife,
sending the bystanders reeling back like the bystanders on
ikons at the Raising of Lazarus. When she marries, a girl is
no longer a member of her own family and sometimes she
never sees them again; she is a slave to her husband and his
womenfolk, a stranger in strangers' tents. It was the rule in the
stern old days that no wife should address her husband in the
first years of her marriage; he, in his turn, would never call
her by name and many years and many births had to pass
before they would converse in public.

Charon* is a permanent presence and the most natural of
companions: 'He is always there,' they say, as Trappist monks
are supposed to do; 'remember him three times a day.' A
nomad that perishes in the mountains goes unhouseled and un-
aneled. If he should perish on the road—and their two yearly
migrations, geared to the slow gait of the flocks, may take
twenty-five or thirty days—he is laid across a pack beast and,

* The spirit of death.

after unloading, a candle is lit for him three evenings running and a cup of wine placed for his soul to drink from. If a *tsellingas* falls mortally ill, the bells are muffled, and if he dies, all the animals, even the bell-wethers, are disarmed in mourning. When men turn fifty and women thirty all the nomads, however hale they are, travel with their *nekrallaxia*, or death-change: a new suit of clothes to be buried in. Clad in its new attire, the body is laid pointing away from the sun on the floor of his hut or his tent with his hands and feet bound together. The young are decked with flowers, and rings are put on their fingers and a wreath round their brows; an ikon is placed at their head and an oil-dip at their feet. Relations watch over the dead all night lest a dog, a cat or a hen should walk over them. Finally the body is wrapped in a woollen blanket or two goats' hair cloaks and then borne away to burial on a bier of branches and leaves. As it is carried out, somebody breaks a wooden spoon, and no one looks back for fear of Charon, who lurks behind them in search of fresh prey. In the old days, they buried the body without a priest: 'he died unchanted' the phrase goes. Before the earth covers him, his hands and feet are unbound and his new clothes are torn, so that he may move more freely 'to where he is going'. If a shrine were handy, there they would lay him; but a shepherd dying in the mountains was often buried below a rock or on the top of a slope whence he could look down on his flocks, should they return another year. His crook was planted nearby and a woman's grave was marked by her distaff with its spindle and thread. She was buried with all her rings and chains and earrings and her festival array of gold coins. When her relations went to dig them up again, after three, five or seven years, to translate the bones in a box or a bag (as they do all over Greece), these trinkets were retrieved, washed and handed on to the children. Occasionally the bones of the skeleton are found to be rigid, 'not to be cut'; this means that the deceased has turned into a vampire, and it calls for priestly intervention and exorcism and the body is left another year to loosen up. Mourning for a dead son lasted for five years, and, to emphasize this sad period, women sometimes wore their clothes back to front. The two traditional hours of the day for the renewal of lamentation are sunset and the dim hour before daybreak when the first crows begin to caw.

* * * *

All this is a far cry from Daphnis and Chloe, a long way from Theocritus and Moschus and Bion. The shepherds of Virgil are farther away still, early milestones on a flowery path that meanders through the scenery of Herrick and Windsor Forest and Fragonard and Watteau to the Petit Trianon and Sèvres. The attributes of the Good Shepherd in the New Testament and the virtuous, rather simple image that the shepherd's calling conjures up in the west are equally irrelevant.

Shepherds that live in the plains have little interest. Those of the mountains are active, lean, spare, hawk-eyed men, with features scooped and chiselled by sun, wind, rain, snow and hail. They give more than an impression, during their occasional descents to the lowlands, of their enemies the wolves, and, still more, of eagles. They live beyond the reach of the authorities, and, as we have seen, the border between pastoral life and lawlessness is often vague. They spell, in fact, independence and inviolacy. Sky and space surround them. When I think of the whiskered, black-clad, booted, turbanned and bandoliered mountaineers of Crete, the word 'shepherd' and all its Western European associations no longer applies. Surrounded by half-wild flocks, they live in an anarchy of landslides and chasms and spikes of mineral. One chances on them suddenly, sitting on ledges of limestone above the ilex-belt and the clouds with rifles across their knees ready loaded against flock-rustlers from a hostile village or family foes bent on the blood feud. All over the Greek peninsula, these men represent exemption; and the most unhampered and nonconformist of all, except for their private and tribal straitjackets of untransgressable behaviour, are the Sarakatsáns. They belong to an older and shaggier scene than Arcadia and Greek Sicily, antedating the idyll and surviving the eclogue by near-eternities.

My first glimpse of them was in December, when I was nineteen, on the Black Sea coast of Bulgaria between Varna and Burgas; I saw them again early next spring in Macedonia, during the 1935 Venizelist revolution, after the battle at the bridge of Orliako.

For reasons too long to expound I was trotting eastwards along the Aemilian Way through the late March afternoon on a borrowed* horse with a friendly squadron of light cavalry in the victorious army of General Kondylis. We were slightly in advance of the main royalist army, which, with its cannon and infantry and trucks and waggons and baggage train, snaked away behind us in a long loop of dust. The march had turned into something of a carnival. After the musketry fire on both banks of the Struma† and the shelling from the hills behind (which I had watched from an empty stork's nest in the top of an elm) and a minimum of casualties on either side, resistance had caved in and our opponents were surrendering or dispersing eastwards. The day had culminated, for my new friends and for me, in the moment when they had drawn their sabres and thundered fast but bloodlessly across the wooden bridge of Orliako against an already vanished enemy in the nearest that any of us would ever get to a cavalry charge. Buoyed along the road by exhilaration and relief, my companions were singing music-hall songs from the Athens I had not yet seen. They unslung their carbines and took pot-shots from the saddle at the birds on the telegraph lines. Beyond the

* Borrowed, indeed, from my kind host at Modi, in the Chalkidike peninsula, Mr Peter Stathatos. It carried me over half Macedonia and much of Thrace, covering more than five hundred miles by the time we got back to his stable a month later.

† Alternatively Strymon.

heads of all these cheerful horsemen, on a high wooded ridge about three miles away, a string of those dark wigwams loomed that had intrigued me in December. I decided to defect from my companions for a night, and (one horseman moving faster than any army) catch up next day by short-cuts across the mountains. After light-hearted farewells and shouted rendez-vous to drink together in Serres and Drama and Komotini, I watched them jingle away, their spurs clinking against the steel scabbards of their sabres; then pounded off towards the hills and the far-sounding goat-bells.

I drew rein towards sunset at the heart of a raucous whirl-pool of half-wild dogs. A *stani* of about fifty huts was scattered among the trees round a spring. The place was alive with bleating and barking and bells, and gold with evening dust. Followed by their shrill young, the ewes and the she-goats were being driven with shouts and whirling crooks and the heckling of dogs and ear-sundering whistles into a semicircular pen of wicker and thatch on a steep slope. Once inside, they were herded towards a narrow lych-gate at one end where shep-herds seized them by their horns or their hind legs and milked them under protest, a few deft seconds for each, into bronze cauldrons. A strange arrival in the country unlooses a friendly hubbub of curiosity and inquisition in Greece. Not so here. The aloof drovers doubled the diligence of their tasks: shouts became louder, the milking more urgent. For the first time, I saw these Biblical men at close range; their black cloaks and their hoods gave them the look of Benedictines who had gone native. There were glimpses—rising from their dim looms and appearing for a moment in the threshold of the smoke-plumed cones and vanishing again—of the stunning magpie geometry of the women. An authoritative old man with a walrus mous-tache and an elaborate crook silenced the dogs and asked what I wanted. I could understand little of what he said: I had spent the few previous weeks, my first in Greece, in snowy Mount Athos, trying to convert imperfect ancient Greek into the rudi-

ments of the modern; and the Sarakatsán dialect was a further
barrier. When they had gathered that, in spite of patched
breeches and puttees, I was not a soldier—no sword or gun!—
in fact a foreigner from England, alone, and too young and as
yet unpredatory-looking to be capable of much harm, their
reserve began to melt. What was going on? They pointed at the
army glinting across the plain through a long cocoon of dust;
the note of a trumpet came softly to our ears. What had all
that noise been about by the Struma? *Bam–boum–boum? Rat-
tat-tat-tat? N'tang n'tang?* . . . I gleaned with surprise from their
half-understood questions that they had only the roughest no-
tion of what was afoot. They knew that there had been a *kinema*
—a movement or revolution—but little more. (Now it occurs
to me that they might have been prudently waiting to see
what sort of a bird I was; what tobacco I smoked, as the phrase
goes.) It seemed scarcely credible that they were unapprised
of events which had taken place so few miles away and split
the whole of Greece in two; as I learnt later, they had filled the
headlines of the world's newspapers for the whole of the last
week. Anyway, eagerly or ironically, they listened to my
stumbling, gesticulating, half-ancient and half-modern onoma-
topoea-laced pantomime of the tidings: the revolt of half the
armed forces in favour of Venizelos, the bombardments in
Athens and Attica, the advance of the government forces
through Salonica to the Struma river, the battle at the bridge;
how the mutinied battleship *Averoff* had sailed away to Crete:
how Venizelos himself had fled, probably to Rhodes, while
the Macedonian leaders retreated to Thrace and, perhaps, into
Bulgaria. A score of hooded nomads had gathered round us
leaning on their crooks and clicking their tongues deprecatingly
at the right moments; joined, in the background, by spinning
papoose-laden women and geometric girls and boys with kids
and lambs slung across their shoulders. When I finished, their
weatherbeaten faces, prompted possibly by the idiom in which
this *communiqué* had been delivered, had lost their sternness;

the blue-grey eyes of the beetling despot who had first spoken assumed a paternal look. '*É! paidí mou,*' he said, with a cheerful expression that clashed with his words, '*kakos einai o polemos* ... war's a bad thing, my child.' Then, over his shoulder, he said, 'The boy must be hungry.' I clambered down, a fair-haired descendant took my horse and another the saddle-bags and the saddle and a bag of oats and we headed through the dusk for the huts.

By the time we had finished the hot milk with black bread broken into it and sprinkled with hammered salt—their only food it seemed, which we all spooned in unison out of the same dish—about forty shepherds were eagerly settled, unshod and cross-legged on the spread blankets, nursing their crooks round a fire of thorns in the centre of the great domed hut. Half a dozen dogs lay panting in the doorway. The old man's oakapple-jointed fingers kept pushing a minute saucepan into the embers; and we hissed and gulped in turn over a single cup refilled with scalding and bubbling coffee. A shepherd sliced handfuls of tobacco leaves on a log with a long knife, then rolled them and genteelly offered the rough cylinders for the smoker to lick shut and light with a twig. The day's halt-ing saga, the oddity of its language evoking friendly laughter from time to time, was demanded all over again and discussed till long after it was dark.

Scarcely anything in the hut had not been made by the nomads themselves. Their household goods hung on pegs and on the looped and fire-darkened stumps of branches jutting from the hut's timbers. Some were neatly piled against the brushwood walls, or spread underfoot: few clues singled out our surroundings for any particular period in the last few millennia: guns, tools, choppers, adzes, spades, billhooks, cook-ing pots, saddles, harness, the tin frills round the ikons and, among a pendant grove of dried and shaggy waterskins, a gleaming branchful of new horseshoes. Otherwise, all was hewn and carved wood or homespun from the backs of the flocks. Strings of onions, garlic, maize-cobs and tobacco leaves hung aloft among the sooty twigs and the cobwebs. Higher still the osier-bound reeds of the thatch converged symmetrically in the apex of the dome. An agreeable and pungent aroma of milk, curds, goats' hair, tobacco and woodsmoke filled the place. The thorns on the fire crackled smokelessly; when a new faggot was thrown on, the flames made the tall hut dance in a gold hollow above a mob of shadows and highlit the bleached and matted hair and those faces shaped by the blasts of winter and the summer solstice. Their features glittered like the surfaces on a flint and whenever my eyes met any of theirs, a smile of welcoming friendliness answered.

I had begun to grasp, in the past few weeks, one of the great and unconvenanted delights of Greece; a pre-coming-of-age present in my case: a direct and immediate link, friendly and equal on either side, between human beings, something which melts barriers of hierarchy and background and money and, except for a few tribal and historic feuds, politics and nationality as well. It is not a thing which functions in the teeth of convention, but in almost prelapsarian unawareness of its existence. Self-consciousness, awe and condescension (and their baleful remedy of forced egalitarianism), and the feudal hangover and the post-Fall-of-the-Bastille flicker—all the gloomy factors which limit the range of life and deoxygenize the air of Western Europe, are absent. Existence, these glances say, is a torment, an enemy, an adventure and a joke which we are in league to undergo, outwit, exploit and enjoy on equal terms as accomplices, fellow-hedonists and fellow-victims. A stranger begins to realize that the armour which has been irking him and the arsenal he has been lugging about for half a lifetime are no longer needed. Miraculous lightness takes their place. On this particular evening the exhilaration was reinforced by other things: my mind was full of the events of the day, the smell of gunpowder, the cannon-fire at dawn which had achieved the innocence of fireworks as the bangs had echoed upstream; the first glimpse, in fact, of warfare. By then I felt I had almost taken part in the battle. The hoofs hammering over the loose planks of the bridge still rang in my ears and the songs on the long ride. On top of this came the beautiful ascent through the foothills, the sunset arrival at the encampment, and now, the voices and laughter and the gold firelit masks of the nomads in this hut in the dark mountains; the tiredness of limb, the feeling of being lost in time and geography with months and years hazily sparkling ahead in a prospect of unconjecturable magic—the fusion of all this made it seem that life, at that moment, had nothing more to offer.

But there was something more, and at once. Yorgo, the old man's grandson who had taken my horse and me under his wing (planning to guide us next morning on a short-cut over the hills to a point where we could swoop down on the army again), fished out a long bone flute. The music that began to hover through the hut was moving and breathless. It started with long and deep notes separated by pauses; then it shot aloft in patterns of great complexity. Repeated and accelerating trills led to sustained high notes which left the tune quivering in mid-air before plummeting an octave to those low and long-drawn initial semibreves. Notes of an icy clarity alternated with notes of a stirring, reedy, and at moments almost rasping hoarseness. After a long breath, they sailed again into limpid and piercing airs of a most touching softness; the same minor phrase recurred again and again with diminishing volume, until the final high flourishes presaged the protracted bass notes once more, each of them preceded and followed by a lengthening hiatus of silence. One can think of no apter or more accurate reflection in sound of the mountains and woods and flocks and the nomads' life.

Less lulling music cannot be imagined. But, overcome at last by the day's doings, I must have fallen asleep in the middle of it. Someone threw a cloak over me. I woke up an hour after midnight to find the hut in the dark except for the embers of the fire and empty of all but the lightly snoring patriarch the other side. Yorgo's hooded departing back was outlined for a moment in the doorway against the stars. A murmur of voices sounded in the cold outside as the shepherds, like monks before the Night Office, assembled for the first milking; this was the equivalent of matins in their pastoral Book of Hours. Then silence fell and after a minute or two, the faint stirring of bells and waking flocks was hushed by the returning currents of sleep.

* * * *

If *I Sarakatsáni* had been written then and if I had read it I would have looked more attentively at Yorgo's flute. Apart from the Greece-wide wooden flute, there are, or used to be, two kinds among these wanderers. One, with a deep and booming note, is a sawn-off gun barrel into which holes have been bored at the appropriate intervals. The other, says *I Sarakatsáni*, is made from the longest bone from an eagle's wing. We know that this bird is abominated. I think Yorgo's flute was one of these. After shooting the eagle and cleaning the wing-bone by burying it, he would have had to neutralize its wicked *mana* by leaving it under an altar for forty days of purification and exorcism before daring to drill the stop-holes and put it to his lips.

To the names of Hoeg and Hadjimichalis, a third must now be added, and this time, an English one. It was this spring, in fleeting refresher-visits to encampments in distant Epirus, that I first started to hear of 'Tzon' and 'Seela'. Always uttered with proprietary affection, these syllables were names to conjure with among the nomads. It took some time to connect these mysterious and almost mythical beings (who, the nomads told us, had lived for years among them in a hut they had built for them, spoke the dialect and accompanied their migrations) with John Campbell* the social anthropologist, and his wife

* Author of *Honour, Family and Patronage* (O.U.P., 1964). A study of institutions and moral values in the Sarakatsán community.

Sheila. But so it was, and, later on, I was lucky enough to find them in Athens. We talked about the Sarakatsáns for many hours, and, to deck this chapter, already reeking of larceny, I have borrowed several precious fragments of knowledge from their Aladdin's cave. Former books, and even these pages, have been at pains to prove some theory of historical origin. This makes a purely anthropological study of the Sarakatsáns, such as John Campbell's, of unique importance and one which students of modern Greece will neglect at their peril.

*   *   *   *

Almost the last Sarakatsáns I have seen are an encampment above Rizani in the foothills of the Thesprotian mountains in western Epirus. The poplars and the shingly bed of the blue-green Kalamos wind westwards through Byronic ranges towards Igoumenitza and the Ionian Sea. The outline of Corfu traverses the jagged V of the foreground mountains like the log that holds the jaws of a captive alligator asunder. It was windy and long after dark when Joan and John Craxton and I reached the little settlement of the Charisis family. Here the password of the name of Campbell did the trick at once and soon we were settled in our stockinged feet on the mat-strewn floor and on divans of blanket-padded brushwood and bracken beside the hearth at the end of the rectangular hut of Yanni the *tsellingas*. It stood among the cones like a small basilica of reeds. The end round the hearth was divided from the rest by a sort of plaited wicker rood-screen. The men all wore black home-spun jackets and tapering trousers; their wives, alas, had abandoned their angular and bi-coloured garb for the universal and funereal black of most Greek peasant women, from which only the stiff pleating of their skirts and the metal buckles of their belts now distinguished them. The strange outfits of the older ones were now stowed away and only produced and admired, once in a while, as precious but obsolete heirlooms. It was another sign of the times that this settlement had become a

semi-permanent winter sojourn. On the way, our torch had
picked out a couple of rows of onions and a few olive saplings:
fell totem-poles of impending stability. In another month they
would be migrating to their mountain pastures above the village of Vitza, high in the bleak and splendid Zagora mountains between Yanina and the Albanian border.

In spite of all this there was no mistaking the utter difference
of our host and of his many brothers and their wives and offspring—all of whom somehow packed into this bright alcove—
from the rest of the world; in dialect, manner, looks, bearing
and turn of phrase. Their hair was fair and unkempt, their faces
hollow-cheeked and aquiline, their blue-grey eyes wide with
alertness and high spirits. The decisive and delicate finish of
jawbone, nostril, nose, cheekbone and brow, all lit from below
like the faces of the apostles at the Feast at Emmaus by the
burning ilex branches and an oil-dip on an iron tripod, looked
almost preposterously patrician. (They were to make the citizens of the gloomy little town of Igoumenitza, afterwards,
seem plebeian and even brutish in our spoilt eyes.) The reckless
tempo of their talk, the dash, humour and ease and the friendliness and lack of fuss of their welcome, were high style indeed,
a text-book example of what Castiglione, in *Il Cortegiano*, calls
sprezzatura, the ultimate distinction of manners. The same held
good of the children—the shadows were argus-eyed with beautiful progeny—and the women who stood in the threshold,
frequently chiming impulsively and un-hierarchically into the
general chat. I noticed that only the husbands called the women
by their Christian names; the others addressed them by the
feminine form of their husbands', 'Yánaina', 'Andónaina',
'Nicólaina', 'Yórgaina': she-John, she-Antony, she-Nicolas,
she-George, and so on.

After bread and milk, the *ouzo* glass was soon whizzing
round at a great rate. To do us honour, they were bent on
killing one of two very young kids which had been brought
into the camp that morning. We refused (probably to their

real sorrow, as they long for an excuse to eat meat); firstly to avoid being a nuisance—mistakenly—and secondly, because we had seen the two kids with their dam in a small hut next door; attractive little piebald creatures that we had not the heart to condemn. We used Lent as a pretext, and they all turned to each other in wonder and sadness, saying, 'Look at that! See how pious foreigners are; not like us!' Knowing how severely they fast, and realizing too late how welcome would have been a breach excused or sanctioned by the laws of hospitality, we felt overcome with embarrassed shame at our hypocrisy, and wished we could unsay our refusal. Andoni, the *tsellingas*'s youngest brother, the handsomest and most spirited of the lot, showed us the cylindrical metal cover, a yard in diameter and exactly fitting the round raised clay ramp of the hearth, under which they baked their bread and their *pittas* and lambs and kids when they got them. We were joined by a dashing boy called Christo Gogola; wintering in a *stani* fifty miles away, he was a neighbour in summer, and had come to invite them all to his wedding soon after Easter. More ouzo circulated, and soon songs in praise of Katsandóni, Tzavellas and other Klepht heroes filled the hut. In time this turned into a session of story-telling, mostly by Andoni, in a thick and intricate dialect with a ruthless docking of final vowels and a slurring of those in the middle that was almost Russian. One had to strain every faculty to follow the drift.* They were fairy tales, rather like those of Grimm, in which talking snakes and wolves and dogs played a great part; there were shepherds who understood the language of animals, too, and enlisted the help of the kingdom of beasts—cocks, donkeys, dogs and swallows—in the settlement of their marital quarrels. Yes, they hated eagles, Andoni said when I asked him, and for the usual reasons. Cuckoos, pigeons and swallows were their favourite birds; they represented summer and the mountains, absence

---

* It took some time to get the meaning of the word he used for 'woman'. It is *gynaika* in ordinary demotic; Andoni pronounced it *y'niák*.

from which in the plains always seems like banishment: 'Once
the lambs hear the cuckoos, we know we're all right.' They
spoke of snakes coming to drink milk by the fire; you must
never hurt such a one—he's the *stoichion*, the genius or daemon
of the dwelling, just as he was in ancient times, and he brings
good fortune to the household. Apart from fairy tales, some
old men were said to understand the language of beasts, and a
case was cited of an ageing shepherd knowing exactly when he
was going to die by overhearing a conversation between a dog
and a cock outside his hut.

'That's all talk,' the *tsellingas* said, a man with a rationalist
turn. 'I've never come across it. Years and years ago, perhaps,
in our grandfathers' time. Not now. . . .'

Wolves, especially up in the Zagorochoria, were a permanent threat, you could see them trooping among the rocks
there in packs of twenty or more, and their howling struck a
chill to the heart. Anyone who shot a wolf cut the head off
and took it round the huts and even down to the villages, and
collected presents of money or eggs or wine. Andoni had come
upon a nest of wolf-cubs three years ago, and tried to bring
them up, in vain: 'Beautiful little creature, but you could tell
by their eyes they were bad. . . .' Jackals, too, were a danger
to young lambs and kids. There were lots of foxes, but they
only went for chickens, so they didn't worry about them. They
sometimes saw deer on the mountains, but you only got bears
much farther east, among the Koutzovlachs on the Macedonian
flanks of the Pindus. 'And then there are *two-legged* wolves,'
the *tsellingas* darkly announced. 'And they don't only go after
sheep and lambs. Some of them stole six horses of mine that
I had hobbled and set to graze on the hill over there. Perhaps
it was the villagers, we're always having trouble with them.
Or Vlachs. I chased them for days but never saw hide nor
hair of the horses again. They probably sold them in Yanina,
or even far away in Thessaly. To the Vlachs perhaps.' They
knew all about Shadowy Ones and Demons, *Skiasmata* and

Daoutis; they were a rotten lot. Andoni touched on something even worse. Through the sierras of the Zagora, beyond Vitza and Monodendri where they grazed their flocks in summer, runs the narrow and terrible gorge of Vichou, falling sheer in a chasm to great depths: a dark chaos of boulders and spikes through which, when it is in spate, a tributary of the Aoös river foams with a noise like faraway thunder. 'When you hear flutes and instruments playing down there,' Andoni said, with his long fingers spreading in the firelight to conjure up this baneful minstrelsy, 'violins and guitars and mandolins—there is no one there, no musicians at all, mind you—it's bad, bad, bad. Bad for the flocks, bad for us, bad for everyone. . . .' The others all nodded in thoughtful and melancholy assent, as though they were sorry the subject had been brought up. Yanina, the provincial capital of Epirus, which, though they had passed nearby with their flocks scores of times, few of them had visited, cropped up in their talk in bated breath, as though it were London or Paris or Babylon, a hotbed of untold luxury and a theme for wild conjecture and hearsay. But whenever their talk veered to their summer pastures in the Zagora, all their eyes lit up like those of the children of Israel at the thought of Canaan, and all spoke at once. That's where we should come and stay with them. What pigeons, what hares! You didn't need wine there—the air made you drunk; and as for the shade, the grass, the trees and the *water*—why the water came gushing out of the living rock as cold as ice, you couldn't drink it it was so cold, and you could drink it by the oka, and feel like a giant. . . . Words failed them.

They implored us to stay. They longed to enlarge on the wonders of their mountains and they were hot for news, too, about the outside world—they so seldom had strangers to talk to. 'Listen to the wind!' they said. But once more, as at Sikarayia, some tiresome reason beckoned us on to Igoumenitza and the sea. We got up to leave at first milking time in the small hours, bidden in chorus, as we emerged, to share their paschal lamb at Easter and to come to the Gogolas wedding and, above all, to visit them in the mountains. Half the company made ready to accompany us back to the main road, 'to keep us clear of the rocks and chasms'. The moon was hidden by a milky mackerel sky. A strong wind blew and a wrack of long silver-rimmed cloud hung in the sky above the sea and the ghostly shape of Corfu. From the hut next door we could hear the two kids bleating piteously. Andoni laughed. 'Listen!' he said, 'they know they've been spared, they're saying thank you! We'll kill a lamb when you come up to the Zagorochória and we'll shoot some hares too, and some pigeons, and some partridges. They are wonderful birds, fatter than the ones they fatten up in cages in Yanina for generals and governors and judges and lawyers and merchants and bishops. . . .'

* * * *

Next day we headed south through the Thesprotian mountains that tower from the Epirot coast between Igoumenitza and Parga, a secluded region full of stony villages with broken minarets and ruined mosques where Albanian beys and agas used to live in lordly halls among plane trees; many of the villagers talk the Cham dialect of Albanian. It is an almost inaccessible world, enclosing sudden grassy plateaux with wild irises and anemones and meadows of narcissi and conical hills and secret lakes with swamps and reeds and flocks of waterbirds. Beyond the steely eastern barrier, the mountains shoot down to the Acherousian plain, where, under the shadow of the great mountain stronghold of Souli, the Acheron and Cocytus meet, two rivers of Hades. Many Vlachs and Karagounis pasture their flocks in this hermetic region. Below a collection of dismal and moulting wigwams on a bleak slope we fell in with some Sarakatsáns from the northern Zagora with a large flock of black goats. Here and there among the flocks near the huts and the folds stood mysterious tapering piles of boulders about eight or ten feet high, over the top of each of which was draped a hooded nomad's cloak. They looked odd and sinister. We asked one of the shepherds what they were for.

'To frighten the wolves away,' he said.

'Do you get many of them here?'

'Ah,' he said sadly. 'That's the sort of place it is. *Tétios éinai o tópos. . . .*'

It looked it, too.

*   *   *   *

Now, a bit reluctantly, I must call a halt to these flashbacks and postscripts—high time, perhaps—and retreat several years, a few hundred miles in space and a score of pages, to the main thread of this narrative, from which we began to deviate among the tassels and the buttoned upholstery of the carriage rocking back with us through the Thracian darkness between Sikarayia and Alexandroupolis.

Not many minutes had passed before the guard worked his perilous way along the duckboard outside and climbed in; not to punch our tickets, but for a chat. We were his only passengers. He was a dark, jovial, round-faced refugee from Smyrna.

'Well,' he said cheerfully, offering cigarettes, 'did you find out where they hide their pots of gold? Any for me? I could do with it, at this job.'

We told him about the wedding. As I had already absorbed one or two hazy notions about the possibility of the ancient descent of the Sarakatsáns, I asked him what he thought about it.

'I don't know,' he said amiably, 'and, what's more, I don't care. I hate the ancient Greeks. We had to learn all about them at school: Plato, Socrates, Pericles, Leonidas, Aristotle, Euripides, Homer—*Andra mi ennepe, Mousa, polytropon os malla polla* and all that stuff. No, I don't *hate* them: that's too strong. But what have they got to do with me? Perhaps we descend from them, perhaps we don't, what does it matter? And who did they descend from, pray? Nobody knows. They were Greeks and so are we, that's all we know. I come from Smyrna—there's an ancient Greek city for you—and I may be more Greek than the Greeks in Athens, more Greek than your Sarakatsáns, for all I know. Who cares? *Greece is an idea*, that's the thing! That's what keeps us together—that, and the language and the country and the Church—not that I like priests particularly, but we owe them a lot. And those old Greeks, our celebrated ancestors, are a nuisance and I'll tell you why. They haunt us. We can never be as great as they were, nobody can. They make us feel guilty. We can't do anything, people think, because of a few old books and temples and lumps of marble. And clever foreigners who know all about the ancients come here expecting to be sur-rounded by Apollos and gentlemen in helmets and laurel leaves, and what do they see? Me: a small dark fat man with a mous-tache and eyes like boot buttons!' He laughed good-naturedly. 'To hell with them! Give me the men of the War of Inde-pendence, who chucked out the Turks, give me Averoff, who presented us with a battleship out of his own pocket, give me Venizelos, who saved us all and turned Greece into a proper country. What's wrong with *them*? If we weren't such fools and always quarrelling among ourselves, if we could have no wars or revolutions for fifty years—fifty years, that's all I ask—you'd see what a country we'd become! *Then* we could start worrying about the Trojan Horse and working out our rela-tionship to Pericles and finding out whether the Sarakatsáns descend from the ancient Greeks!'

I saw his point. For some, the ancients are a source of in-spiration and vague pride; the outside world sets so high a price on them; to others they are a perpetual irritation. What about Byzantium? that's where our traditions date from, a modern Greek may think; not from Pericles holding forth on the Acropolis, not from Diogenes's barrel or the tent of Achilles.

What's Hecuba to him or he to Hecuba?

CHAPTER 2

The Monasteries of the Air

The Greek summer dies slowly. October was melting into November, but only the earlier dusk, the sudden mists, the chill mountain air and the conflagration of the beech trees had hinted, as we advanced from Macedonia down the eastern flank of the Pindus, that autumn and winter were on their way. Here, where the Peneios falls into the Thessalian plain and saunters off down its broad and pebbly bed, not a leaf had fallen from the plane trees. Behind us climbed the Pindus, the road branching steeply westwards over the Metsovo pass to Yanina and Epirus. But to the east the Thessalian champaign expanded from the mountain's foot as smoothly as an inland sea, its distant shores of Olympus and Ossa and Pelion invisible in the early autumn haze.

In the flurry of impending arrival in Kalabaka and the screeches in Vlach as the truckload of migrants assembled their babies and poultry and their bundles, the Meteora went almost unnoticed. Only when we were nearly in the streets of Kalabaka did we gaze up at the tremendous spikes and cylinders of rock that soared for perpendicular hundreds of feet into the sky. There was nothing to halt the upward path of the eye, except, here and there, an irrelevant tuft of vegetation curling from the rock-face on a single stalk; or the straight damp smear of some spring's overflow, shining like a snail's track from the eagle-haunted regions to the outskirts of the grovelling village. One immense drum of stone ascended immediately overhead. Behind, separated by leaf-filled valleys, the pillars and stalagmites retreated in demented confusion, rising, curling and lean-

64

ing, tapering to precarious isolated pedestals (on the summit of one of which the wall and the belfry of a monastery, minute and foreshortened, could just be discerned) or swelling and gathering like silent troops of mammoth halted in meditation on the tundra's edge.

We gazed upwards in silence for a long time. Even the Koutzovlachs, blunted to this phenomenon by their migrations to and from their summer villages in the Pindus and their Thessalian winter-pastures, seemed lost in wonder. They only sank their glance at the cry of some fellow-villager making the month-long journey by road with the village flocks. For the streets were a moving tide of sheep, and the air was full of golden dust and baas and shouted greetings in the strange Latin dialect of these black-clad shepherds. Through the assembly of homespun cloaks and whiskers and crooks and the fleecy turmoil, a tall monk advanced. He was a head and shoulders taller than anyone else, and his high cylindrical hat increased his height to the stature of a giant. 'There you are,' the driver said. 'There's Father Christopher, the Abbot of St Barlaam.'

Could we stay at his monastery for the night? Of course we could, or two or three. His assent was underlined by a friendly blow on the shoulder and smile on that long saturnine face that radiated the wiry strands of his beard in a bristling fan. Half an hour later we were advancing westwards on either side of his mare. A satchel of provisions hung from one side of the saddle bow, a wicker-caged demijohn of wine from the other. In the middle, loose and easy in the saddle, puffing at his short pipe, talking, or quietly humming to himself, rode the hospitable abbot. The greetings of passing peasants, as we ambled westwards, prompted a response of humorous and squire-ish banter or an occasional mock-threatening flourish or a jovial prod with his great stick. The shadows in the astonishing rocks were broadening, and all, in the second village of Kastraki, was mellow and golden. Then the last houses fell behind, and as we rounded the vast central tympanum of conglomerate, a deep gorge opened before us, that dwindled and climbed along a chasm between the mountains. The white walls of the monastery of the Transfiguration appeared on a ledge far overhead and soon, the outline of St Barlaam. My heart sank at the height and the distance. It seemed impossible that we should ever reach that eagle's nest. . . . At that moment, the sun dipped below the serrated edge of the Pindus. The mountains ahead turned greyblue and cold and threatening and sad, and every trace of cheer seemed to die from the world. Those Greco- and Mantegna-like rocks might have been the background for the desert macerations of St Jerome, the Agony in the Garden of Gethsemane, or the Wilderness of the Temptation.

As night fell, the road insensibly climbed. At the foot of the rock of St Barlaam, a great square chasm, choked with undergrowth and rock, disappeared into the mountainside. 'The cave of the dragon,' the abbot said, pointing through the dusk, with a quiet and slightly grating laugh, 'safely stowed away under the monastery.' The road turned into a narrow flagged ascent between overpowering volumes of rock, winding among boulders and twisted plane trees and opening at last into a slanting world from which all glimpse of the plain was locked out. We were deeply engaged in this improbable geology. But a turn of the path led from our labyrinth into the most brilliant moonlight, and the mountains were suddenly robbed of their menace and their weight. All was silver and light and magical and miraculously silent. The plane trees were as still as the gleaming precipices themselves, as though each leaf had been rolled out of precious metal and beaten thin and then wired to the silver branches. Fathoms above, the reception platform of St Barlaam and the jutting tiles of its eaved penthouse projected into the moonlight in a galleon's poop, from which, like an anchor at the end of its cable, the great hook hung. The smooth sides of the cliff were not only perpendicular, but at many points they curved outwards and overhung their base, as naked of projection or foothold as the glass mountain in a fairy tale.

High in the void, the fabric of the monastery overflowed its monolithic pedestal in a circle of jutting walls and eaves and storeys.

The abbot drew rein and let out a roar. The echoing syllables of the name 'Bessarion!' dwindled and died down the valley. High above, on the ledge of the monastery, a pale spectacled face peered over the bar of the penthouse and a faint greeting came sailing down. 'Let down the rope and come and look after the mare,' the abbot's voice boomed up. The hook, taking two minutes on the way, revolved down to us as the thick steel cable was payed out. This, until the steps were cut in 1932, was the only way into the monastery. In those days, the traveller squatted in a net whose topmost meshes were hitched over the hook, which then floated gently into the air and, revolving and unwinding on itself, was slowly hauled up to the platform on a winch. The net, on its arrival, was fished in with a hooked pole and lowered to the boards. The traveller was then released. In the past century a rope as thick as a man's wrist was used. Answering the query how often it was changed, a former abbot is reported to have said: 'Only when it breaks . . .'

The Deacon Bessarion, breathless from his run down the steps, helped the abbot secure the luggage and supplies to the hook, unsaddled the mare, and led her off to the stable on the flank of the opposing rock, joining us then in the long climb. The staircase twisted back on itself again and again under the overshadowing rock from which it had been hollowed and brought us at last, panting and tired, to a heavy iron doorway. This opened, through a hole, into a dark stepped grotto through the heart of the rock. We rose at last into a courtyard of the monastery that was only divided from the gulf by a low stone wall. A spacious loggia, paved with square black and white slabs, lay at the top of another short ascent, built out at a recent date from the Byzantine brickwork of the monastery. A cypress tree, stooping in the wind, miraculously flourished there. The tiles and the cupolas of the church in the light of the moon, the patina and disorder of the monastic buildings looked domestic and human after the chaos of rock through which we had come up. Turning round, the abbot—a portentous figure on the top step, with his beard and his robes blown sideways in the sudden tramontana—opened his hands in an ample gesture of welcome. Then, leaning over the rail of a penthouse which shook with every gust of wind while Father Bessarion toiled at the windlass, we watched the burdened hook ascending. The luggage, the saddle and the demijohn were safely unloaded on the planks. Leading us into the chapel, the abbot lit a taper at the sanctuary lamp and the gold and silver of the iconostasis and the innumerable haloes of frescoed saints twinkled among the shadows. Making the sign of the cross and kissing the main ikons, the abbot and Father Bessarion retired. We followed them out into the moonlit yard. There was nobody about and no lights in the windows. The buildings appeared aloof and spellbound.

★　★　★　★

I half remembered the details of the guest-room, as Father Christopher turned up the wick of an oil-lamp, from the few days I had spent there four years before the war—the table with a glass bowl full of the cards of visiting ministers and prelates and Byzantologists, the sofa under the window, the faded Russian print of a panorama of Jerusalem. It seemed curious that anything as human and welcoming as this golden lamplit chamber could exist on so windy and austere a height. But soon Father Bessarion was cutting up apples and goat's cheese for a *mézé* to accompany the ouzo with which the abbot replenished the little glasses the moment they were emptied; and when we sat down together to a frugal supper of beans, the great demijohn was uncorked. By the time the two monks were lighting their pipes, we were thick in conversation about the war and the problems of Greece and the decay of Orthodox Monasticism. They made an interesting contrast—the shy, diminutive

Bessarion with his ragged cassock and soft skull-cap, the eager benignity of his eyes behind thick lenses, and the abbot's great stature, his shrewd and humorous glance, the lean sardonic features repeated on the wall in a gigantic shadow embowered in clouds of smoke. A thread of raciness and worldly-wisdom ran through his discourse. His family had been priests in Kalabaka for centuries. Quitting this traditional sequence of the secular clergy, he had become a monk of St Barlaam at the age of thirty-two, and then, which sounded unusually swift, he had been ordained deacon and priest and appointed archimandrite and abbot three months later. He was now seventy-six, and had never suffered more than a few days' illness in his life. His remedy for an occasional cold or a touch of fever was, he maintained, infallible—five days up in the mountains with the flocks belonging to the monastery, innumerable okas of wine, sleep every night in the shepherds' brushwood huts, and then—he extended his vast hands in the gesture of Samson embracing the columns of Gaza—he felt as strong as a giant once more. Father Bessarion, he hoped, would succeed him in his abbacy. Stroking the great tortoiseshell tom cat in his lap—there were two in the monastery, Makry, now sleepily purring, and a little black female with a white face and a red ribbon round her neck, called Marigoula—he described the monastery in winter, when the mountains were deep in snow and the jutting timbers stalactitic with icicles. 'Some of them are many yards long and more than two feet thick. When the thaw starts, they break off and tumble into the valley with a noise like cannon fire. Sometimes the clouds are so thick that Bessarion and I bump into each other in the church while singing the office. . . .' How strange and lonely this bachelor life sounded! Other monks were mentioned, but we only saw one during the whole of our stay, a man of unbelievable age who tapped his way slowly into church one morning with a walking-stick.

After the hard planks on which I had been sleeping in the villages of the Pindus, the bed in my white-washed room was a great luxury. When the wind dropped I could hear the deep level breathing of the sleeping abbot in the room next door, and, occasionally, a sigh of contentment. Then the wind began to moan once more round our tapering mattress of rock. Outside, the moon rimmed the tiled cupolas of the church, filling the empty slanting leagues that ran southward from these columnar mountains with a pale and glimmering lustre.

★　　★　　★　　★

At luncheon next day, the abbot's chair was empty. He had risen in the dark and ridden off to harangue some charcoal burners working in the monastery woods on the slopes of the Khasian mountains; a journey involving six hours in the saddle each way. We were alone with Bessarion. Outside the extreme severity of Mount Athos there seems to be no distinction of sex in the hospitality offered by Orthodox monasteries, and Joan was as welcome a guest here as any of the male visitors. Bessarion's large eyes kindled behind his glasses as he told the stories of the local saints of Thessaly—the miracles of St Dionysius of Karditza and the death of the patron of his native place, St Gideon of Tyrnavos, martyred just over a century ago by Veli Pasha, son to Ali, the famous tyrant of Yanina. His own life story was interesting enough. After our retreat from Greece in 1941, he had hidden two British soldiers for a number of months in the foothills of Mount Olympus, later increasing their number with a wing-commander who had baled out of his burning aircraft on to the Thessalian plain. When this became too dangerous, he escaped with them by submarine from Trikeri, south of Mount Pelion, to the Middle East, where he served with the Greek Army from El Alamein to the final Greek triumph at Rimini. But he had always longed to be a monk, and, on his release, he had spent a number of months in various Athonite cloisters and hermitages. Then he stayed for a while in the monastery of Dousko on Mount Khodziakas, but, feeling unable to settle there, removed to the Meteora.

'This is the place for me,' he ended up. 'I will always stay in St Barlaam.' He pointed to the blue waste of sky outside the window. Nothing else was visible. 'Up here,' he said, 'one feels nearly in Paradise . . .'

Vocations for the monastic life of the Eastern Church have become less frequent in recent decades. Now, they are very rare indeed. From the early centuries of the Christian era when the immense numbers of ascetics in the Thebaid were organized into communities by St Pacomius, Greece, Egypt and the Levant have always been a fruitful region for monasticism. It was for an international host of monks that the great St Basil, in the writing of his Rule (the forerunner of that of St Benedict which is the corner stone of monasticism in the West), legislated from his cypress groves on the Pontic shores. There is still only one monastic order, St Basil's, throughout the Orthodox world. It is divided, however, into two observances: the Cenobitic, or communal, in practice comparable to the life of the Benedictines; and the Idiorrhythmic or individual, which may be roughly likened to the life of the Camaldulese and the Carthusians. The latter live and eat apart, and only meet each other in church. But, in spite of the early hours and the frequency of the fasts, the life is far less severe and secluded than that of the orders of St Romuald and St Bruno; and the rigours of the Cistercians are unknown. Eastern monasticism prospered and proliferated through early Christian times and the Middle Ages, and there was scarcely a desert without a stylite or a mountain-top without a monastery. The highest peaks were usually dedicated to the Prophet Elijah, their elevation being symbolic of his assumption to heaven; but all the great monasteries of the East seem to have been built on amazing sites. The monasteries of Mount Athos, the volcanic cones of Cappadocia, the peaks of the Meteora, St Catherine on Mount Sinai and St Ivan of Rila in the southern Bulgarian heights, illustrate what was happening on a smaller scale throughout the Christian East. The humanism of the Renaissance failed to shake the

timbers of Orthodoxy, likewise the Great Heresy and the New
Ideas of the Encyclopædists. Those remote storms, which
rocked the Western Church to its foundations, were muffled
by distance, by an alien culture, and by Turkish occupation.
For the Turks, though scornful, were, on the whole, tolerant of
the religious life of the rayahs. Monasteries were allowed to
multiply. Their outburst of racial ferocity against the rebellious
Greeks served to strengthen the position of the Church, and the
Church, alongside the language, became the outward symbol,
the talisman, of Greek survival. (And so it has remained.)
Greek monasteries were thriving and populous communities
during the last century and for much of this, and I think their
decline is due to economy and legislation rather than to religious
doubt or controversy. The Russian revolution was a severe
blow to the strength of the Orthodox Church in general and,
in particular, to the revenues of many Greek monasteries. The
nationalization of church property in Rumania also stripped
them of many estates granted in past centuries by the hospodars
of Wallachia and Moldavia. The reforms of Venizelos caused
further secularization of conventual property; and war, occupation, burning by Germans, looting by Italians and sporadic
destruction by rebels have all done their work. Little remains.
Empty monasteries, ruined by neglect and disaster, gutted by
time and now, perhaps, used only as a fold for goats and sheep,
are as essential a part of the Greek landscape as the countless
fortresses left by the departing Franks. Many are no bigger than
a peasant's farmhouse. A few kind and hospitable old men still
linger in some of them, tending their poultry and half an acre
of corn or a grove of olive trees, only exchanging their
patched and tattered habits for black robes and a cylinder hat
when they ride to market on their donkeys.

Another reason for the lack of monastic vocations is the recent
impact of the materialistic civilization of the West, which for
the Greeks still possesses all the charm of novelty. The Greeks
are restless, positive, individualist and enterprising, and, with

what justice I do not know, they often accuse modern monks of being lazy. Monastic life in Greece, which, especially in Athos, has hardly changed since the early days of Byzantium, has little appeal for a generation enthralled by the appliances of the industrial West. Abstractions are rare themes in Greek conversations, and the contemplative life is profoundly alien to them. The change that has come about is thus the result of no intellectual struggle, but of an easy and automatic defection. In the West, perhaps because of the satiety, disgust and fear of the civilization it has engendered, a revival of monasticism is taking place. In Greece it is the reverse. Life, if it were not for wars and economic distress, would be complete without the anodynes of either religion (except in the villages, or in the towns as a national symbol) or philosophy.

The abbot, over dinner, gloomily echoed this sentiment of monastic decay. 'St Barlaam alone possessed three village-farms, but they were all lost under Venizelos in 1928. They're done for. We used to have thousands of acres too. . . . And, up till the war, hundreds of sheep and goats—hundreds of cows, sixty horses . . . the Germans and Italians and rebels did for them. There were hundreds of monks up here, battalions of them—battalions, *Mihali!*—in the old days—and a hermit in every hole in the rocks, like hives full of bees. . . . Look at us now! Ah, *parakmí, parakmí!*' The last word—'decline'—was to become familiar during the next few days. 'The young don't want us any more.' He poured out the wine pensively, and then, with his sudden rather Pan-like smile, repeated the words of the Greek Testament about wine making glad the heart of man, and touched our glasses with his own.

*   *   *   *

I was woken up in the small hours of next morning by the clanging of bells. The air reverberated with the semantra of the surrounding monasteries. The sound of these flat beams, each of them several yards long with a waisted middle for the monk on

73

duty to grasp with his left hand while he strikes the flat surface in sharp accelerating strokes with a little mallet in his right, carry for miles. The blows are scanned in threes in commemoration of the Trinity. Some say this instrument was invented by Noah in order to summon the world's fauna to the Ark. It made us think how similar to the Ark were these monasteries, each poised on its private Ararat. Just outside my window, the loud clank of the bell of St Barlaam drove away the last fumes of sleep. I remembered that yesterday had been the vigil of St Demetrios of Thessalonika and, shovelling on my clothes, I made my way by striking matches along the catwalks and staircases to the little church of the monastery. Only a few pale slits in the dark sky predicted a new day.

The church, which is scarcely larger than the oratory of a castle, is dedicated to All the Saints. A lowered sanctuary lamp and the tapers that lighted the breviaries of Father Christopher and Bessarion dispelled a little the surrounding shadows. But outside their narrow pools of light, all was dark. I leant in one of the miserere-stalls that lined the small semicircular bay on the right of the chancel. The corresponding apsidal concavity on the left was lost in gloom. The three of us were alone in the church. As Bessarion chanted the office, I attempted to follow the neumes and flexions and quarter-tones in the oriental-sounding monody by the dots and the rise and fall of the slender curves and pothooks in scarlet ink above the text on the taper-lit page. The hair of both the monks, usually twisted into buns and tucked under their headgear, now tumbled in long twists half-way down their backs. From below, the candle-light threw peculiar shadows on the waxen features of Bessarion and sharply defined the deep eyesockets, the fiercely bridged nose and quizzically wrinkled brow of Father Christopher, when, censer in hand, a magnificent colossus in splendid and threadbare vestments, he emerged from the altar. His deep voice groaned the responses to the higher pitch of Bessarion. At a pause in the liturgy, the deacon swung the pyramidal lectern round on its pivot, turned the pages, and began intoning the panegyric of St Demetrios. Makry the tom cat stalked slowly into the church and up to the rood-screen; the light from the central arch cast his elongated shadow portentously across the flagstones. Nimbly he leapt on the high, mother-of-pearl-inlaid octagonal table supporting the lectern and, curling his tail neatly round his haunches, sat gazing at the page. Without a break in the chanting, Bessarion pushed the raised paw away from the margin and gently stroked the tortoiseshell head as he sang; and slowly the long liturgy unfolded.

On the curved wall above Bessarion's small island of light, the extremities of frescoed saints were faintly discernible: the bare brown shanks of a desert father, the pattern of black crosses on the end of a patriarch's white stole, the bunioned swaddlings and thongs of a canonized peasant, the purple buskins of an emperor, a hero's red-gold greaves, the rusty swirl of a martyr's robe and an archon's pearl-sewn mules; all vanishing into the dark. Higher on the wall, at the end of elongated and invisible trunks, the embossed gilding of their haloes reflected the candle-flame in a dim theatre of gold horse-shoes. Only with the slow growth of the pallor of dawn through the eastern lunettes did they begin to emerge, one by one. Shaggy St John Prodromos, oddly winged, held his own head in a platter, half-nimbused with a rainbow of glory. St Demetrios leaned on his lance. St George was a centurion with sword and buckler. St Procopios swaggered with half-drawn falchion. St Govdelaas was attired in a red robe, a fillet con-fined his hyacinthine locks. St Anais ambiguously gesticu-lated in a cloak lined with a pattern of small black eagles. Higher still, more elaborate scenes were depicted: a beautiful Falling Asleep of the Virgin on a scarlet couch; a Nativity; processions of penitents labouring uphill and each bearing a cross; towering castles, sieges with the sky full of missiles, pitched battles and shipwrecks. Every soffit, every spandrel and pendentive and coign was peopled by a heavenly host that climbed at last to the great Pantocrator inside the central cupola. On the sides of two of the main pillars were frescoed the brothers who re-built much of the monastery in 1511; SS Nectarios and Theophanes, members of the archontic Apsaras family of Yanina. They were identical figures in dark hoods and robes and immeasurable beards, both gazing heavenwards and each holding in one hand a scroll and in the other an exact replica of the church in which they are painted. On the flank of a column of the narthex, dressed in a lemon-yellow dalmatic, a black scapular and a mauve cape, stood a tall figure haloed and darkly bearded, his flowing locks crowned with a royal or imperial diadem. He had been pointed out the day before as the Emperor John VI Cantacuzene—one of the founders of St Barlaam, my cicerone had explained.*

It was broad daylight when the service ended, and I wandered into the narthex, or antechamber, to look at the rest of the frescoes. The painting of the katholikon, or nave, was completed in 1548 and those of the narthex in 1566, by a certain Frankos Katellanos and by Father George, his monkish brother. It is strange how little, to an inexpert eye like mine, the

---

* I think this was a mistake, and that the fresco probably represents John Ourosh Palaeologue, King of Thessaly, virtual Despot of Epirus and Abbot of one of the Meteora; a man, according to chronicles, renowned for his holy life. This would explain the royal *and* the saintly attributes, only the former of which could be applied, even by the most charitable iconographer, to Cantacuzene. The error, if it is one, is understandable, as the Emperor, retiring at the end of his stormy career to a monastic life on Mount Athos, adopted the same conventual name as Ourosh Palaeologue, i.e. Ioasaph or Jehosaphat. (Ioasaph was also the monastic name of John VII Palaeologue.) The name is written beside the fresco. Also, *Antony* Cantacuzene was a founder of the neighbouring monastery of St Stephen, though his link with the Emperor's family is not determined; which increases the confusion. John VI was mentioned to me as a founder by monks in three of the Meteora and his fresco is designated as such. Chronicles, though, as far as I have been able to discover, do not record the fact. He was almost certainly a liberal benefactor, and may have visited the monasteries during his campaigns in Epirus and Aetolia in 1340.

Byzantine formula changes. Except for the Cretan renaissance, the same plastic technique prevailed, on general lines, for well over a thousand years, and a stranger would attribute these paintings to a far earlier date. Like the Orthodox religion today, Eastern iconography remained, until very late indeed, spiritually a part of the Byzantine Empire. Long, indeed, after Byzantium had ceased to exist as anything more than a sacred vision in the minds of the Greeks.

The pillars were again painted with saints' figures. Many of them were ascetics of the desert. The torsos of SS Agapios and Daniel the Stylites projected from boxes built on corinthian capitals, and the beard of a naked hermit aproned in pale green leaves fell below his knees in a swaying white stalactite like melted sealing wax. The nakedness of the more fortunate Makarios, identically bearded, was covered with thick smooth hair growing all over him in a suit of silver fox. Only his hands and feet emerged and his knees, which had worn holes in the thick pelt by constant kneeling. The walls were devoted to wild scenes of martyrdom—inverted crucifixions, flayings, impalements, draggings by wild horses, tearings apart by bent saplings, brandings, mutilations and, above all, beheadings. Phalanxes of splendidly clad figures knelt or lay prostrate with blood gushing from their headless trunks while their heads, still haloed, rolled away over the sad plain.

There was something immensely pleasing about the chapel of the Three Hierarchs hard by. Basilican in shape, with a low wooden roof divided up in a Mexican-looking pattern of black and white chevrons and faded orange, it was paved with mellow brick-coloured slabs. Led by the triumvirate of Doctors—SS John Chrysostom, Gregory Nazianzen and Basil of Caesarea—the holy company trooped round the walls with the only Koutzovlach saint bringing up the rear—Nicolas of Metsovo, who was burnt at the stake by the Turks in the market place of Trikkala. In the death-bed scene of St Ephraim of Syria, the saint lay swathed in a grey shroud on a wicker-work bier, and a fellow-ascetic lowered his bearded face for a valedictory kiss while another embraced his swaddled feet. An affluence of crutched elders streamed from the neighbouring hermitages, some carried on each others' backs and some in primitive sedan chairs. Next door, an army of virgins and matrons and censer-swinging sages encompassed the death-bed of St John the Divine. The Evangelist, tonsured in the manner of the Western Church, reclined in a pink and gold palace on a catafalque draped with green and mauve set about with tall gold candle-sticks. The faded colours of all these frescoes, the primitive technique, the arbitrary perspective and the literal punctilio of the detail, give them, although they were painted as late as 1637, an infinite charm. The insane mountains of the Meteora them-selves must have been the inspiration for the background to the life of Christ that surrounded the upper walls—those narrow pinnacles of stepped and toppling table-mountains, shooting, in the Betrayal, right across the sky from either side, and almost forming a bridge. Most memorable of all was the oblong cartouche containing the Last Supper. On benches of gold and polygonal stools Our Lord and the twelve apostles were seated in a ring, with an embroidered communal napkin across their knees. There is a faint glimmer of the Renaissance in the architecture of the background and in the yellow and black striped awning draped from gable to gable. A great round table is tilted out of perspective to display its burden of slender candlesticks, goblets of wine, cruets, egg-cups, dishes, elegant waisted ewers with curling spouts, knives, loaves of bread and, scattered here and there, large white radishes still trailing their bright green leaves. The company at the Mystic Feast, clad in gay togas and tunics of red, white, green and lilac, turn to each other in animated discourse with light-hearted gestures. The atmosphere is that of a symposium or a banquet from the Decameron.

I returned to the main church once more, catching a glimpse on the way of Bessarion kindling a fire of thorns in the sooty depths of the kitchen. A blaze lit up the lenses of his spectacles and the minute bronze saucepans for Turkish coffee with which he was busy. Beyond, over the lintel of the outer door of the narthex, the souls of the dead were being weighed in great painted scales. On one side, the righteous were conducted to paradise by angels. They floated heavenward on rafts of cloud, and the interlock of their haloes receded like the scales of a goldfish. But on the other side, black-winged fiends were leading the damned away haltered and hand-cuffed, and hurling them into a terrible flaming gyre. This conflagration, peopled with prelates and emperors, swirled them into the shark-toothed mouth of a gigantic, glassy-eyed and swine-snouted monster. Giant dolphins and herrings and carp, each one with human limbs sticking out of its mouth, furrowed a stormy sea in the background. Below were four compartments. In the first, the bodies of the writhing victims crawled with small white objects: 'The worm that dieth not', the legend read. The second was filled with tearful heads, their teeth bared and brows racked with anguish: it was called 'Weeping and gnashing of teeth'. Naked figures huddled despairing in a penumbral cellar in the third: this was Tartarus. In the fourth, labelled 'The Outer Darkness', the vague shapes of the lost ones were just outlined in a rectangle of murk.

Something pressed my shoulder. Looking round, I saw the great horny hand of the abbot resting there and, above and beyond it, his eye-brows raised high. 'There you are,' he observed severely, 'Hell' (he pointed at both in turn) 'and Heaven.' His index-finger was aimed at the ascending airborne swarm. 'Let's hope *that's* where you go.' As he turned towards the stairs, I thought I could divine the ghost of a wink. 'Up we go,' the abbot continued, 'Bessarion's ready with the coffee.' We halted half-way up the stairs. In my preoccupation with the frescoes I had forgotten to look down into the gulf. The lower world was hidden beneath a snowy mass of cloud that rose in a solid waste to the edge of the parapet. Only the monasteries emerged like outposts in a Polar wilderness, as if one could cross the half-mile to the Transfiguration on snow-shoes. The bridge, the tiles and the rotunda of St Barbara were just visible. The rest was snowed under. St Stephen and Holy Trinity rode high on the pale billows, and a bell sounded over the intervening distance like the signal of an ice-bound ship in distress. Towering high above this white desert, the giant blue monolith next to St Barlaam was hooped with three perfect smoke-rings of cloud.

*　　*　　*　　*

Distances between the monasteries are not so great as they appear from the plain. In half an hour the winding pathway from the foot of St Barlaam led us down to a shallow saddle, then up a steep hill opposite and under some plane trees to the foot of the Transfiguration. Three-quarters of the way up the rock of the monastery's pedestal, the cliff curves slightly back-wards from the perpendicular and a narrow bastion of masonry, growing in thickness as the mountainside recedes, climbs for a hundred feet so that its platform may overhang the pathway in a clear drop. The rotting remains of a ladder, jointed every few yards, hung from a hole under the jut of the monastery. Before the steps were cut, this precarious approach was an alternative to the net-ascent. It was withdrawn at night-fall up a channel of rock, and the foundation remained as im-mune as St Barlaam from the outside world. From below it looked just as forbidding and inaccessible. A flight of steps and a little doorway at the base now lead through a narrow cavern cut through the rock to the beginning of the stairs. They finally brought us, out of breath and with thumping hearts, into the entrance to the monastery—a vast arched and dusty place. It was traversed by mote-speckled sunbeams that fell on old wind-lasses and baskets and piles of winter firewood. Through the rickety floorboards, vertiginous vistas dropped to the dim vege-tation that still flourished on the unhewn rock face enclosed by the tower's three projecting walls. A slanting lane led away, through great pillars and high semicircular arches, over changing levels of flagstone and cobble into what might have been the purlieu of a town of immense age mysteriously poised here above the level of the clouds. But the narrow thoroughfares—except on one side, where the *Platylithos*, or the 'Broad Rock' of the monastic charters, swelled into a small hill—advanced into the sky. The monastery buildings, in spite of the four churches they contain, were crammed into a compass smaller than a village green.

Worm-eaten semantra and heavy iron hoops and arcs for the same purpose were suspended on chains under a colonnade along the flank of the main church—the Metamorphosis, or the Transfiguration of Our Saviour, from which the monastery, with the name of Meteora (since extended to include the entire mountain colony), takes its name. It is not only the greatest of the monasteries, but it is built on the highest rock, and it enjoyed or arrogated to itself some sort of primacy over the rest of the Meteora: a privilege or pretension that was contested now and then by sharp and unseemly battles between monks of the rival foundations.

Scholarship and the recording of history played a less important part in Eastern monasticism than it did in the West. Records about the Meteora are scarce. Contemporary documents are surprisingly uninformative, and the outlines of their story must be pieced together from the occasional notes of a more historically-minded monk in the mildewed monastic libraries and from the Synodal Judgements and, above all, the chysobuls of founders and benefactors. These voluminous documents inscribed on parchment and appended with heavy seals, are drawn up in Rumanian in the case of Moldo-Wallachian voivodes, and those—the vast majority—in Greek are a tortuous maze of Byzantine abbreviations and ligatures ending, when they are from an emperor, with complex and calligraphic vermilion signatures sprinkled with gold dust and cinnabar.

The first ascetic of the Meteora appears to have been the hermit Barnabas who, in A.D. 985 founded the little skete of the Holy Ghost in the rocks above Kastraki, something over a mile south of St Barlaam. Many zealots followed his example during the eleventh century, and, by 1162, they had formed a miniature Thebaid centred on the skete of Dupiani or Stagoi,* where the scattered athletes of God would congregate for Mass on Sundays. In the fourteenth century, monasteries began to appear on the loftier summits and the Meteora slowly changed into the phenomenon they have remained ever since. Perhaps the first impulse was the advent of St Athanasios the Meteorite. The details of his life are based principally on an anonymous and undated manuscript from the library of the Transfiguration. He was born in 1305 in Neopatras on Mount Othrys. Captured by the Grand Company of the Catalans who were ravaging central Greece, he travelled to Athos, Byzantium and Crete. Finishing his novitiate in Mount Athos under the tutelage of a venerable monk called Gregory, Athanasios and his instructor left the Holy Mountain in flight from an invasion of the corsairs that infested the Grecian coasts. Drawn by reports of the many miracles performed at the foot of the Meteora, 'which', the Bishop of Verria informed the pilgrims, 'are only inhabited by the vultures and the crows', and by the triumphs of asceticism achieved there, they wandered south and established themselves in a cave on the summit of the Stylos, or the Rock of the Column, where they devoted themselves to prayer and weaving and basket-work. These rigours, however, proved too fierce for the elderly Gregory, and Athanasios conducted him over the mountains to the refuge of Salonica, returning alone to find that the monk who had replaced him on the Stylos had died there, his body remaining, as he had wished, to be devoured, like that of a Parsee, by the birds. A scavenger with a

* Stagoi, the hierarchic name of the bishopric of Kalabaka (cum Trikke, or Trikkala), is contracted from the words eis toushagious, ' all the Saints'.

finger in its beak was the first sight that greeted the returning saint. He then settled on the crest of the rock where his monastery now stands, surrounding himself shortly afterwards with fourteen monks, and building a church there with funds supplied by 'a powerful personage belonging to the race of the Triballes'. The first great monastery had been established.

The Triballes, in the high-flown language of Byzantine documents, are the Serbs. The decline of the Byzantine Empire, during the middle of the fourteenth century, had gathered speed. The wars of the rival emperors, John V Palaeologue and John VI Cantacuzene (during which the Turks made their first ominous entry into Europe), had left its western regions exposed to the ambitions of Stephen Dushan, the Serbian kral, who occupied north-western Greece. By 1345, nearly the whole of Thessaly was in his hands. Mimicking the style of the Empire which he hoped to overcome, he placed his general Prealoumbos as viceroy in Trikkala with the Byzantine title of Caesar.* It seems likely that this was the powerful personage who backed Athanasios. On the death of Stephen in 1355, his half-brother Symeon Ourosh usurped the Kingdom of Thessaly from Stephen's son. The advance of the Turks in the Balkans soon cut off the old Serbian Kingdom from its newly acquired Greek provinces and Symeon remained King of Thessaly with Trikkala, that dusty lowland town by the winding Peneios, as his capital. To add colour to his imperial aspirations he adopted the family name of his mother (Palaeologue again: she was Maria, daughter of the Despot John, brother of the Emperor Michael VIII who delivered Constantinople from the Latins) and married a Greek princess, Thomaïs, the daughter of John II Ducas, the Despot of Epirus. The children of this marriage were virtually Greek and they appear to have been eager to forget their barbarian origins. The daughter, Maria

* No longer the exclusive appanage of the Emperor, but second in the imperial hierarchy.

Angelina* Ducaina Palaeologina, reigning as Despotess of Epirus, discarded her Serbian patronymic, preferring to stiffen her Epirote dignity with the names of three imperial dynasties acquired in the female line, which she occasionally further reinforced with that of a fourth, Comnena. Her brother, John Ourosh Ducas Palaeologue, succeeded to his father's crown in 1371. But, long before his accession, he had become a monk in Athanasios' monastery of the Transfiguration, and there, except for a short period at Mount Athos, he remained under the name of Father Ioasaph till his death. Resigning the transactions of his Thessalian kingdom to the Caesar Alexis Angelos, he frequently advised his sister on the conduct of her thorny Despotate beyond the watershed of the Pindus. He seems to have been as wise as he was holy, and it is to him as much as to St Athanasios that the Transfiguration owes its pre-eminence and its beautiful buildings.

SS Athanasios, Ioasaph and Barlaam (who established himself on the neighbouring peak at the same period) are the three dominant figures in the monastic triumphs of the Meteora. The saintly king died long after the Turks of Sultan Amurath had defeated the Serbs, his distant and putative liegemen, on the field of Kossovo;† long after Bajazet the Thunderbolt had annihilated both Greek and Serbian sway in Greece.‡ Several different dates are ascribed to his death, but it must have been within a decade or two of the final destruction of the Byzantine Empire in 1453. The new-moon and horse-tailed banners were slanting across Europe.

The original church begun by St Athanasios and completed by Father Ioasaph now forms the hieron, the part behind the rood-screen reserved to the officiating priest. The main body of the church—the katholikon and the narthex—was reared

* Angelina is not a Christian name, but the feminine of Angelos, which is also the surname of a former Byzantine imperial family. Ducaina and Palaeologina follow the same process.

† 1389. ‡ 1393.

nearly two hundred years later in the reign of Suleiman the Magnificent, Queen Elizabeth's contemporary. Built in the Athonite cruciform style with the transepts ending in apses lined with wooden stalls, it is much larger than the other churches of the Meteora. The height of the pillars, and of the central dome of the Pantocrator and the shafts of sun falling through its numerous windows on the predominantly blue background of the beautiful frescoes leaven the thick Byzantine masonry to an almost miraculous lightness. We were joined in our scrutiny of the icons by a sad and elderly monk who seemed to derive little pleasure from our visit. We accompanied him to the old hospital and a fine barrel-vaulted refectory. The long table was smashed and the floor was littered with rubbish, but, in a bay at the end, a massive circular table of stone marked the seat of the abbot and his symbouloi. It had plainly once accommodated a large number of monks. Asked if it was ever used now, the old monk tilted his head back in the Greek gesture of negation.

'What could we do with such a place? There are only four of us left . . . *Parakmí, parakmí . . .*'

His fellow-monks were wavering at the doors of their cells in a long gallery; with one exception, they were aged and fragile men. One, seeing that we were about to leave, ambled indoors and returned with glasses of raki and half a dozen walnuts lying with their shells already broken in the palm of his hand.

'There, my children. I'm sorry we can do no better; but times have changed. Once . . .'

The ghost of poverty inhabited the beautiful place, but the tradition of hospitality is slow to disappear. His message of decay accompanied us on our journey to the windy edge of the rock, where a few autumn crocuses flourished round a little pavilion.

We regained St Barlaam by another path over a smooth plateau of rock where we found Bessarion chasing the abbot's mare, which had broken loose. Haunted by visions of the poor animal plunging into the gulf, we helped him round her up and lead her back to her stall and we all three climbed to the monastery together.

Seated with the two monks by the window of the guest-chamber that evening, I asked how St Athanasios the Meteorite could possibly have ascended the Broad Rock. Bessarion looked at the abbot and then out of the window.

'They say,' he observed tentatively, 'that he flew there on an eagle's back. . . .'

Father Christopher had opened his snuff-box. He prepared the snuff himself from powdered tobacco and herbs and spices. It smelt like pot-pourri.

'That's what they say,' he repeated absently, and took a large pinch.

Bessarion began to describe his journey from Greece to the Middle East by submarine.

*   *   *   *

The Convent of St Barbara, or, as it is more commonly styled, Roussanou, projects from the side of the basin which is roughly girded by the taller spires of the Meteora, on a sharp leaning blade of rock. It is as compact as a swallow's nest. The masonry and the mineral imperceptibly blend and the convent sails into the air like a little Danubian keep; expanding below the eaves in a circuit of beam-stayed wooden balconies, the tiled upheaval of its roof swelling in the centre to an elegant cupola. We descended in a wide half-circle from the foot of St Barlaam and climbed down the hillside through thickets of thyme and cystus and tamarisk. The cleft between the crag of Roussanou and the adjacent peninsula of the massif is spanned by a narrow iron bridge running like a diving board from the top of a steep triangle of stone steps, built out from the moun-tainside, to the monastery door. Father Chrysanthos, the last monk of St Barbara, died there long ago and it is now the home of a minute company of nuns. The two that were living there greeted us as we entered and led us into a golden empty expanse of low wooden ceilings and undulating floors whose worn planking was suspended from wall to wall as uncertainly as a cobweb. Everything trembled at the softest footfall. The light streaming through the wide balconied windows and from the chinks in the woodwork resembled that of the deck of a sailing ship under an awning. Banistered ladders climbed to still higher regions overhead and disappeared through hatchways into the bowels of the convent. The chapel, a small flagged chamber with a domed square rising on four pillars to the saucer shaped hollow whose tiled convexity we had seen from above, is embedded in the timbers of the conventual buildings. Judgements and martyrdoms, more bloody than any I have ever seen,* flowed across the narthex walls. But inside the whole universe was displayed. Seas and mountains unfolded, forests stocked with strange denizens, an entire zoo: peacocks with their tails spread, camels, lions, antelopes, serpents, wyverns and hippogryphs. Dragons traversed the sky trailing smoke like skywriting from their nostrils and the elements were represented by dripping icicles, storm-clouds, hail, rain, ice and snow. Equinoxes, eclipses, the sun, the moon and the planetary system joined in a diminishing ring above the girdle of the zodiac. The regions of paradise, peopled by thrones and dominions and powers and many winged seraphim ascended the drum of the cupola in celestial zones to the tall golden figure of the All-Powerful.

In spite of their simplicity and gentleness, there was little trace of Western conventual aloofness, of the recluded and downcast custody of the eyes, about the two nuns of Roussanou. The faces under the black head-kerchiefs were round as apples, and they addressed one as 'my child' in the familiar and friendly Greek fashion. Mother Ekaterini, the abbess, settled

* Except perhaps those in the church of St Nicholas on the lake-island of Yanina.

in one of the sunny window seats and unfolded her sewing with a sigh while Sister Kyriaki prepared a meal on a little table—*pitta*, a salad of onions and tomatoes, and, on each folded napkin, a loaf of bread with its crust embossed with a cypher of our Lord's initials and St Constantine's cross from the Milvian Bridge with its message of victory. Smoothing out the needlework in her lap, Mother Ekaterini told us that the monastery had been founded five hundred and sixty years before by a Princess Marina of Russia. She knew little about her, except that she had fled from Russia when she was still a beautiful girl and settled here as a nun for the remainder of her life. I wondered what descendant of Rurik or great boyar's daughter of Kiev or Novgorod she might have been.*

While we ate, they asked us about England; was it across the sea? Was America part of England, as Thessaly was a part of Greece, or was it the other way about? Sister Kyriaki wondered whether there were any nuns in England. Before we could answer, the abbess spoke in tones of gentle admonition.

'Of course there are, thousands and thousands of them. If they have them in a small country like Greece, do you think they wouldn't have them in a great place like England?'

Far below the window the road unravelled through the rocks to the edge of the plain, of which only a fragment appeared through a causeway of the Meteora. The small monastery of St Nicholas, ruined and empty and St Barlaam's first sojourn, mouldered on their spikes. Then the rocks came to an end except for a sudden resurgence by the strand of the Peneios, where a massive blue-grey outcrop rose like a basking whale.

---

* The abbess's words were the only mention of her I ever found. Perhaps I have not come across all the sources. The records say that Roussanou, the faint Russian sound of whose name the Abbess attributed to this problematical hyperborean foundress, was instituted by the monks Nicodemus and Benedict—a very strange name for an orthodox monk—in 1380, and restored in 1545 by two monks from Yanina, Maximos and another (and final) Ioasaph. It seems always to have been a male foundation.

An eagle, soon followed by his consort, floated languidly round the pedestal of St Barlaam, their motionless feathers almost touching the precipice. The midday sun struck their still wings and stretched their long perpendicular shadows down the rock face. I repeated Bessarion's words about the trajectory of the Meteorite. Sister Kyriaki was astonished. 'Just fancy,' she said, crossing herself in wonder, 'on the back of an eagle!'

'Well, he was a saint,' the abbess said, threading a needle with authority. 'How should he travel?'

*   *   *   *

To a stranger accustomed to the discipline and the quiet activity of the monasteries of the Catholic Church (those rigours destined to organize monastic life so that its central purpose may be fulfilled in greater peace and silence), much in the monachism of the East, and especially in these reduced communities on the Meteora, seems haphazard and improvised. When one remembers that scarcely a dozen monks now inhabit a region which was once the home of many hundreds, it will become more understandable. Foreign travellers observed the symptoms of decay a hundred years ago.* Now, even in the inhabited monasteries, all that remains is a handful, perhaps only a couple, of monks, one or two peasants devoted to the service of the monasteries, and a tiny floating population of shepherds. The best impression of Orthodox monasticism as it must have been in its apogee (though even here the symptoms of decline are not lacking) must certainly be sought in the great monasteries on the slopes of Athos and from the dwellers in the solitary hermitages, approachable only by rowing boat and rope-ladder, excavated in the face of the mountain high above the Aegean waves.

*   *   *   *

* *Monasteries of the Levant* by the Honble Robert Curzon and *Excursion dans la Thessalie Turque en 1858*, by Leon Heuzey, are the most interesting of the numerous accounts.

The monastery of St Stephen is the most accessible of the Meteora, and for this reason it may have been the first of the great rocks to harbour an ascetic, a twelfth-century hermit called Jeremiah. Though it is one of the highest, only a little draw-bridge separates its ivy-mantled walls from the bulk of the mountain. A climbing cobbled pathway led us obliquely from the entrance under a dark vault into the courtyard. The place, except for the youngish monk who had answered our tugs on the bell-wire, seemed deserted. The cobblestones, the wooden galleries and the fig tree with its fading leaves were drowned in sunlit sleep and only towards the evening did we explore the buildings. The late eighteenth-century church of St Charalambos appeared strangely naked and blank after the jostling frescoes to which we had grown accustomed. There was nothing there except the fine Epirote woodwork of the iconostasis and the throne, where censer-swinging mannikins and cranes with vipers caught in their bills could be singled out from the hewn foliage. The church is the guardian of the head of St Charalambos, an inch of whose pate is visible through the silver-work of a reliquary. This resembles, in craftsmanship, the casket in which the monks of the Transfiguration preserve fragments of the True Cross, the Sponge and the Winding-Sheet. The Meteora are rich in relics, vestments, mitres and jewelled crosiers and also in manuscripts and chysobuls and codices, many of them of great beauty. I remember studying with wonder the detail of their illuminations before the war. Most of them remained hidden for a long time in their war-time caches; some are in the National Library.*

The old church of St Stephen, after the whitewashed planes of St Charalambos, seemed immensely old: a dark, low basilican chamber of which the walls were once entirely covered with ochreous and smoky paintings. Wall inscriptions speak of an

* When Thessaly was liberated from the Turks, the monks and the sur-rounding villagers rose in arms to resist the attempts of the Athenian authori-ties to transfer their manuscripts to Athens.

early monastic benefactor, Mitrophanes, and of a late restorer living in the early sixteenth century, called John of Kastraki. The church must have been built in the fourteenth century, successor to the original foundation of Jeremiah. Tradition maintains that its great benefactor, Andronicus Palaeologue the Younger, stayed here a while in 1333. The monastery and church were looted by Italians who carried away the bells; German machine-gun bullets and mortar bombs, fired from the plain on the suspicion that the monastery was harbouring guerrillas, pierced the east wall of the church and destroyed nearly all the fourteenth-century frescoes, the fragments of which, with the broken woodwork, now lie about the floor in pathetic heaps of rubble. The frescoed lineaments of the founder, Antony Cantacuzene, are one of the few mural survivors of this attack. The outlines of the shadowy prince emerged by the light of a taper held in the abbot's wavering fingers.

The pale face and wide open eye of the abbot, in their setting of dark hair and beard and eyebrows, were full of indefinable distress. I wondered, as we followed the slight shuffle of his limp from the pretty white guest-chambers to the lamp-lit refectory, what the cause might be. Father Anthimos had been abbot for a number of years, and his kind face lit up at any word of praise for his monastery. Towards the end of supper, he told us how, during the fighting a few years before, the monastery had been attacked by a body of E.L.A.S. guerrillas; owing, perhaps, to the presence of a post of three gendarmes in the monastery. The iron gate by the bridge was first blown open with a bazooka. Then the invaders swarmed in, seizing two of the gendarmes and cutting their throats at once. The third ran across the open space outside the monastery to throw himself over the precipice, but, brought down by a rifle wound, he met the same fate as his colleagues. The abbot was stripped naked and beaten and one of his legs was smashed with a blow from a rifle butt; and his foot remains twisted at a strange angle. In other ways, this experience had plainly left lasting effects on the abbot. He covertly dabbed his eye with a napkin as he finished the story.* Then, with hardly a pause, he began a long account of the origin of the legend of the Evil Eye when Solomon was building the great temple of Jerusalem.

St Stephen is the easternmost of the Meteora, and the Thessalian plain spreads eastwards from the foot of its rock in an expanse that no eminence interrupts. Seen from the ledge of the monastery next morning, it looked unending. Its eastern limits were the haunt of the centaurs and of the Myrmidons of Achilles, and Trikkala (invisible at the end of the unwavering road and the loops of the Peneios) sent its contingent to Troy. It has always been a battlefield. Caesar defeated Pompey on its southern limits, the Byzantines marched and countermarched, the Bulgarians swamped it in a flood of Slavs, Vlachs proliferated. Not long after the first hermits settled, Bohemond defeated the Emperor Alexis Comnene here, shortly after Bohemond's countrymen had conquered England. Franks and Teutons and Catalans imported the alien and cumbersome apparatus of Western feudalism. For over a century, it was again the scene of the wars and the jangling dynastic claims of caesars and despots and sebastocrators and krals. The Turkish advance was only halted by Bajazet's defeat in Asia Minor by Tamburlaine; and then the Ottoman tide swept forward. The themes of Byzantium were hewn into pashaliks and vilayets and sanjaks, submerging the Greeks, except for the irredentist struggles of the armateloi and the klephts, for over five hundred years. I remember peering up at the Meteora from a Bren-carrier in our harassed retreating column in the spring of 1941, and thinking, in spite of the plunging Stukas overhead, how remote and detached they looked, and how immune. The verse I heard in St Wandrille returns to my mind. *Altissimum posuisti refugium tuum, et non accedet ad te malum.* . . . And indeed, since the earliest anchorite, for almost a thousand years of tur-

* I heard it again next day from the inhabitants of Kalabaka.

moil and war and occupation, no harm came near them. Only in the last twenty years have they been touched by the high-leaping waves of universal trouble.

*　　*　　*　　*

The last day in the Meteora was nearing its end. The steep path down to Kalabaka and the lower regions uncoiled from a dead tree at the foot of the rock. But it was hard to leave the last of the monasteries. Holy Trinity, with its row of white columns and arches, the grey confusion of walls and rose-coloured tiles, the dome and the tall dark mast of a cypress tree above the deep ravine, looks, more than any of its fellows, like the structure of a dream. None of the monastic rocks can have been harder of access, and speculation as to how the first monk, the almost legendary Dometios, first scaled it, would be a re-statement of the conundrum of St Barlaam and the Transfigura-tion. The landing stage and its hook overhang a narrower chasm than any of the others and the cutting of the steps, during the episcopate of Polycarp of Trikke and Stagoi, must have been an even harder feat. Nobody knows when the monastic church was built, nor when the little chapel of St John the Baptist was scooped from the rock, though the names of sub-sequent restorers and benefactors—Parthenios, Damascene and Jonah—are commemorated on the walls. The iconography is dark and indistinct.

Holy Trinity was the poorest of all the monasteries of the Meteora. It is uninhabited now. The monks left before the war, and none has returned. Some of the doors of the empty cells hung open. Others were closed with twists of wire, and last year's leaves blew about the wide wooden halls. In the little garden, an old shepherd with bright blue eyes, long matted hair, and a spade-shaped beard like that worn on vases by Ajax and Agamemnon, was sitting on a rock with a tall crook over his shoulder. He was shod in cowhide moccasins and dressed in a kind of sheepskin hauberk caught in by a belt. He looked as wild and solitary as Timon of Athens, but over the rare luxury of a cigarette he admitted that he got lonely in Holy Trinity, and added that he was about to abandon the flocks to become a postulant of St Stephen. Delving into a past that seemed almost as remote and nebulous as that of the monastery's foundation, he recounted his experiences during a short-lived emigration to Louisiana as a hand in the municipal slaughterhouses of Baton Rouge.

From the plain's brink at St Stephen, we had turned back into the heart of the monastic regions. Only the descending pathway gave a hint of egress to the outside world. Dispersed among the rocks where monasticism still subsisted—Roussanou, St Stephen, St Barlaam and the Metamorphosis, isolated survivors of a scattered metropolis of twenty-six foundations—crumbled the shells of the extinct monasteries. Poised on their pinnacles, they are no longer accessible. No steps ascend and no monks are left to cast their nets into the surrounding gulf. They disintegrate in mid-air, empty stone caskets of rotting timber and slowly falling frescoes that only spiders and owls and kestrels inhabit or an occasional family of eagles. How distinct the rocks of the Meteora appear from all that surrounds them! They have a different birth, and bear an alien, planetary aspect, like a volley of thunderbolts embedded in the steep-sided hollow. The flanks of the nearest pillars were as smooth as mussel-shells, striped in places with yellow lichen or with moss as dark as submarine foliage and the straight ascending flight of the conglomerate sides was only broken here and there by a frill of evergreen. As they retreated, all these colours resolved themselves to a universal blue-grey gunmetal hue.

Here, on the edge of the precipice of Holy Trinity, we were on a level with all the monasteries except the towering Transfiguration. Lying on the grass among autumn crocuses and cyclamen and anemones, we watched the shadows darken. The great columns, as slanting and horizontal creases appeared, seemed to be on the move; to climb and twirl like melting sticks of barley sugar, thrusting their burden in spirals into the still and watery evening. A slender Jacob's ladder of pale gold sloped among the monasteries from a bright-rimmed cave among the changing clouds, singling out half an acre of mountainside and the minute strolling figures of Father Christopher and Bessarion on the raft of St Barlaam. The faint tap of a semantron sounded across the darkening chasm, followed soon by the sad clanking of hesperine bells from the Metamorphosis. As the shades of evening assembled, the monasteries began to float as if they had sailed to the surface of some private element. Their massive supporting pillars became irrelevant appendages: wavering tendrils that tapered and dwindled and vanished in the dusk until the clusters of domes and cypresses and towers, like little celestial cities, seemed only to be held aloft in the void by the whirring and multiple wings of a company of seraphim.

CHAPTER 3

The Helleno-Romaic Dilemma
and Sidetrack to Crete

'Romiòs eísai?'

A glance of surprise accompanied the question. It was long past midnight and I had stopped at an open-air bar on the way back to my hotel in Panama City. The three barmen were taking their orders in Spanish but shouting them back to the whiskered cook in Greek; and when my turn came, I asked for something in the same language. Hence the question: *are you a Greek?* The place was run by a family from the little port of Karlóvassi in Samos. They were the fourth Greeks I had met during nearly a year in the Caribbean and the Central American republics: one was a business man in Haiti; another, on the plane between Havana and British Honduras, a grocer; the last, a lonely innkeeper in Cordova, on the shores of Lake Nicaragua opposite the volcano of Momotombo. (Greeks, so widely scattered all over the world, are scarce in these parts. The nearest settlement was a little sharkproof colony from Kalymnos in the Dodecanese who dive for sponges off the Florida reefs.)

How incongruous, among the languid Panamanians and Lascars and Chinamen, these three alert islanders seemed! When the time came to pay, it was impossible. This encounter was a sudden shaft of light and cheer in a rather dispiriting sojourn, and, as I made my way back to my quarters through the trams and the mosquitoes and the racy invitations murmured in the lanes, I meditated with homesickness about the faraway archipelago and the language and the country which we all knew well; and also about the wording of their question: why, in their momentary delusion about where I came from, they had used the word '*Romiòs*' instead of the more usual 'Hellene'.

*   *   *   *

The answer carries us back two-third of the way to Pericles. When Constantine founded a second capital for the late Roman Empire, Constantinople was not meant to be the successor to the ancient metropolis on the Tiber, still less a substitute or a rival. The mushroom city was the twin capital of an undivided State. But within sixty years, different emperors ruled as administrative partners over the two regions. The eastern city expanded; the western, beset by barbarians, declined; and, in less than a century, almost by mistake, it was extinguished by the Goths, leaving the Empire shorn of its western half, but once more subject to a single city, the New Rome on the banks of the Bosphorus. And so it remained until 1453, when it was destroyed by the Turks. The eastern outlived its amputated western half by twelve dynasties, eighty-four emperors and just under a thousand years.

The world in which Byzantium–Constantinople–New Rome grew up was Greek. So were the surviving Roman citizens and soon the emperors too. Athens had fallen into a decline, and Constantinople was now the heart and centre of the Greek race. When theological discord about the Holy Ghost divided the East and the West the newer imperial city became the metropolis of the Eastern Christendom as well, and remained so for all its millennial span. So, for a thousand years, the Greeks were *Romaíoi*—Romans—as well as Hellenes; and the word *Romaíoi* soon meant a subject of the Empire and an Orthodox Eastern Christian in rather confusing contrast to the Western Christians with their spiritual capital in Old Rome. The word 'Hellene' came to mean a pagan, and when, after Julian the Apostate's brief revival, paganism disappeared, the word 'Hellene' went into abeyance too. Much later, for a freak decade or two, a Byzantine élite, influenced by the neoplatonist cosmogony of Gemistus Plethon—alas, lost—seriously thought of themselves as 'Hellenes'. It was a faint, entrancing Renaissance echo of Julian's throwback, and, the times being what they were, the word 'Hellene', one suspects, had more than a dash of its old pagan meaning. Radiating from Mistra in its last days, the revival was as fleeting and ill-starred as the school of painting that flourished by its side. (I wish I had been there.) Dire events blew those brief candles out. Afterwards only *Romaíos* remained. To the Moslem races—the Persians and Arabs and, later, the Turks—the Empire was known as Rūm. By the time Byzantium fell, and for the following four centuries, all Greeks, in Islam, were *Rūmis*. The grander word *Romaíos* dropped out of everyday use, and Greeks themselves used the more familiar word *romiòs* (a half-Graecized form of *rūmi*) in referring to themselves and their countrymen.*

The spoken Greek of everyday—the language of popular poetry, songs and proverbs, the living tongue, in fact—came

---

* The Roman imperial mantle on Greek shoulders has led to a splendid confusion; for the word '*Rūm*', on Oriental tongues, referred not only to the Christian Byzantines—they are so styled in the Koran—but, for a century or two, to their conquered territory in Asia Minor; it designated the empire of the Seldjuk Turks in Anatolia with its capital at Konia (Iconium), reigned over by the 'Sultans of *Rūm*'. To tangle matters still further the word *Romania* was often used in the West, especially during and after the crusades, to specify the parts of the Eastern Empire which lay in Europe; the Turks extended *Rūm* into 'Rumeli', ('land of the Rumis') to cover the same area. One still finds the confusing word 'Rumelia' on old maps. (In Greece, Rumeli now specifically applies to the great mountainous stretch of continental Greece running from the Adriatic to the Aegean, north of the Gulf of Corinth and south of Epirus and Thessaly.) The Turkish word for the ancient Greeks is 'Yunan'—'Ionian'—and they now call Greece Yunanistan. The Greeks themselves thought of the Italians and the Western Catholics, especially after the schism had split Christendom into an Eastern and Western half—as the 'Latins'—followers of the Latin rite—or, more generally, after the Crusades, as 'the Franks', a word still

to be called Romaic. Opposed to this was the archaizing literary idiom of theology, chronicles, official documents and the liturgy, which grew steadily more artificial as time passed: a language of scribes. The deviation began long before Byzantium fell; both are versions of the universal *koinē* of the Hellenistic world, and undisputed heirs of ancient Greek. But Romaic, or Demotic, Greek was spoken by everyone; the other, 'Katharévousa', the 'Pure', was written by a few, spoken by none. One was familiar homespun, the other, ceremonious brocade. When, for a combination of political and religious reasons, the Greeks stopped thinking of themselves specifically as 'Hellenes', they didn't cease to be Hellenes, even if they thought of themselves as *Romioi*. When Greece regained its freedom, the old name of Hellene was once more in the ascendant and *Romios* fell into disfavour among the revivalists. Today, the two words carry definite and different undertones.

'Hellene' is the glory of ancient Greece; 'Romaic' the splendours and the sorrows of Byzantium, above all, the sorrows. 'Hellenism' is symbolized by the columns of the Parthenon; Byzantium, the imperial golden age of Christian Greece, by the great dome of St Sophia. Were one compelled to find an emblem for the more complex meaning of *Romiosyne*—the Romaic World, 'Romaic-hood'—perhaps it would still be St

---

sometimes applied to north-western Europeans by both the Greeks and the Turks: inhabitants of Frankiá, or Frangistan.

The most famous single use of the word *rūmi* is its appendage to the name of Mevlana Jellaludin, the great Moslem sage, mystic poet and the founder of the whirling Dervishes. For, though a Persian, he settled in Konia under the Sultans of Rūm.

A final pitfall: none of all this must be confused with the Holy Roman Empire invented by Charlemagne and endorsed by the Pope in A.D. 800, and destroyed by Napoleon at the Federation of the Rhine. What an influence the idea of Caesar's name has exerted on history! The Byzantines wore it by right, the Holy Roman Emperors adopted it. 'Tsar' is a slav form of the same word, and, until recently, the Kings of England, as successors to the Great Mogul, bore the title of Kaisar-i-Hind.

Sophia; but a St Sophia turned into a mosque filled with turbans and flanked by minarets, with all her mosaic saints hidden under the whitewash and the giant Koranic texts of the occupying Turks; the Greeks meanwhile, exiles in their own land, celebrate their rites in humbler fanes.

A few years ago I asked George Theotokas, the distinguished Greek writer, why the word *Romiós*, used in certain contexts, has a derogatory sense. He thought for a long time, and then said 'I suppose because it means our dirty linen. *Einai ta aplyta mas . . .*' In this subsidiary meaning, it not only conjures up the tragedy of the Fall, but the helplessness of subjection and the strands of Turkish custom which inevitably, during an occupation lasting centuries, wove themselves into the web of Greek life. It suggests the shifts and compromises with which the more intelligent Greeks outwitted their oppressors. Under the Ottomans, only the Greek Orthodox Church, and their wits, were left to the Greeks. These they used to some purpose. The Oecumenical Patriarch, the Sultan's single go-between with his Christian subjects, held the Greeks together as a family till better days should come. Turkish scorn of languages and their artlessness as negotiators led Phanariot Greeks, as Dragomans of the Sublime Porte, to play a considerable part in the foreign policy of the Empire. Greek Phanariot princes reigned vice-regally from the vassal thrones of Moldavia and Wallachia; Greek bankers handled finance; Greek mountaineers—the Armatoles—'guarded' the mountain passes; Greek seamen manned the warships of the Turkish fleet.*

Most of them laboured in secret to lighten their country-men's lot. The administration was fierce, but it was also idle and corrupt. Under these conditions ruse and compromise became virtues. Flexibility and quick wits were the keys to survival and the road to riches. (*Nés dans le serail*, as it were, *ils en connais-saient les détours.*) This is where the word *Romios* begins to take

* As a concession for these services, Greek vessels from Hydra and the islands handled the entire carrying trade of the Mediterranean.

on its pejorative sense. It implies that, the enemy once removed, a deposit of the wicked arts by which the Greeks had out-witted him for ages, still remained: weapons now aimed at their fellow-countrymen. Abetted by the untamed customs of the mountains, they slowed up the smooth conduct of a re-generated and sovereign state. Indeed, the phrases 'romaïka pragmata!' and 'romaïkes douliès!'—'Romaic things!' and 'Ro-maic doings!', always accompanied by a series of disapproving clicks of the tongue—mean 'slovenly goings-on' or, worse still, 'dirty work'.

*   *   *   *

The Turkish occupation is a boundless limbo. But it is full of wonderful stories of Odyssean ruse, picaresque adven-ture and the skilful exploitation of chaos. Tales abound of soaring careers and distant wanderings in search of fortune which can vie with anything in *Gil Blas*, *Hadji Baba* and the *Arabian Nights*. *Romiosyne* at its humblest and most comic level, is epitomized in the shadow-play of Karayiozi. This fascinating dramatic tradition is thought to have begun in China; at all events, it held sway for centuries in many lands from Man-churia to the Adriatic Sea and in each country it moulded itself to the ideas and manners of the inhabitants. In some parts of the Orient it was rabelaisian and lewd. Among the Greeks, it took on a lively, witty, parabolic turn. It has become pro-foundly and inalienably Greek.

The actors are transparent silhouettes cut out of camel-hide and coloured, jointed and manipulated by the invisible puppet-master and his apprentices on long rods which flatten and ani-mate the figures against a stretched white linen screen lit from behind. The scene, often adorned with palaces, mosques and seraglios, is laid in Constantinople or in occupied Greece at any time in the last two or three centuries. The one-act plays per-formed there, of which there are over a hundred—a fixed canon varying slightly according to the skill and imagination of the puppet-master—aim only to amuse; but they do much more: they depict, by comedy, caricature, parody and farce, the entire Romaic predicament.

The protagonist and anti-hero is the Karayiozi himself. He is the epitome of the poverty-stricken and downtrodden rayah; his home is a wooden hut on the point of collapse. ('Karayiozi's hut' all over Greece, is synonymous with a hovel.) He is small, bald and hunchbacked; one of his arms, apt for the whole range of Greek gesticulations, is preternaturally long, a survival of the phallus which has such a bawdy role to play in the Arabian Karaguz. Ragged, barefoot, illiterate, nimble and versatile, he is a fast, pert and funny talker, and his speech is full of comic mistakes. Though he is a willing thief—*Romaïka pragmata!*—he is often caught; he is bold and timid by turns, skilled in subterfuge and disguise, volatile, restless, resilient, irascible and pugnacious, soon dashed, swift to recover. His schemes nearly always go awry and bring on a harvest of blows. Talking, jumping, gesticulating, arguing, he darts about among his towering and more static fellow-shadows with the restlessness of a firefly. However absurd and monstrous his behaviour we are always on his side. He is deeply likeable, a comic David surrounded by Goliaths. A small man pitched against intolerable odds, he corresponds to something in all of us; a pin thrust again and again into the balloons of vanity and self-importance; he is a perfect manifestation of the passion of the Greeks for mocking themselves and each other. The laughter of the audience is directed against themselves by proxy, and they know it.* He is the essence of *Romiosyne*.

Karayiozi, then, is a *Romios*. But 'Romios' covers a wider field than the candle-lit quadrilateral that confines his antics. It suggests, as we have seen, the ghostly splendours of Byzantium, the sorrows of servitude, the 'dirty washing', and the absurdities of the shadow play. It also bears a meaning which is

---

* I mentioned the prevalence of this Greek characteristic a few days ago to Niko Ghika, the painter. He said: 'They never do anything else.'

free of any sad or derogatory undertone. It conjures up feelings of warmth, kinship and affection, of community of history, of solidarity in trouble, of sharing the same hazards and aspirations, of being in the same boat. It is the emblem of membership of the same family, a thing that abolishes pretence and explanation and apology. A Greek recognizing another Greek in adversity or exile or emigration, salutes him as a fellow-*Romios* and stands him a free meal or a bed and lends him a helping hand.

In spite of the intervening lustre of Byzantium and the woes of foreign domination, consciousness of descent from celebrated ancestors in the ancient world survived, however dimly, among even the humblest *Romioi*. All this, for modern Greeks, is caught up in the word 'Hellene'. Though time, among the un-lettered, may have driven this feeling into the subconscious or reduced it to the irrelevance of an obsolete legend, it was always there; even though circumstances removed the word from general currency for centuries. Scholars and men of letters, sadly reduced in numbers, kept this heritage alive and when the Turks were driven away at last, it was not a revived Roman Empire of the East, centred on Constantinople, which emerged, but Hellas with its capital (after a period of indecision) in Athens. The dome of St Sophia retreated—(not very far; it still hovers beguilingly in the awareness of all Greeks)—and the Parthenon, neglected for many centuries, sailed aloft as a new lodestar for their national life; and it was not as Byzantines or Romaics that the Greeks, perhaps rubbing their eyes with won-der, began their new life, but as Hellenes. It may be compared to the revival of an old, forgotten, but authentic title long in abeyance. *Romiosyne*, as we have seen, had the pungency of the familiar and the immediate; Hellenism has the glamour of an idea. They are two aspects of the same thing.

It would be hard to fire the blood of an English road-mender with the names of Boadicea, Caractacus or Cadwal-lader, or a French grocer's with that of Vercingetorix. At the rebirth of Greece, the inhabitants were suddenly, so to speak, taken in hand by rulers and hellenizing poets and scholars and by professors who had studied in the universities of the West, and introduced to a whole museum-load of forgotten marble relations. They were pleased; they were also overcome with shyness. These gods, philosophers, generals and heroes filled them with awe. They had always known about their grand kinsmen in a half-apprehended fashion; even though the only one they knew by name was Alexander the Great, the connection was a source of vague pride. The ancients were now presented as exemplars, almost as Confucian cult-objects. The modern Greeks, thought the classical innovators, had only to take them to their hearts for an emulous new Golden Age to begin and outshine the reign of Pericles.

It is hard to blame them. They lived in an age of wonders. The marvel of liberation had happened. There was much to be criticized in the recent Romaic past, many alien barnacles to be chipped away, modes of thought to be rooted out and impurities to be purged from the noble Greek tongue. . . . It was too early for them to understand that their fellow-countrymen's descent from the ancient Greeks (and from a Greek past far remoter than the fifth century B.C. they had arbitrarily singled out as their starting point) was more convincingly asserted by hundreds of humble customs and superstitions that seemed backward and barbaric to their mentors, than it was by the rather charming neo-classical stucco buildings which began to spring up in Athens. It was impossible for them to grasp that the despised demotic was the rightful heir to the speech of the ancients, while the 'pure' idiom in which they wrote—for *Katharévousa* has never been heard on human lips*—was, for all its noble descent, stone dead. Perhaps the words 'Hellas' and

---

* This is not quite true. I have heard it attempted, unforgettably, once, by an abbess in Mistra; uttered in a nasal and halting delivery and packed with marvellous blunders. It was very strange. Other cases exist, all of them cited and imitated as extreme instances of pedantic absurdity and always

'Hellene' sounded as awkward and unreal to them, at that moment, as 'Britain' and 'British' still do, after a century or so of empire and commonwealth, to the inhabitants of the British Isles: words only used by sovereigns, politicians, passport officers, journalists, Americans and Germans; and no one else; least of all the Welsh and Cornish, the only islanders entitled to them; only, quite correctly, by the inhabitants of Brittany.

The ancients were a theme for pride; they were also a cause for self-reproach. How could the Greeks compete with these antique resurrected wonders? (How can any of us?) Their inadequacy suggested a hopeless falling-off; those stony faces were a standing rebuke. An inspiration to some, to others they were a source of bewilderment, and for a few, a subject for resentment, almost for anger: why not blow up the Parthenon? The new trends seemed to put the whole of *Romiosyne*, all that made life worth living, in the wrong. Anyway, the Romaic Pantheon was full. The spirit of Byzantium was en-

---

provoking laughter. It has the incongruity of Plato with a top hat and an umbrella.

Yet it is impossible not to have a sneaking respect and liking for this hieratic mandarin language with all its euphuistic artificialities and its archaic syntax. *Katharévousa* has even been used now and then (a feat of unnatural virtuosity) as a medium for poetry; some of the poems of Calvos have a curious fabricated beauty, and there are elements of *katharévousa* in Cavafy: cunningly placed bits of whalebone in the more sinuous demotic. It is elaborate and forbidding, but it is precise: indispensable, its champions say (which its opponents bitterly deny), for legal, scientific or mathematical definition. *Katharévousa* is an expensive faded leather case stamped with a tarnished monogram, holding a set of geometrical instruments: stiff jointed dividers and compasses neatly slotted into their plush beds. *Dimotiki* is an everyday instrument—a spade, an adze or a sickle—the edge thinned and keen with honing and bright from the whetstone; and the wooden shaft, mellow with sweat and smooth with the patina of generations of handling, lies in the palm with an easy balance. Partisanship for the two idioms has led to rioting in the Athens streets, to bloodshed and even death.

throned there, and Constantine and Helen and Basil the Bulgar-Slayer and the last Palaeologue; a whole phantom parade of emperors whose City was still in bondage. There, too, were the Virgins, the saints and the martyrs of Orthodoxy: their icon lamps burned in all their houses; their frescoes, dark with incense and blurred by the kisses of a thousand years, covered the walls of their churches. It was not for their mystical significance that this painted army was loved, but for the miracles they wrought, and their ghostly succour in dark days. To these had been added the mountain chiefs and the sea captains of the War of Independence: Kolokotrones, Karaiskakis, Athanasios Diakos, Miaoulis and Kanaris and many others. These whiskered heroes were *Romioi* to the backbone. Apotheosis crowned them; theirs were the yataghans, the long guns and the fireships that had delivered Greece from the Turks. Leonidas and Miltiades, meanwhile, could look after themselves. They had performed brave deeds against the Persians, it was said. But it was such a long time ago.*

*   *   *   *

There is a purpose behind this preamble: to lull the reader into receptivity before launching a private theory of my own which I shall call the Helleno-Romaic Dilemma. The cornerstone of this theory is the supposition that inside every Greek dwell two figures in opposition. Sometimes one is in the ascendant, sometimes the other; occasionally they are in concord. These are, of course, the *Romios* and the Hellene; and for the sake of the present theory, the word 'Hellene' is distorted to mean only the exact antithesis to '*Romios*'. All Greeks, according to my theory, are an amalgam, in varying degrees, of both; they contradict and complete each other. But it is the antagonism of the two which concerns us here, not their possible synthesis. 'Two souls, alas,' my hypothetical Greek might exclaim with Goethe, 'live in my breast.' It suggests a lifelong

* See page 63.

Zoroastrian war in which the Hellene is Ormuzd and the
Romios, Ahriman. I advance all this with diffidence. Greek
friends on whom I have tried out the Helleno-Romaic Dilemma
were interested and amused by the idea and thought there
might even be something in it. The easiest way to present it is
by drawing up two parallel lists of characteristics, allegiances
and symbols taken at random from a larger catalogue which
could cover many pages. Some, for the sake of illustration, are
purposely slight and frivolous. Here they are.

	THE ROMIOS	THE HELLENE
1	Practice	Theory
2	The Concrete	The Abstract
3	The real	The ideal
4	Private ambition	Wider aspiration
5	Argument	Rhetoric
6	Concentration	Diffusion
7	Instinct	Principle and logic
8	Improvisation	System
9	Empiricism	Dogma
10	Love for the recent past	Love for the remote past
10a	Admiration for Western material progress, distrust of Western theories	Admiration for European civilization, rooted in ancient Greek liberal ideas. Some distrust of Western materialism
11	Retention of Romaic customs	Adoption of Western customs, abhorrence of Romaic orientalism
12	Distrust of the law. Readiness to bypass it by manœuvre, favouritism or by any of the bad old short-cuts	Respect for the law. Hesitation, on principle, to bypass it by the means opposite
13	Self-reproach about Greece's material limitations	Self-reproach about Greece's Romaic blemishes
13a	Respect for learning as a means to advancement	Respect for learning for its own sake
13b	Belief in quick returns	Reliance on the long view

	THE ROMIOS	THE HELLENE
14	Reliance on inherited precedent and proverb	Search for analogy in the ancient world
15	Seeing the outside world as a field to be exploited	Travel in search of knowledge or legitimate commerce
16	Evaluation of things in terms of money	Admission of other values
17	Reluctance to admit ignorance	Admission that there are things beyond his range of knowledge
18	Compulsive labelling of everything, whether accurate or not★	Compulsion to define, explain and classify
19	Looking on Greece as outside Europe	Looking on Greece as a part of Europe
20	Seeing Europe as the region of alien 'Franks'	Europe the region of fellow-Europeans
20a	Reaching agreement by bargaining	Settlement by negotiation
21	Belief in the sacredness and indestructibility of *Romiosyne*	Belief in the destiny of Hellas
22	Strong regional loyalty, distrust of people from different provinces, e.g. Crete *v.* Mani	Centripetal tendency towards Athens. Contempt for provincial rivalries and limitations
23	Certainty of every Romios of his own suitability for the office of Prime Minister	Decent self-confidence
24	Shrewdness, impaired by (*a*) credulity and (*b*) needless suspicion	Circumspect acumen
25	Tendency to resolve political difficulties by revolution	Belief in constitutional method, with revolution only as a last resort
26	Lack of scruple to gain personal ends	The soul of honour

★ E.g. in solving the conundrum of a solitary foreign traveller, by regarding him as (*a*) an omniscient sage, (*b*) a millionaire, (*c*) a lunatic, (*d*) a spy. Sometimes all four simultaneously. See end of (32).

27	Fatalism	Philosophic doubt
28	Quick wits	Lively intelligence
29	Marriage wholly determined by dowries and parental bargaining	Milder version of the same, modified by romantic and aesthetic factors
30	Blind tribal allegiance to a political party, based on regional bias or personal allegiance to a figurehead	Strong political partisanship with a greater chance of its being based on private deliberation
31	A passion for newspapers, especially the political sections	A passion for newspapers, especially the political sections
32	Unquestioning belief in the printed, as opposed to the written or spoken, word. This is corrected intermittently, by the remark: 'Nothing but lies in the newspapers.' The attitudes are often reconciled by the paradoxical ability to believe two contradicting statements simultaneously	A stricter approach, and a reduced capacity for the reconciliation of opposites
33	Abhorrence of a naked fact, and haste to clothe, amplify and elaborate: 'The mythopoetic faculty'	Comparative absence of this bias
34	Daemonic capacity for exertion under stimulus of enthusiasm, interest, patriotism, friendship, ambition	The same, tempered by 7, 8, 9
35	Tendency to flag if stimulus and urgency are removed. Dread of boredom	The same, corrected or mitigated by 7, 8, 9
36	Procrastination due to 34, and lack of sense of time. Dislike of routine	Climatic influences, corrected or mitigated by 7, 8, 9
37	Trust in improvisation (8) and the tendency to allow things to fall into decay through feeling	Belief in maintenance and upkeep, due to greater hope for establishment and security

THE ROMIOS	THE HELLENE
of impermanency of human affairs	
38 Sensitiveness to insult, which leads to rash, violent and self-destructive acts, or enduring and implacable feud	Same sensitiveness, but reaction less violent and calling for milder sanctions
39 Despair and melancholia (*stenachoria*) if things go wrong. May be mitigated in time by fatalism, proverbs and a saving resilience	Same tendencies considerably reduced, corrected by comforts of philosophy
40 Fondness for *leventeiá*, i.e. the dash and fire of youth, a cheerful temperament, courage, speed, quick reactions, good looks, skill in singing, dancing, marksmanship, capacity for wine drinking and fun, often accompanied by *meraklidilíki*, its sartorial expression	An acknowledgement of the characteristic with a distinctly more restrained and sober approach
41 Importance of *philotimo*, 'honour-love', i.e. honourable conduct between humans, in chaos of *Romiosyne*, and, above all, private *amour propre*, like the Spanish *pundonor*, or personal dignity. It is wounds to this— 'he touched my *philotimo*'— which must often lead to 37	Honour regarded as a precious legacy from the ancient Greeks
42 *Bessa:* a word of Albanian origin, meaning the inviolability of an oath, especially in guerrilla warfare. The opposite of treachery	Probably the same as above
43 Settling the world's problems over endless cups of Turkish coffee in cafés	Settling the world's problems over endless cups of Turkish coffee in cafés

44	Fondness for cards, backgammon, etc.	The same
45	Sobriety and frugality relieved by dionysiac interludes	Interludes likely to be less dionysiac
46	Addiction to *amané* songs, i.e. wailing, nasal rather melancholy melopees in oriental minor mode	Violent abhorrence of *amané* as alien and barbaric survivals
47	Urban addiction to *rebétika* songs and dances: i.e. Athenian low-life, fatalistic, near-apache hard luck stories, accompanied by special stringed instruments. Supposed to have originated in hashish dens. Complex solitary dances, perhaps from Asia Minor. The choreographic expression of the songs	Distaste, based roughly on the same reasons as the foregoing. Tendency towards Western music
48	Rustic devotion to mountain, island and country dances (usually a chain of dancers led by a solo performer)	Toleration of these as 'wholesome' and as part of heroic tradition and folklore and for their possible descent from the ancient Pyrrhic dance
49	Rustic devotion to *klephtika* or Klepht songs: long, fierce and semi-oriental in style, celebrating mountain warriors' feats of arms	Toleration of the same in theory if not in practice, as humble mementoes of Hellenism's triumph over barbarian occupation: 'Wholesome': unlike *amané* and *rebétika*
50	Outward disapproval, but secret sympathy, in the distant past, for brigandage and piracy; survivals of a lively and anarchic life	Understandable condemnation of these as stumbling blocks to government and the functioning of a European state: '*Romaikès douliès*' at their worst

THE ROMIOS	THE HELLENE
51 Fondness, among the old, for smoking narghilés	Disapproval, for obvious reasons
52 Addiction to the *komboloi*: amber beads strung together like a rosary, and clicked rhythmically as a nerve-settler, like chain-smoking	Faint disapproval, even if addicted
53 Fondness of a small, raffish minority (urban low life *rebétika* world, see 47) for occasional hashish smoking, as accompaniment to singing and dancing	Proper abhorrence of this oriental survival
54 Belief in miraculous properties of certain icons	Enlightened disbelief
55 Resort, among isolated rustic communities, to magical remedies administered by old women. Retention of many pagan superstitions, practices and beliefs	Scorn of obscurantism, even though magical practices and superstitions are of ancient descent. Trust in medical science
56 Indifference to ethical and mystical content of religion, but semi-pagan attachment to the Orthodox Church as the unifying guardian of *Romiosyne* in times of trouble	Comparative indifference to ethical and mystical content of religion, but tolerance of Orthodox Church as symbol of Hellenism
57 Strict observance of religious fasts and feast days and instinctive, tribal retentions of many of the external signs of Orthodoxy	A tendency to disregard these, except at holidays of Christmas and Easter
58 Patriotism based on 21 (R), and inspired, in wartime, by the memory of the Klephts	Patriotism based on 21 (H), and inspired, in wartime, by the heroes of the ancient world
59 War seen in terms of guerrilla	Military science
60 Rule of thumb	Text book

61	In general, impulsive readiness for anything that is not vetoed by some hallowed taboo	More restraint and a more cerebral approach to the problems of life
62	Homesickness for Byzantine Empire	Nostalgia for the age of Pericles
63	Demotic	*Katharévousa*
64	The Dome of St Sophia	The columns of the Parthenon

Should one add up the attributes of each column and mould them into people, two lop-sided freaks would emerge. Fortunately neither exist; each is a function of the other. Only enclosed in the arena of a single breast do they come to life. They are permanently, more or less, at loggerheads, and there is a wide range of contingencies for friction in which the actions of their host depend on which of them wins. After each of these bouts, he might paraphrase Gibbon: 'I sighed as a *Romios*, I obeyed as a Hellene'—or the other way round.

It seems wrong to write of this conflict without mentioning some of the attributes which are common to both sides. It would leave the picture badly out of focus.

Emotional feeling for Greece is the country's deepest conviction. Affronts, threats and the danger of invasion are the things that not only fling the *Romios* and the Hellene into each other's arms—several things can do this—but reconcile all the internal differences of the country. Courage, self-sacrifice and endurance reach heroic heights. When the emergency passes, cohesion too dissolves, and political rivalries rage as fiercely as ever (no wonder the verb *stasiazo*, 'I am in a state of faction', was one of the earliest verbs one had to learn at school); parties abound and factions flourish but such is the individuality of the Greeks that the country is really made up of eight million one-man splinter-groups reluctantly forced into a series of temporary coalitions.

Other traits leap to the mind: self-reliance; the belief that effort and cleverness, backed by luck, can accomplish anything; intelligence, rapid thought, alertness, curiosity; thirst for fame;

restlessness and extreme subjectivity; a passion for news; eloquence, the knack for expressing thought in words; the
impulse to express thought in action; energy and enterprise;
enthusiasm and disillusion; a deep-seated feeling of confidence
and of absolute equality not only with other Greeks, but with
the whole human race, and of superiority to many; lack of
class-consciousness or snobbery; strong family feeling; im-
patience with political opposition, corrected by tolerance of
human shortcomings and fallibility; an easy-going moral code
modified by rigid and puritanical notions of family honour;
sensitiveness, especially to irony or affronts to personal dignity;
quick temper, which can interfere with this; hatred of solitude
and scorn for privacy, the need to sharpen the mind by conversation. Opinion is shaped by newspapers and by talk, seldom
by private reading or un-utilitarian study; abstract philosophy
and metaphysics are absent from Greek life. Talk is an addic-
tion and it is conducted with invention, great narrative gifts,
the knack of repartee, the spirit of contradiction, the question-
ing of authority, mockery, self-mockery, satire and humour.
Love of pleasure emerges in the pan-hellenic passion for sitting up late eating and drinking and singing whenever the
slightest excuse crops up.

The Greeks are famous for their financial acumen. Their
knack of spinning the air into gold is mercifully unpolluted by
its accompanying blemish: meanness is scorned and almost
non-existent; they prize and practise generosity whether or not
they can afford it, and the laws of hospitality are as deeply
rooted as the most sacred feelings of patriotism or Orthodox
pietas. I think the Greeks have a much sharper awareness than
Western Europeans of the flux of events and the instability of
human affairs. In spite of interludes of Romaic sloth and pro-
crastination, they feel compelled to take time by the forelock,
exploit favourable currents and wrest fortune from un-
promising circumstances; a tendency which can lead to bold
and sudden undertakings and sometimes to opportunism. They

have the keener sense, which poor and barren countries instil, of the existence of disaster and tragedy. But, though they may see many things in tragic and melodramatic terms, stoicism and humour are at hand to deflate them. Humour, indeed, runs through their whole story in a saving lifeline. Similarly the self-imposed code of *philotimo*, or private honour—a whole apparatus of ancestral scruples—mitigates anarchic impulses and sets a codifying bridle on Romaic short-cuts and personal solutions. To contravene these laws marks the offender with a more shameful and indelible brand than any sanction that the law can inflict.

Two items close this long list. The first is the conviction that a stranger feels here that he is surrounded by people of ancient and civilized descent. This feeling grows in force the lower one plunges in the economic scale; not because it is absent in bourgeois circles—far from it;* but primitive surroundings place it in higher relief. The last of these Greece-wide attributes is an orientation towards virtue. This may be rooted in the qualities which the ancients prized or in the Christian ethic. Perhaps natural and physical influences are responsible. Chthonian demons drove the ancients to acts of darkness and horror; rage and violence sometimes harry their descendants. But the luminosity which surrounds them does much to exorcize the principle of wickedness and confute the dogma of original sin. In a world where the law's retribution is looked on as bad luck and life after death holds neither hope nor terror, the existence of this quality is especially remarkable. The bent towards virtue may waver, but it exerts as powerful an influence on the Greek subconscious mind as the north on a compass needle.

*　　*　　*　　*

* Sudden riches and the accumulation of luxurious and unfamiliar appliances and an alien set of social values are no more exempt from raw and barbaric blemishes than they are in other countries; but the assimilation is notably shorter and less painful.

These sweeping remarks abound with contradictions, and so they should. It is also clear that the lists of Romaic and Hellenic characteristics represent different strata as well as opposed principles. The Romaic list enumerates humbler traits. The Hellenic idiosyncrasy affects every degree of the Greek ladder but spreads more amply as the rungs mount and the Romaic heritage thins out. The Dilemma is not only a struggle between the Old and the New, but between the East against the West as well.

The result of the tug-of-war is easy to predict. The old is breaking up, ancient customs are dying in scores, landmarks are vanishing, everything is changing with bewildering speed.

In Athens, particularly, the innovations of the West are welcomed with uncritical joy: incongruous skyscrapers spring in stooks, wirelesses deafen, sky signs fidget, neon scatters its death ray, trams clash, giant American taxis like winged and elongated boiled sweets screech and squeak along the sweltering asphalt with Gadarene urgency. The fever of demolition and rebuilding has the Athenians by the throat. Streets gape as though bombed, masonry crashes, the dust of a siege floats in the air and the clatter of pneumatic drills has replaced the little owls' note as the city's *leitmotiv*. Rusting whiskers of reinforced concrete prong the skyline: new hotels soar from the rubble like ogres' mouth-organs. Athens is in a state of headlong flux.

On every return, I discover that a fresh crop of cafés, taverns, restaurants and bookshops, all of which had seemed as firm as the pyramids, has vanished, and the reshuffle of landmarks sends me careering from street to street like a fox with all his earths stopped. A few years ago, after only six months' absence, I arrived from the Piraeus and headed for a corner of the Syntagma—Constitution Square, the agora of modern Athens—intending to alight at my old refuge, the oddly named Hotel New Angleterre. (This was a dilapidated yellow building in the engaging neo-classical style of the reign of King Otho, at the pillared and pedimented door of which Victorian travellers would assemble on horseback for the journeys to Sunium, Marathon and Delphi. Flaking plaster caryatids supported the balcony, a stubborn lift groaned within, the hall ceiling was frescoed with centaurs, and along cobwebby vistas eccentric plumbing ran wild.) But it had gone, vanished as completely as if djinns had whisked it away, and there stood a gleaming cube of concrete and a brand-new café full of tubular chairs whose backs were strung like harps with plastic thongs:

Thank God, thank God that I wasn't there
When they blew off the roof of the New Angleterre . . .

I crossed the blazing Syntagma to the Hotel Grande Bretagne thirsting for a consolation drink. Nothing would have changed there, I thought. But I was wrong. The old hall had acquired the vast and aseptic impersonality of an airport lounge. (Greek architects have forgotten the saying of their ancestor Isocrates about man being the measure of all things.) Beyond it, the bar, the noisy and delightful meeting place of many years, had become a silent waste dotted with lost and furtively murmuring customers dwarfed by their habitat into air-conditioned skaters on a rink of marble. Only the old barmen were unchanged. They looked puzzled and wistful. . . . (At the moment of writing, this bar is closed yet again for its fifth alteration in the last three decades. I wonder what Babylonian phoenix will emerge.)

It is the same everywhere. The Athenians look on this constant change with a mixture of abstract pride and private bewilderment. Much of this architectural restlessness may spring from the sudden boom in tourism. One's first reaction to this new windfall is delight: Greek economy needs these revenues; one's second is sorrow. Economists rejoice, but many an old Athenian, aware of the havoc that tourism has spread in Spain and France and Italy, lament that this gregarious passion, which destroys the object of its love, should have chosen Greece as

its most recent, most beautiful, perhaps its most fragile victim.
They know that in a few years it has turned dignified islands
and serene coasts into pullulating hells. In Athens itself, many
a delightful old tavern has become an alien nightmare of bas-
tard folklore and bad wine. Docile flocks converge on them,
herded by button-eyed guides, Mentors and Stentors too, with
all Manchester, all Lyons, all Cologne and half the Middle-
West at heel. The Athenians who ate there for generations
have long since fled. (Fortunately, many inns survive unpolluted; but for how long? The works of writers mentioning
these places by name should be publicly burnt by the common
hangman.) Greece is suffering its most dangerous invasion
since the time of Xerxes. Bad money may drive out good, but
good money, in this case, drives out everything.

In dark moments I see bay after lonely bay and island after
island as they are today and as they may become. The present
vision is familiar enough: rough slabs with bollards and cap-
stans, crescents of sand or white pebbles where the fishermen
toil barefoot at their nets, caulk and careen their boats, repair
their tridents and weave complex fishtraps of wicker and twine.
The ribs of caïques assemble above the froth of shavings like
whales' skeletons. Humorous, sardonic, self-reliant men live
there, lean from their war with the elements, ready to share
their wine with any stranger. At nightfall they assemble under
the branches outside the single ramshackle taverna. Now and
then, after a good catch, if musicians are handy, one of them
performs a slow and solitary dance for his own pleasure, and
then rejoins the singing and the talk. Sponge fishing and storms
and far travel and shipwrecks and half-a-dozen wars, and sometimes smuggling, play a great part in their conversation; laughter often interrupts it. After dark, beyond the caïque masts,
the water a mile or two out is scattered with constellations
where other sailors are laying their nets from little acetylene-
lit fleets or craning overboard to lunge with their long fish-
spears. Behind them the alleyways descend the hillside in rivu-

lets of cobbles between archways and escalading whitewash. The smell of basil and rosemary fills these lanes, competing with the salt, tar, sweat, resin, fish scales and sawdust of the waterfront. Their life is rigorous to the point of austerity and sometimes of hardship; but there are a hundred things to make it worth while. There is no trace of depression or wage-slavery in the brine-cured and weather-beaten faces under those threadbare caps. The expression is wary, energetic, amused and friendly and their demeanour is a marine compound of masculinity, independence and easy-going dignity.

Then the second vision assembles. The shore is enlivened with fifty jukeboxes and a thousand transistor wirelesses. Each house is now an artistic bar, a boutique or a curio shop; new hotels tower and concrete villas multiply. Battalions of holidaymakers agleam with lotion relax under striped umbrellas. The roar of the speedboats sometimes drowns the transistors, sirens announce fresh steamerloads, helicopters clatter. The caïque-building yard has long been cleared away to make room for a row of bathing huts and a concrete lavatory; the spotless Tourist Police stroll past in couples. Somewhere at the edge of this scene, round a table of tubular metal, the old fishermen sit; they approve of the boom but they are slightly at a loss to know why they are not enjoying themselves any more. The Tourist Police tell them that last week's directive from the ministry forbidding bare feet and narghilé-smoking has been reversed: the tourists find them more picturesque. The mayor observes that his new hygiene-order is being enforced: no donkey is unequipped with the regulation net under its tail to catch the droppings; when the new and unnecessary road is finished and the first blasts of exhaust-smoke and klaxon set the final stamp of civilization on the place those obsolete animals will have to go. The struggle for life is over. The old fishermen's sons have jobs as waiters, knick-knack-salesmen and guides. The more personable fulfil a pliant role similar to that of gondoliers or Capri boatmen, while alms keep the little ones supplied with bubble-gum.

No tubular tables in the old taverna. One of a score now, the *boîte* is redecorated with old ships' timbers. Here, by neonrise, candles in bottles gleam from barrels turned into tables, each with its painted skull-and-crossbones; nets are draped from anchors and tridents, the bulbs hang in lobster pots, while another old fisherman's son in fancy dress twirls on the dance floor in an arranged and stepped-up dance based on the *zeibekiko*. Beaming and sweating in carefree clothes, conducted tours accompany the simplified beat with massed clapping and their own electric guitars and accordions. Cameras flash; Westphalia and the Midlands send up their acclaim.

But all is not well. Bronzed by long sojourn and gazing sadly into their highballs and away from the freckled and steaming influx, the older settlers are at bay. Who could have foreseen all this three summers ago; when their yachts first dropped anchor here; when the first village houses were bought and converted, the earliest cocktail cabinets borne ashore, the first property acquired and developed? The gloom of the fifth century A.D. weighs on them; the dismay of Gothic patricians, long-Romanized, at the sight of their kinsman fresh from Illyricum swarming through the Aurelian walls. It is time to weigh anchor again and seek remoter islands and farther shores and pray for another three years' reprieve.

This vision of the future is coming true. But only a few places are affected and the islanders have so far withstood the impact with considerable dignity. Perhaps they will take it in their stride. If they do, it will call for heroic qualities. It would be sad if Greece went the way of Italy and the South of France. She deserves a nobler destiny. Let those who are responsible see what five years have done to the south coast of Spain, and tremble.

* * * *

The Helleno-Romaic Dilemma seems a small affair beside the tremendous new forces of change; but it is from the two poles of the Dilemma that the strongest resistance will come. The traditional framework of life in the mountains acts as a barrier or, at the least, a series of obstructing hurdles, against innovation. The roads are few and the mountains high and the influence of the plains and the cities can only scale those ranges after long delay. At the other extreme stands the Neo-Hellenic tradition. Its votaries, after a century, regard the wholesale westernizing and innovating spirit of their ancestors, so eager and well-intentioned at its outset, with more caution now. They discern and deplore the accompanying dangers and, though they cannot defeat them, at least they set up a mental opposition. Somewhere between these extremes the weakest point lies.

Imagine a sheet of graph paper. At the top of the left side is a point labelled *Islands and Mountains* and equally high on the right, *Athens*. From each of these points a curve falls steeply and then crosses the page in a shallower sinking arc, and meets the other curve in the centre close to the bottom. Not at zero, however, as the curve beginning at *Islands and Mountains* can also be called *Rustic Romiosyne*, and the other—*Athens*—is also *Urban Hellenism*; the first always has an inchoate inkling of the second, and the second a vestigial residue of the first. The two curves, now forming a single line from left to right, are the psychological journey of a villager, drawn from his range or his island by the city's magnetism, and point D, the half-way intersection point, stands for Danger. By the time he reaches it, the patriarchal defences have fallen nearly to zero and the ascending trend is not yet under way. This point is situated in the outskirts of large towns and above all, of Athens itself, the brightest lodestar of these lonely itineraries. Disarmed and unequipped, the stranger gropes across a no-man's-land. Should all not go well, disappointment and cynicism take possession of him. It is now that the materialism of the West shines its brightest and the propaganda of the East falls on the most un-questioning ears. It is the moment when the instinctive Greek virtues are most in need.

The eclipse of *Romiosyne* will carry off some bad old ways, but much that is precious and venerable. There is something patronizing and unfair in the opposing spirit. It lays claim to all that is virtuous in rustic Greece; all that is backward, super-stitious, lacking in scruple, unpolished or uncivil it groups under Romaic things. This creates an insipid picture of Greece, reducing rustic life to innocuous folklore and whittling the countryman down to an evzone doll. The Greeks are very con-scious of foreign opinion: they tend to shepherd foreigners towards the conventionally acceptable things and away from the backward and the obscure. They need not have these fears. The strangers who form the deepest regard for Greece are not the ones who are bear-led; they are the solitaries whose travels lead them, through chance or poverty or curiosity, along the humble and recondite purlieus of Greek life. The monuments of the past evoke their deserved wonder, but it is not these that finally win pride of place in the memory and affection; it is the live Greeks themselves: not the Greeks as they were two-and-a-half thousand years ago, nor as they will be or could be or should be one day, but as they are.

* * * *

'Really!' I can hear some Athenian exclaim at this point. 'Are we to stop progress for the sake of an occasional eccentric traveller? Undo the work of a hundred-and-fifty years? Bring back piracy and reinstall the brigands, encourage armed faction, civil war, assassination, malaria, illiteracy? What else? Sloth, bribery, dirt, disease, poverty; lawlessness, superstition, stone-age agriculture, the whole wretched inheritance of Ottoman times—all to supply a refreshing change from the sophistication of the West? You seem to forget how poor the country is. Are we to call a halt to industry and tourism? Stop building roads, opening up communications? What about the mountain people for whom you profess such fondness? Ask *them* what they think . . .!' Were I engaged on the task of demolishing my own argument, I would begin on exactly these lines; for he is right, and his questions are unanswerable.

'And,' the hypothetical Athenian might continue, a little wearily, and with equal justice, 'there is little sympathy, I notice, or only a few grudging and perfunctory words, for the terrible difficulty that confronted us; little praise for the efforts of the Neo-Hellenists, the Modernists, the Westernizers, or whatever we are, to deal with it all. You seem to forget the size of the task when we got rid of the Turks. We needed whatever inspiration we could find: why not Ancient Greece? I think'— and here I detect a tolerant smile behind the voice—'we have as good a right to it as the rest of the world. And we are not really quite the philistines or pedants you imply. It is true that many things of value are being sacrificed. We know it and we regret it. It is inevitable, and the same is happening everywhere. But surely the gain outweighs the loss . . .?'

His words are true and as they die from the air I realize how severely they damage my case. The civilized tones of this imaginary Athenian also remind me of the growing number of Greeks who are sadly aware of the predicament: men who must feel the hopelessness of the imbalance with an anguish far deeper than anything that can affect a foreigner. I remember, too, painters like Ghika, poets like Seferis, and a whole world of literature and the arts which has not only assimilated the ancient world and tapped deep sources of inspiration in the world of Byzantium and *Romiosyne*, but absorbed all that the West has to offer as well. They have almost—though not entirely, I hope, in the interests of human variety—reconciled the Helleno-Romaic Dilemma.* But, above all, the invisible

* A couple of months ago I was expounding this Dilemma theory to just such a Greek friend. He was entertained by the idea, and we were wondering what figure could symbolize the two warring principles. A wrestling

speaker brings home yet again the ineluctable doom of *Romiosyne*; by underlining the blessings that accompany its passing, he almost reconciles me to it.

And yet...

And yet, stubborn, unregenerate and irreducible, the pro-Romaic bias lingers. It can be condemned as backward and selfish and dismissed as obsolete; but it thrives as robustly as a field of tares planted by years of wandering and too deep-rooted to uproot. Those distant ranges and archipelagos instilled me with the conviction or the illusion of approach to the truest and most interesting secrets of Greece. Every region has con-tributed to this: the great temples and ruins and the famous summer islands which are the common experience of all visi-tors; but also Macedonia, the Pindus, the Rhodope mountains of Thrace, the midwinter cordilleras by the Albanian border, the rocky hamlets of the Zagora, jagged Epirus, the Thessalian foothills, the hinterland of Roumeli, the Peloponnesian water-sheds, roadless Tzakonia, the ultimate wilderness of the Mani and a whole solar-system of islands. They are not only the background for dilettante wanderings in summer and spring, but for winter too, when life, tormented by wind and rain or hushed by snow, shrinks from its autumnal expanse to huddled lamplit circles in huts and caves: at moments it is a world of wintry chaos, exhilarated by advances and victories and racked by defeat, occupation and discord.

These regions are not empty landscapes but the mineral back-cloth—stage, stage-wings and proscenium—of a theatre flung

---

match between Plato and Kolokotrones? We discarded this for a similar grapple between Pallas Athene and Psorokostaina ('Mangy Betty', see *Mani*, page 208), the poor, ragged old woman who, in the early days of Greece's liberty in the last century, became a satirical but affectionate nick-name for the woebegone aspects of the new state. 'I've got it!' my interlo-cutor said at last. 'It would be Karayiozi's eye peeping through the holes in a mask of tragedy!'

up for the Greeks themselves: diminished when the cast withdraws, validated by their entry. Piranesi and Lear place figures about their scenery for scale or decoration or local colour or corroborative detail. It is not so here. Each pair of eyes and each voice is anarchically distinct. Isolated against horizontal and zigzag, magnified by a lens of light, sharpened by the sun's behaviour, fragmented above blazing thorns or transfigured by lightning, every face in turn is the protagonist of its own drama.

* * * *

Crete gave my retrogressive hankerings their final twist. In spite of the insular pride of the inhabitants, their aloofness from the mainland and the idiosyncrasy of their dialect and their customs, this island is an epitome of Greece. Greek virtues and vices, under sharper mountains and a hotter sun, reach exasperation point. It is, in the unpejorative sense with which I have been trying to rehabilitate the word, the most Romaic region of all; the last region the Turks relinquished. In another sense it is the least; Crete fell to the Turks two centuries later than the rest of the Byzantine Empire. This reprieve was the last half of four hundred years of restless subjection to Venice. In 1669, after a long siege, Candia fell to the Turks, and for two hundred and forty-six years Crete was the worst governed province of the Ottoman Empire and the one where the conquering race was thickest on the ground. It was the fault of the Great Powers, not Crete, that her liberation was so long delayed. Revolts against the Venetians had been leavened by interregna of literary and artistic activity. But her history under the Turks was a sequence of insurrections, massacres, raids, pursuits and wars almost without a break. Enosis with Greece was only achieved in 1915.

Like certain ranges of Epirus and the Mani, the Cretan mountains were never entirely subdued. The struggle could only have been carried on in a land of wild mountains by people of exceptional vitality and determination. There is hardly a village where the old men are unable to recall at least one rebellion and remember with advantages the deeds they did. (Until a few years ago, an old woman in the nome of Retimo still survived from the siege of the Abbey of Arkadi. Having turned it into a fortress and refuge against the besieging Turks, the abbot, when supplies at last ran short, touched off the powder magazine and sent himself and his fellow-defenders sky high.* One tiny swaddled girl, blown a couple of furlongs, landed in a thicket and lived. . . .) The memory of these times was still fresh in 1941, when the island was invaded by the German parachutists. Following the instinct of centuries, the old men and boys and women (for the retreat had marooned nearly everyone of military age on the mainland) leapt to arms and fell on the invaders alongside their allies. Instead of three years of docile subjection these acts ushered in bitter resistance.

The grandeurs and miseries of the occupation are well known. But that is not, here, the point. It is this. When, with a scattered handful of other Englishmen, I found myself involved in these doings, the ranges strung between Ida and the White Mountains were our refuge; the people we lived among were mountaineers, shepherds and villagers living high above the plains and the cities in circumstances which exactly tallied with the life and the background of the Klephts in revolt at any time during the past few hundred years. Modern life had only found the most hazardous foothold; many of the blemishes of lawless mountain life ran riot. There were leaders of guerrilla bands who were paragons of courage and unselfishness; a few, equally brave, were as ruthless and ambitious as Tamburlaine. The habit of centuries, as we have seen, impelled resistance to the occupation at all costs. It had also bequeathed lawless customs which now wreak havoc among the Cretans them-

* The event, which occurred in 1866, was celebrated by Swinburne in his poem about 'rent Arkadion'.

selves. They are virtually weaned on powder and shot; every shepherd goes armed, and a worship of guns and great skill in handling them dominate the highlands. The rustling of flocks, though it is on the wane, still goes on. Marriages sometimes begin by the armed abduction of the bride by her suitor and his friends, and blood feuds, initiated, perhaps, by one of these two causes or by an insult, by rage or an exchange of shots, can decimate opposing families over a space of decades and seal up neighbouring villages in hostile deadlock. Harsh and terrible deeds are done in the name of family honour. The wildness of the country puts these things beyond the reach of the law and fills the mountains, even in peacetime, with a scattered population of outlaws; in war, when all shadow of authority except the hostile and impotent writ of the enemy was swept aside, lawless ways doubly prospered. In spite of the occupation, in which these mountaineers were so resolute and determined, private vengeance (especially in Sphakia and Selino) laid many villagers low.

All this is confined to a few regions and it is on the wane. Obviously, it is the duty of the state to stamp out these fierce customs. Yet I can never hear or read of a Cretan mountaineer being hunted down and brought to book for participating in one of these mountain feuds without a feeling of compunction: the juxtaposition of modern law and those eagle-haunted wildernesses seems somehow as incongruous as the idea of Orestes bundled into a Black Maria. For many of these tragedies are, by age-old standards, innocent; they are prompted by feelings of duty and conducted with honour.* There was much

---

* They have nothing to do with the extinct horrors of brigandage. These customs are deplored by all except the very small minority who practise them; some villages have a very bad name. But the general attitude may be likened to the reciprocal cattle-reaving which held sway on the Scots and English border, or in the Highlands before their pacification. (The two atmospheres are related in more ways than one.) They are not in any way comparable to the sinister murders of the Mafia or the Camorra, which are rooted in squalid urban greed and enforced by terrorism. Most

to deplore; much more, however, to admire; in particular their courage and the compassion that prompted them to shelter, clothe and feed the straggling army of their marooned allies. For this hundreds of Cretans were killed in reprisal massacres, and scores of villages were burnt to ashes; and, when their protégés were safely spirited away to Africa, their ardour was poured into resistance, and, most mercifully for us, into backing up the handful of foreign emissaries who had been dropped into their midst to help carry on the secret war. It was no mean thing for these solitary allies in their midst to feel that they had the support of a dozen mountain-ranges and of several hundred villages; indeed, if need be—and there was need, now and then—of the whole island.

But, apart from these general qualities, so propititious to the struggle which was afoot, it was the detail and the structure of their life—in which we aspired, in speech and manner, to drown ourselves—which invited fascination and respect.

Little in these crags and ravines had changed for centuries. One felt that each village must have existed since Minoan times. There was little there but a church filled with flaking Byzantine frescoes and a slanting maze of stepped and cobbled lanes; but there were subtle differences in the weave and the pattern of blankets and knapsacks and the way that men tied their fringed headkerchiefs, and in the cut of their hooded capes, and in some of them, a distinguishing accent, a variant of the Cretan dialect, and even of physical appearance. However often these villages had been sacked and burned they were always built again and according to an unbreakable formula. I remember sitting on the flat roof of a friend's* house in Anoyeia, on the slopes of Mount Ida, and, as I gazed at the

---

of the killers in American gang warfare are of Southern Italian and Sicilian origin, while the Greek contribution, as far as I can make out, is nil.

* My godbrother Stephanoyanni Dramoudanis, killed in 1943. He had been arrested by the enemy for helping us. He made a break for it, with his hands tied behind his back, but was shot down as he leapt a wall.

moonlit jigsaw of roofs and houses all round, calling to mind Aristotle's ideal for the capitals of the Greek states: cities small enough to hear the voice of one herald.

We seldom stayed in villages; not through fear of treachery, but lest innocent garrulity should endanger them. The houses contained little: a semicircular arch across the living-room, a smoke-blackened hearth, a low ledge of divan round the walls spread with coloured blankets, a loom, a wooden table and stools, the icons and their lamp and a pitcher with thorn twigs in the mouth against flying insects. Onions, garlic and tomatoes hung from the cobwebbed beams; faded pictures of Venizelos looked down from the walls and enlarged sepia photographs of turbaned grandsires armed to the teeth. Hens, pecking their way indoors, were always being shooed out, and swallows dived to and from their nest in the rafters with a swish; when we were there, rifles leaned in the corner and lay across the tables; some were adorned with silver plaques and cartridge-belts heavy with flashing clips festooned them. The thick embrasures of the windows and the doors framed downhill cascades of olives and a canyon twisting between dovetailing scarps; often these vistas ended in a triangle of the Aegean or the Libyan Sea; they were nearly always commanded by the upheaval of Ida or the White Mountains. Sometimes, with sentries posted, after a banquet with the Olympianly bearded priest, the mayor and the village elders, we would stay the night. At these meals, the women, coiffed and clad in black—saviours of numberless British, New Zealand and Australians—served and stood near with arms akimbo; they joined in the conversation spiritedly but, in this masculine and patriarchal society, seldom sat with us. In villages like this I was treated for small maladies now and then—for rheumatism, due to constant sleeping out in wet clothes—and for persistent headaches. The universal remedy of cupping was followed, in every case, by darker therapies administered by clever old women: many candle-lit signs of the cross were performed over the afflicted part; incantations accompanied them, and oil dropped slowly into a glass of water in ritual quantities. Once a beautiful young witch knotted a pinch of salt in one corner of my turban and murmured spells for half an hour. Impossible to discover the words: '*mystiká prágmata! Kalá prágmata! Vaskaníes!*' was the only answer, through lips across which forefingers were conspiratorially laid; words followed by peals of laughter from the women and the girls who gather at such times: 'Secret things! Good things! Charms . . .!' They worked at once.

But the high mountains, for nearly three years, were our real home. It was there, at the end of hours climbing and higher than the dizziest village, that devotion to the Greek mountains and their population took root. We lived in goat-folds and abandoned conical cheese-makers' huts and above all, in the myriad caverns that mercifully riddle the island's stiff spine. Some were too shallow to keep out the snow, others could house a Cyclops and all his flocks. Here, at ibex- and eagle-height, we settled with our small retinues. Enemy searches kept us on the move and it was in a hundred of these eyries that we got to know an older Crete and an older Greece than anyone dreams of in the plains. Under the dripping firelit stalactites we sprawled and sat cross-legged, our eyes red with smoke, on the branches that padded the cave's floor and spooned our suppers out of a communal tin plate: beans, lentils, cooked snails and herbs, accompanied by that twice-baked herdsman's bread that must be soaked in water or goats' milk before it is eaten. Toasting goats' cheese sizzled on the points of long daggers and oil dewed our whiskers.* These sessions were often cheered by flasks of raki, occasionally distilled from mulberries,

---

* Before beginning, all signed themselves with the cross, their thumb and two first fingers conjoined to honour the Trinity, the cross-bar going from right shoulder to left in the Orthodox way; and, at the meal's end, before storing away any fragments of bread left over, they would kiss them in memory of the Mystic Feast.

sent from the guardian village below. On lucky nights, cala-
bashes of powerful amber-coloured wine loosened all our
tongues. Over the shoulders of each figure was slung a bristly
white cloak stiff as bark, with the sleeves hanging loose like
penguins' wings; the hoods raised against the wind gave the
bearded and moustachioed faces a look of Cistercians. turned
bandit. Someone would be smashing shells with his pistol-butt
and offering peeled walnuts in a horny palm; another sliced
tobacco on the stock of a rifle: for hours we forgot the war
with talk and singing and stories; laughter echoed along mino-
taurish warrens.

Few of the old men could write or read, those in middle age
found reading hard and writing a grind; the young were defter
penmen, but, owing to their short time at school and the disorder of the war, they were not advanced in the craft, apart
from an occasional student on the run from the underground
in one of the towns. A by-product of this scholastic void was a
universal gift for lively and original talk; the flow and style of
their discourse were unhindered by the self-consciousness which
hobbles and hamstrings the rest of us. They had astonishing
memories. These often reached back to their great-grandfathers'
day, and, by hearsay, far beyond. In an island of long lives, this
made all the past seem recent: compelling proof of the con-
tinuity of history. It reduced the war to just another struggle,
the worst and the most recent of many, with which we were
perfectly able to deal, and, though the Germans had overrun
Greece and driven the British back to El Alamein, win. 'Never
fear, my child,' some greybeard would say, prophetically prod-
ding the smoke with a forefinger like a fossil, 'with Christ and
the Virgin's help, we'll eat them.' All agreed, and the conversation wandered to the First World War and Asia Minor and
arguments about the respective merits of Lloyd George and
Clemenceau, to Bismarck and the assassination of Abraham
Lincoln, or the governments, constitutions and electoral sys-
tems of different countries. Then the level of this far-ranging

chat, much of it far beyond the scope of their literate equivalents in England, might suddenly be reduced by another old man, simpler than his fellows, asking, and evoking general derision and amusement by his question, whether the English were Christians or, like the Moslems, polygamous. . . . Intelligence, humour, curiosity, the rapid assimilation of ideas and their quick deployment, an incomparable narrative knack, arguments resolved by a sudden twist, the inability to leave facts and ideas undeveloped—they are objects to play with like nuggets—all these graces flowered in this stony terrain. The Cretan dialect, with its ancient survivals and turns of phrase and a vocabulary that changed from valley to valley and an accent unpolluted by the metropolis, was an unstaunchable fountain of delight and fascination.

Their clothes, however ragged and patched, were emblematic of the dash and spirit they prize so highly: black boots to the knee, baggy, pleated, dark-blue trousers—breeches among the young*—wasp-waisted at the middle by a twisted mulberry silk sash eight feet long in which was often stuck a long dagger with a branching ivory hilt and an embossed silver sheath; above this came a black shirt and sometimes a blue waistcoat as tight as a bullfighter's, stiff with embroidered whorls. A black silk turban with a heavy fringe was twisted at a rakish tilt round every brow. Bandoliers and a slung gun came next—fittings which often accompanied the frocks of abbots, monks and priests—and over them, in winter, the white hooded cape. A curly handled stick, never a crook as on the mainland, with as many wriggles along its shaft as could be found, finishes everything off. All, however tattered and frayed by mountain life, is taut and streamlined, a garb in which, as I well know, it is impossible not to swagger. This bravura was accentuated among the old men by the odd archaic cut of their beards;

* Cretans of the towns and the lowlands who had abandoned this mode were referred to, with some scorn but more pity, as *makrypantalonddes*: 'longtrousermen'.

shorn under the jaw-line, they jutted from their chins like the beards of ancient warriors on vases. This look was underscored by their deceptively frowning eyebrows and the high hawklike bridges of their noses. The ferocity of those swooping brows was contradicted by the eyes beneath. These are seldom wary and reserved, as they are in the Mani: alert, confident, wide, humorous and unguarded, they blaze like lamps.* Everything about these men spells alacrity and vigour. They are lean, sweated to the bone, strong and resilient; the old are as hard as the limestone that surrounds them, the young as fast across the mountains as Hurons, as untamed as ibexes. Nowhere in Greece is the quality of *leventeiá* so clearly manifest. This attribute embraces a range of characteristics: youth, health, nerve, high spirits, humour, quickness of mind and action, skill with weapons, the knack of pleasing girls, love for singing and drinking, generosity, capacity to improvise *mantinades*—those intricate rhyming couplets sung with a sting in the second line —and 'flying like a bird' in the quick and violent dances. *Leventeiá* often includes virtuosity on the *lyra*: it is universal zest for life, the love of living dangerously and a readiness for anything.

Rather unexpectedly, this supercharge of energy and extroversion is shot with a most delicately poised sensitiveness, sometimes by a touchiness, where a mishap or a slight, even an imaginary one, can turn the world black and drive its victim into melancholy and languor, almost to pining away. It is the task of friends to diagnose the anguish and exorcize it; not always an easy task. This lurking demon, resembling the *tribulatio et angustia* of the Psalms, the Greeks call *stenachoria*.

---

* The island was captured from the Byzantines by the Saracens of Spain in the eighth century, and turned into a nest of corsairs. Rather more than a century later they were driven into the sea; the island was seized for Byzantium again by Nicephorus Phocas and seven half-legendary princes. Here and there, especially in the south, one can detect a line of nose, a curl of brow, that may ultimately spring from this piratical sojourn.

But the problem acts both ways: should distress assault one, they recognize its symptoms with an almost feminine intuitiveness and try, with tact and solicitude, to resolve it; and even if they are mistaken about the cause, this kindness may allay the effect. Their need and their talent for friendship is the obverse of implacable hatred for enemies.

Stenachoria finds them helpless; but, with the major calamities that shower down upon them, they are better fitted to deal; ancestral reactions come to the rescue. The loss of a kinsman in a mountain affray or a reprisal holocaust would unloose grief and rage which, ungovernable at first, the longing for vengeance would channel and the anodynes of fatalism slowly allay. The Cretans see life in tragic and heroic terms. This being so, it is fortunate that their feeling of comedy is also pronounced. They are preternaturally quick at locating the ludicrous aspects of things; they seize the point and throw it back in a different shape. (The gift for laughter in Greece becomes still more remarkable when we think of her neighbours. Turkey, the Slav states, Albania and Southern Italy weave a dark garland of literalness and scarce jokes. . . .) This blessing lightened many of our troubles. It gave a marvellous zest to those long troglodytic sessions which, especially in winter, often kept us pent.

These were the times when one heard how to foretell the future by dreams and by gazing at the markings on the scraped shoulder blades of sheep and learnt about the superstitions and beliefs which still survive there; about gorgons and nereids and vampires; of the 'light-shadowed ones', who can see more than ordinary mortals; of how an ancestor of the Manouras family fought with a dragon outside his village, and how, at each anniversary of the Battle of Frangokástello, phantom hosts of Greeks and Turks—'the people of the dew'—complete with guns and cannon and banners, are seen to fight the battle all over again. The hours were often whiled away with singing *mantinades*. Some of us even learnt to improvise them ourselves, which was considered a feat for strangers, and hailed with applause. There were many songs. But *ta rizitika*, 'the foothill ones', were far beyond our scope, so intricate are they, so unseizable in key and rhythm and changes of tempo. One called *Chelidonáki mou gorgó*, 'my swift little swallow', especially sticks in my memory. . . . The *lyra* often accompanied these songs; it is a three-stringed instrument a foot-and-a-half long, propped upright on the musician's knee and played with a bow. Beautifully hollowed and carved out of walnut, this smooth and polished instrument is light as a feather and capable of a great range of moods. Exciting and violin-like, the melodic line swoops, soars, twirls, laments and exults with a manic-depressive fluidity. It was good luck to have a *lyra*-player in one's party, not only for the sake of the music; the players are great fun, as a rule, fast runners, and crack shots; nonpareils of *leventeiá*, in fact.*

The lucid memory of the old men made a century or two ago sound as recent as yesterday. Take the *Erotókritos!* This poem was written by a shadowy figure called Vincentios Cornaros from the east of the island. A Cretan, in spite of his august Venetian name (perhaps, but not certainly, of remote Venetian origin), he lived in the early seventeenth century during the last decades of the Venetian occupation. The poem, nearly twelve thousand lines of fifteen-syllable rhyming hexameters, is written in deep and wonderful Cretan. Romantic and epic in style, its Arcadian and mediaeval background suggests Orlando Furioso and the dream region of Shakespeare's wood near Athens. Mountains tower, seas rage, battlements frown from crags, horns resound, glades echo to the cry of hounds, hawks hover, throne-rooms glitter, bowers and chambers are

---

* The instrument is only to be found in Crete, but a similar one, though it is narrower in shape, used to be played by the Laz-speaking Greeks of Pontus, near Trebizond on the Black Sea in the confines of the Caucasus. One can still hear it now and then in those villages where Pontic refugees have been settled, mostly in Thrace and Macedonia.

lulled by lute strings, swords clang together, lance after lance is splintered in ceremonious and deadly tournaments. It is the background for the thwarted and ill-starred loves of the hero, Erotókritos and Aretousa, the king of Athens' daughter; ill-starred, that is, until the happy ending, by which time fabulous beasts, witches, spells and terrible steel-clad rivals and a thousand hazards in castles, ravines and forests have all been overcome. This chivalrous and magical world of fable was just as remote from the author's period as Cervantes from the books that Don Quixote read. Unknown outside Greece because of the deep vernacular that enshrouds it and its daunting length for a translator—though many, including me, have longingly toyed with the idea—it is one of the great epic poems of Europe.

In Crete, this tremendous metrical saga plays the part of the Homeric cycle in Dorian times. Everyone knows it, all can quote vast tracts, and, astonishingly, some of the old men in the mountains, though unable to read and write, could, and still can, recite the whole poem by heart; when one remembers that it is nearly a thousand lines longer than the Odyssey, this feat makes one scratch one's head with wonder or disbelief. They intone rather than recite it; the voice rises at the caesura and at the end of the first line of a couplet, and drops at the end of the second; now and then to break the monotony, the key shifts. During our winter vigils, it continued for hours; every so often another old man would take over; listening, I occasionally dropped off for an hour or two, and woke to find Erotókritos in the thick of yet another encounter with the Black Knight of Karamania. (He symbolized, at the time the poem first saw the light, the threat of the Ottomans; Turkey had already conquered the rest of Greece, and was soon to submerge Crete itself.) The rhythmic intoning might sway on till daybreak, with some of the listeners rapt, others nodding off or snoring; or until a runner broke in from the dark like a snowman in a gyre of flakes; the news of arrests in Herakleion,

Retimo or Canea or the alarm of a mountain battalion advancing up the valley jerked us all into motion.

*　　*　　*　　*

Life was not always dark and speluncar. When the snows melted we would pitch our ephemeral quarters on ledges of rock among cedars twisted by the wind, or in high and lonely folds of the mountains far from the eyes of all but initiate shepherds. We exchanged the hut roofs and the cave ceilings for a low and enormous procession of stars or a moon so bright that when it was full the colour of the sea, the mountains, the trees, the thorns and the faces of our companions all showed, as in a reduced daylight, darker replicas of their diurnal colour. The valleys, the foothills and the answering ranges beyond had the gleam of sheet-metal hammered into angles. A blink and a refocus of the eye would bring them close and interleave and volatilize them into a floating and insubstantial universe where only the shadows looked solid: shadows that rocketed in wide spikes up the flanks of the peaks, zigzagged down ravines and spread like immobilized forked lightning along the torrent beds; rock-faults, invisible by daylight, slanted in stripes; the void between the beetling sides of chasms rose in dark obelisks; tapering clefts pitched illusory pyramids: convex and concave changed places. The shade thrown by the nearby fissures, grottos, branches, eyebrows, rifle barrels and scabbards loomed from the insubstantial radiance in geometric figures. They were bars, parallelograms, triangles, lozenges and polygons of darkness; Cubist scenery in which each clump of aloes and cactus rose in a still vortex.

This night life is lodged all the more firmly in my memory because for a long time it was only then that we could move about the island. Night became day. 'Look,' a Cretan said, as the upper rim of the moon appeared behind a screen of hills, 'our sun is rising. Time to set off!'; and another nocturnal journey began. This was sometimes a caravan of mules loaded with arms and explosives dropped from the sky or disembarked in a lonely cove; sometimes we headed for plateaux where, after days of postponement, the momentary quincunx of our bonfires would bring fresh supplies thudding round us; unless, that is, no miscalculation or sudden wind or confusion of landmarks in the pilot's eye scattered them among the enemy. More often these travels were undertaken alone except for one companion. Cavemen released, free to leave the mountains at last, and bound for some faraway meeting or gathering of guerrillas, we would descend to the foothills and lose height down glimmering staircases of olive and vineyard. The villages through which we stalked with our guns cocked were silent and unreal as fictions of snow and ivory. We tiptoed under their arches and down lanes that twisted round the corners in paper fans of steps. Sometimes we stopped with circumspection at the shutter of a friend's house, and after a brief entry and whispered confabulation, continued on our way. Metallic chestnut woods gleamed; the oleanders and poplars were doubly silver by the beds of shrunk streams. The water had dwindled to a net of quicksilver in a waste of boulders that Venetian or Turkish bridgebuilders had spanned with pale arcs of masonry. At a loop in a valley, hundreds of frogs drowned the nightingales, the drilling of crickets and the little owl's hesitant note. We heard dogs in the villages and brief jangles as flocks woke and fell asleep again in folds half-way to the sky. These sounds strung a thread of urgency and collusion through the peace of the night. Sometimes we would lie flat with held breath in a cactus clump or among the rocks or flattened against a wall under an archway till the footfalls of an enemy patrol died away; noticing that the boulders, the dust and the white plaster were still warm from the daylight hours of midsummer basking. The smell of many herbs filled the air. (A fragrance so powerful that it surrounds the island with a halo of sweet smells several miles in radius; it told us when we were stealthily approaching Crete by sea on moonless nights from the stinking desert, and long before we could descry the great silhouette, that we were getting near.) Advancing through the warm night, we had the sleeping island to ourselves and a thousand charms hung in the air. We reached our rendezvous before dawn; a broken-down water mill, a small monastery thinly monked by warlike brethren, a solitary chapel, a circular threshing floor, or a lonely goat-fold on a high ledge. There would be challenge and answer, a scrape of hobnails on rock and a clinking of arms as dark figures rose gleaming from the shadows into the moonlight; then salutations and fifty whiskery embraces. When the moon set, the sky lifted a wing of radiance at the other end of the heavens. The shafts of the sun sloped up into the air from many clefts between the eastern vertebrae of the island. When the beams fell horizontal, our meeting place was anchored like a flying carpet in the line of their advance. We killed the microbe of the night with swigs of raki and watched these massed prisms of light shooting beyond us for overlapping leagues until they hit and ignited the white ibex-haunts in the west. The peaks all round us sent darker volleys of shadow along their path, all of them streaming westwards and tilting down into the canyons until the whole intervening labyrinth was filled with early light.

*　　*　　*　　*

The Cretans have many backgrounds. Visions, accumulated over nearly a thousand nights and days, drop into the brain and replace each other with the speed of lantern slides: darting scattered through olive trees, firing from behind rocks and walls, then running forward again; cursing at wounds, stoically dying; in flight from blazing and exploding villages, uttering promises of vengeance through their teeth; executing, on a lonely plateau, apprehended traitors; sitting, at peaceful moments, relaxed under the great plane tree of a village; gathering grapes into giant baskets; treading out the wine; watching the women harvest the olives by beating the branches with poles of reed and bringing the berries pattering on the bright blankets spread below; loading mules with cheeses like millstones; raising dust clouds at the dance to the *lyra's* frenzy; assembling at midnight in a church set about with sentries while some proscribed foreigner stands godfather to the child of a friend; feasting afterwards on a roof and emptying their pistols into the air to bring luck to the newly-baptized little girl.* There are battle scenes, dramas, genre pictures, conversation pieces, kermesses and eclogues, all subdivided into close-ups which pin this world down and make it jut and recede in its proper dimensions.

Were my feelings for the island planted by insufficient and subjective causes? The circumstances of war and the exhilaration of youth have much to do with it; also, perhaps, some chance affinities with the Cretan temperament, abetted by an interest in remote communities and language. The emotions of gratitude and of brotherhood-in-arms and community of purpose all play a part; the Greek bent for hospitality, too, and the universal wish to please. My sentiments may have been affected by our position in their midst. After all, we were isolated links with the headquarters on which all of our military fortunes depended, lonely swallows presaging summer; magicians, almost, who could summon arms and gold from the sea and the sky. But any straggling allied soldier, from whom nothing could be expected but death and destruction as the punishment for harbouring him, was welcomed and cared for as warmly; and all their sacrifices were prompted by an imperious sense of duty; some of them were, quite literally, saints. They not only risked everything to help their solitary allies; they made them members of the Cretan family. Best of all, they forgave our mistakes.

In a place where all is violent and extreme, faults must abound. The passion for arms, the dashing costume, the im-

---

* E.g. my pretty goddaughter Anglia, child of Chariclea and Stephanoyanni Dramoudanis of Anoyeia. See p. 128 (note).

mense and articulate local pride sometimes degenerate. A
damaging minority of *pallikarádes*, as they are called—armed
braggarts or bravos, as opposed to *pallikária*, or warriors—
and of *pseudokapetanaioi*—'false captains'—does exist. Some of
them proved, surprisingly, as good as their wildest boasts.
Others vapoured about the foothills on their own or attached
themselves until they could be got rid of to the fringe of
guerrilla bands; useless mouths to fill and a burden to their
commanders. (It is a type of Cretan which, in Athens or on the
mainland, gives a bad name to the island in communities that
do not know Crete itself.) Mistrust of the truth clouded matters
now and then, and the ravines were smooth channels for
rumour—it murmured there as unreally, sometimes, as the
noise of the sea in the whorls of a shell. Internal suspicion and
jealousies were frequent stumbling blocks. Collaboration with
the enemy was miraculously scarce, treachery rarer still. Head-
strong wills sometimes collided, anger flared, the canyons
echoed with ultimata. 'Ah, *Micháli mou*,' an old Cretan said to
me at such a moment. 'We've only got to put a glass roof over
this island, and there's a first-class lunatic asylum for you. . . .'
But in spite of all these things, there must be a deep underlying
wisdom that guides the island in time of stress: the resistance in
Crete, under an occupation of great savagery, was one of the
best organized in Europe. It was resolutely maintained and
unanimously backed; and, in spite of the island's name for discord and insurrection, it was one of the few parts of occupied
Europe which was not, after the liberation, mangled by civil
strife. Political differences were sunk. The movement was
launched beyond recall from the moment the Cretans took up
arms at the invasion; it absorbed all the best in Crete. All that
was good, brave, wise, tough, enterprising, spirited, dangerous
or amusing was on the same side; every Odysseus and Pheidip-
pides, all the Hectors, Ajaxes, Nestors, Lancelots, Merlins,
Rowlands, Herewards, Robin Hoods, Maid Marians, Friar
Tucks, Dick Turpins, Hiawathas, Kims and Mowglis, were

ours. Communist organizations wrought chaos on the mainland; when, later on, they attempted to do the same in Crete,
only the scum was left for them to recruit. Negligible in
numbers and deplorable in quality, they were soon scattered.

* * * *

The island has always abounded with marvels and portents
and the exaggeration of the mountains casts an overpowering
spell. Insanity and genius vibrate in the air. It is no wonder that
the spirit of early Greece, surfacing in the Minoan world, took
so odd a twist here, or that this should be the birthplace of Zeus
and the setting of the myths of Pasiphae and the Minotaur and
Daedalus. Nobody who knows the lines and the mood of these
mountains can be surprised that they gave birth to the most
brilliant of the Greek schools of icon painting; those crags
almost turn El Greco into an explicable phenomenon.

The islanders' passion for their country turns the island itself
into the heroine of most of their songs: 'Crete, my beautiful
island, crown of the Levant,' runs one of the couplets they often
sing, 'your earth is silver and your rocks are diamonds.' This is
more than a flowery trope: the metamorphic limestone mass,
especially where it soars above the tree-line in a wilderness
where nothing can grow, does shine like silver and lend to the
great peaks, even in August, an illusion of eternal snow; and the
sharp-edged and many-faceted rocks throw back the light with
a dazzling and adamantine flash. In ravines and hollows at midday, when the sun has drained every shadow, a hint of fear is
present. There are no trees for the cicadas, no goat bells to be
heard across the stagnant air; the far-off ricochets of an invisible
shepherd practising against a boulder, stop. Sound expires with
a gasp; the only hint of life is a horned skeleton lying among
the rocks, as though an ogre lived not far off. The world becomes a hushed and blinding wilderness. Colour ebbs from the
sky; the hot mineral shudders; all is haggard and aghast. It is
the hour of meridian fright and an invisible finger runs up the

nape of the lonely traveller there and sets his hair on end. At
moments like these the island stands in the sea like an anvil for
the inaudible strokes of the sun.

Then pinpoints of shade expand. There is a jangle, and a
waking hoof, unloosing a small landslide and an echo, puts an
end to this catalepsy. Afternoon divides the ascending gorges
with diagonals of light and flutes the overhangs of rock.
Shadows accumulate in corridors frilled with dittany. Narrow
enough for spiders to span, they wind for miles at the bottom
of precipices that almost close overhead. At last the walls begin
to yawn and fall apart. The gap is full of wheeling kestrels and
a causeway opens on the hollow evening universe.

Below, in the gold and powdery radiance, village follows
village down the flanks of Canaanitish valleys. Their western
walls descend in tiers of light. If it is spring, a mist of green corn
bright with poppies almost brushes the olive branches. Later,
the lanes are pulpy with fallen mulberries; flocks trail their
shadows along the slant of the light in a score of tinkling dust-
clouds. But, in the years of which I have been speaking, we had
to turn away from these georgic scenes and climb into a landscape as different from them as another star. In those giant
apocalyptic regions the sun lingered long after the lowlands
had been invaded by dusk. Lit still by the remains of the day,
the rocks flared ochre and apricot and orange, with shadows of
electric green and ice- and magnesium-blue. The edges of the
crags and the tilted rock-blades turned saffron and mauve as the
last light filled those barren glades and slid upwards out of
reach. Then in the wolf-light, the colours would soften and
deepen and merge and each dying stone disputed the advance
of the dark with its own private glow. The world became
legendary. Oracular caves gaped, chasms of delusion fell away,
each canyon was the Valley of the Shadow. Sinais, and the Eternal
Rocks in the background of Cretan icons, soared. Solemnity
invaded everything. We were in the landscape of St Jerome's
hermitage, of *trecento* Temptations and Agonies. High above,

on the uttermost pinnacle, the last of the daylight would linger like a Transfiguration, then glide aloft and disperse in the fainting and darkening sky. It was night. Our red cigarette ends would brighten as we sat on the rocks before the final weary scramble and the exchange of whistles in the dark that would tell us that we were home again.

Stop press

A last word on *Romiosyne!* In 1901, the writer Argyris Ephtaliotis published a book called *A History of Romiosyne.* The name was pounced on at once and Hellenism instantly found a brilliant champion in the academician, archaeologist and writer, George Sotiriadis.* Reviewing the book, he demanded that the word *Romios* should henceforth be used only in one specific and pejorative sense: 'a mean, vulgar and sordid man'—Greek is understood. His fiat evoked distinguished opposition; a giant rose from the shadows: Kostis Palamas, no less. (The place of Palamas† among Greek poets exactly matches that of Victor Hugo and Tennyson in France and England, and homage to his supremacy is sometimes rendered with a trace of Gide's famous reluctance about Hugo.) The poet, in seven persuasive pages, goes to the opposite extreme from Sotiriadis. Some form of the word *Romios,* he urges (quoting Krumbacher), was the ordinary word for a Greek from the reign of Justinian to the time when he, Palamas, was writing. It was the identity of the Eastern half of the Empire with Christianity which drove the word 'Hellene' from everyone's lips. Among Christian Greeks, the word now meant only a compatriot who clung to the pagan faith, an idolator, and when the gods went underground into folklore, the name of their votaries dropped into disuse too. Outside scholarship, the word only dimly survived in folk tales and fairy stories, where the word 'Hellene'

* Father and father-in-law of old friends, Roxani and Shan Sedgwick.
† 1859–1943.

still carries a suggestion of supermen and giants.* Perhaps they
are a survival from the stories about the titans still lingering on
dimly in country minds, the ghosts of ghosts. The resurrection
of 'Hellene', says Palamas, is dust flung in the eyes of foreigners;
(surely this is too harsh?); *Romios*, reality.

The word he urges, is anything but shameful. It may not,
like 'Hellene', be garlanded with the victor's wild olive from
the Olympic games, but it is wreathed with the thorns of
martyrdom and redolent of thyme and gunpowder. The name
conjures up the glories of Byzantium, but also its fall and all the
ensuing sorrows. And now, writes Palamas, the martyrdom of
the *Romios* still continues: on his back all the new sins of the
liberated and constitutional Hellenes are loaded. He is frog-
marched into the alien role of the vulgar pseudo-politician
bawling in the coffee houses of Athens, the paunchy gasbag
and the know-all—the 'average Greek' of Athenian caricatures
—who is always bragging about how he would fix things in
the new kingdom, if he had his way. In a passage of great skill,
Palamas deftly switches the blame for the now restricted and
pejorative interpretation of *Romios* to the vices and pretentions
of the resuscitated Hellenes.

It meant, he continues, something different to their ancestors.
The name was worn like a mantle of glory. It was emblematic
of a lonely aristocratic pride, a possession not to be exchanged
for all the principalities of the Orient and the West. He cites
the klephtic song of Vlachavas, the last of the great armatoles
of the Khasian crags between Olympus and the Meteora:
'*Romios ego gennithika, Romios the na pethano*' he says in the song,
before he was slowly cut in small pieces, without a single groan,
by the executioners of Ali Pasha: 'A *Romios* I was born and a
Romios I shall die.' Palamas then brings up a damaging battery
of quotations, in each of which '*Romios*' is synonymous with
honour and warlike courage. He begins with a mediaeval song
in which the Greek soldiers cry 'Dragons and the children of

* See p. 39.

dragons are the Romaic warriors.' 'Bulgars and Albanians and Serbs and *Romioi*,' wrote the poet Rigas Pheraios, urging the Balkans to unite against the Ottoman rule, 'are girding on their swords.' 'Behold the *Romioi*, the stout pallikars,' says a Cretan, describing some ancient siege, 'little reck they for the arrows and the shot, the culverins and the lances!' Daskaloyannis, the Cretan hero, 'yearns in his heart for the day when enslaved Crete shall be *Romiosyne*', and urges all the *Romioi* to rise up 'and devour the Turks'. In 1792 Lambros Katsonis, the great seaman who harried the Turkish fleet all over the Aegean, refers to the 'renowned company of Romaic fighting men who represent the Hellenic race'—a significant juxtaposition! When the great Kolokotronis himself, in his *Events of the Hellenic Race*, opposes the Turks to 'the Romans', he does the same. The death of the hero of Souli, Marko Botsaris, in the battle of Karpenisi, was lamented at once in klephtic verse:

> 'And when the Romioi learnt the news, and when
>   they heard the tidings'

(curious how reminiscent of the Songs in the Old Testament, and especially of the Psalms, is this rephrasing of the same statement!)

> 'they dressed themselves in clothes of black, they clad
>   themselves in mourning.'

This is heavy artillery. Nothing vulgar, mean or sordid here. After vindicating and setting free the word he found so bitterly wronged, he counter-attacks with vigour: What about the word 'Hellene'? Is it not obsolete and artificial, and, with its lingering hints of the pagan world, inaccurate? Is there not something ceremonious and sluggish about it—pompous, in fact? Mr Ephtaliotis was right to entitle his book as he did: 'historical accuracy demanded it'. 'And surely,' he argues in his peroration, 'there is a purer and deeper linguistic feeling, something musical and poetical in *Romiosyne*, something spirited and light and winged, which, I think, is lacking in "Hellenism" with all its heavy and immobile magnificence.'

Romiosyne has lost more ground in the six decades since he wrote.* I can't follow Palamas all the way in his attack on Hellenism; I am too fond of both. But the argument reflects the struggle which is this chapter's theme. It is an overt symptom of the private wrestling match which I think is taking place in eight million arenas. No foreigner can say which side is right. The conflict involves not only reason and history but atavistic, subconscious and tribal instincts too deep for any stranger's reach. But, as things are, the Hellenic lion beats the unicorn of *Romiosyne* all round the town; confusion begins to rob the strange creature of substance; oblivion looms about it like a wood, its outline blurs as the branches multiply. But even though in a few decades its beautiful name may be no longer uttered, I hope *Romiosyne* won't vanish for ever. The Hellene and the *Romios* need and complete each other. Long live both of them; or perhaps it would be safer to say, since these last pages have split the *Romios* into two antagonistic halves—long live all three.

* It is now strictly for internal use; not for foreigners, however fluent and seasoned. A few days ago, a blacksmith friend cut short the involved rigmarole of a customer with the words: '*Pes to romeïka re adelphé, dia na se kataldvoume*' ('Say it in Romaic, brother, so we can understand'—meaning, 'put it simply'). Later I asked him whether a passer-by were Greek, using the word '*Romios*'; and got a black look. Modern times have made it suspect in a stranger's mouth; but, still more, the word is too loaded, precious and private for foreign use. I was an outsider usurping a secret family password.

CHAPTER 4

North of the Gulf

'Are there any lobsters?'

Without looking up from the front page of the *Akropolis* and swatting irritably at the whirling flies, the keeper of the taverna clicked his tongue against his palate, tilted his head wearily backwards and lowered his eyelids in the economical and uncompromising negative that runs east from the Drin and the South Danube Bend to the Great Wall of China.

'Why?'

'There are none.'

'No lobsters?'

'None at all.' Then, after a pause, he said, 'There are some lobsters in the sea.'

'Yes, I know. But I meant, to eat.'

'Only in the sea.'

'Don't they ever catch any?'

'Never. Very rarely. It's not the custom. *Den to synithízoune.* Only every few years.'

'Then why is the town called Lobster?'*

'It's just a name, like Athens or Preveza.'

'A funny name for a town with no lobsters.'

'It's just the name they call it by.'

The *Akropolis* claimed him and he went on deciphering the headlines to himself in a low and halting monologue. A crone in clogs who was scraping dirty plates with a ladle, came to the rescue. 'I've never even seen one,' she said. 'Only in a photograph once, in a book, and I'm over seventy.'

* *Astakos*, the name of the town, is 'Lobster' in Greek.

'I wonder why it's called Astakos?'

'It was named after a king's son. Long, long ago. Long before the Turks even.' She made a gesture with her spoon. 'Perhaps a hundred years ago.'

There was no fish either, she went on. No red mullet, even? No. Only in the sea. The sea glimmered tauntingly at the end of the street. We ordered fried eggs and chips and settled under an acacia among the cats. Even at nine in the evening, the town was hardly cooler than at noon, and the taverna and the streets were deserted. As the local vineyards seemed as unhelpful as the sea, we sipped hot beer.

It had been a day of heat, glare, loss, breakdown and illness. Only a splendid dinner and a flood of wine could have effaced its memory. Deluded by the name of our destination, we had consoled ourselves with the prospect of lobsters; now this prop had been smitten away. The cats, which had been prowling round the table like Midianites, sat and waited and so did we. After half an hour the old woman clip-clopped out of the shadows with a plate in either hand.

'I'm sorry they've been so long,' she said kindly. 'It's not the cooking,' she sighed, 'it's the cooling that eats up the time.'

'The cooling?'

'Hot food is bad. It makes people ill.' I remembered that this belief prevails in certain remote regions. Hot fried eggs are especially dangerous and a prudent cook sets them aside until they seize up. The yolks stiffen to discs of yellow cardboard in a matrix of white glacé kid islanded in cold oil that must have been poured from the sanctuary lamp of a disaffected shrine, and beside them the pale prisms of fried potato form an elastic and frigid magma. So it was now: time had changed our two plateloads, the only cold things in Astakos, into collectors' pieces of freak geology. We asked for goats' cheese and bread; then, prising the eggs loose and fragmenting them, we covertly scattered the shards among the cats. Fifteen leapt forward; a few moments' scrutiny dispersed them again. Their eyes were wide with disillusion. One long black cat of more commanding aspect remained behind and a suppliant forepaw touched my knee as he fixed us with a gaze of injury. A mew of desolation went up, too harrowing to be borne; a massed wail followed our departure. From my room I could hear them turning on each other in recrimination, as if each one were telling his neighbour that had he played his cards differently, all might have gone well. They too wanted lobsters.

* * * *

The little port of Astakos lies in a wide inlet of Acarnania, the south-westernmost province of Roumeli. Ithaca, Cephalonia, Levkas and Zante blur the western skyline, and to the south, the other side of the entrance to the Gulf of Corinth, the north-west corner of the Peloponnese shoulders its way into the Ionian. A tortuous journey had brought us here. The minarets of Yanina, the storks' nests and the mountain-reflecting lake were a long way behind us now. Moving by slow stages, we had gazed at the ruins of Dodona and halted, like Byron and Hobhouse, at the monastery of Zitza and penetrated the Pindus as far as Metsovo; we crossed the Thesprotian plain to the mouth of the Acheron and Parga. Taking to the mountains again, we climbed to Souli, the wrecked stronghold of the Epirot Klephts against the armies of Ali Pasha. Two days' trudge over the mountains of Epirus had brought us to the enormous precipice of Zalongo. (It was here that the Souliot women, in flight from their burning home and the Moslems of Ali, had flung themselves to their deaths in one of the strangest hetacombs in history.) The valley of the Louros, flickering with trout under its giant planes, led us downstream to Preveza and the waters round Actium where Antony, like a doting mallard, breaking off the battle against Augustus to follow Cleopatra's fleeing galley, had changed the history of the world. Thence, our road followed the reedy and bird-haunted shore of the Ambracian Gulf to the many-legended bridge of Arta. Here, among the giant Frankish debris and the Byzantine churches of the Despots of Epirus and the croaking of frogs, we halted for a day or two's reading and exploration.

In the ranges we had crossed and the villages where we slept, nothing substantial had changed since the pilgrimage of Childe Harold and little enough since the reign of Pyrrhus. Pleasure and exhilaration had attended every mile of unhurried progress. But, with our advance into Acarnania, our luck turned. Khaki undulations shuddered in the heat of the solstice, the villages were few, nondescript, mantled by dust and thinly and listlessly peopled; crestfallen dogs skulked across the middle distance and the threadbare donkeys looked near to death. Sparse fields of maize and sunflowers straggled on either side of the track and mean crops of tobacco drooped. The sun trampled over us roughshod, all was shadowless and bereft of colour, and we could almost hear the crackle of the withering and the death of every green thing. Greeks call the region Xeromeros, 'the dry place'. . . . It was a wonder, I thought, as we rocked along beneath that burning-glass of a sky, that the curling tobacco leaves didn't catch fire and smoke themselves there and then; why wait to be gathered and redundantly strung up to dry and then rolled into cylinders in the wicked town of Agrinion? What could the cicadas find to feed on? Whenever we stopped for a glass of cloudy water in a village or for a puncture, their shrill noise, without the engine's competition, became deafening. How odd that their preliminary notes—those tentative scrapes at daybreak, soon joined from tree to tree—can wax to this all-pervading clatter! Among olive groves, it is the very voice of the Mediterranean summer; one misses them when they vanish in autumn, leaving nothing but their ghostly shells along the twigs like celluloid violin-cases; but here they were a malediction. Could this be what is meant, in the last chapter of Ecclesiastes, by the words 'and the grasshopper shall be a burden'?

The road uncoiled through a waste of nonentity far beyond

the point of no return. But, as the afternoon hours wore on, a spark of hope kindled. A mirage of auspiciously-named Astakos, our journey's end, began to dance in our brains like the thought of Mecca among pilgrims crossing the Empty Quarter. We began to describe to each other the cool anticipated town: the tables along the lighted waterfront, the jolly priest, the benign mayor, the schoolmaster versed in antiquarian lore, the friendly taverna-keeper emerging from a promising vista of barrels with a lobster clicking and snapping in either hand. . . . There were welcoming burghers and perhaps the twang of guitars and nimble fishermen treading out the Butchers' Dance. . . . But the sunset guided us into a different kind of town. We swerved to avoid a dead dog which must have lain there for days and a cloud of flies swallowed us up. New houses of scorching concrete were already falling into ruin; others had been abandoned, half built. Huge cubes of cement littered the shore, destined to be assembled one day into a mole; they now sealed the sea from sight as though it were a drain. Surlier than a turnkey, a whiskered slattern showed us the dark chambers into which the melancholy little hotel was subdivided and we began to understand how wide of the mark our imaginary goal had been.

Now the ghost meal was over, prostrate in my dungeon, I tried to read a chapter of *Edwin Drood* by a bulb hanging faint as a glow-worm in the middle of the ceiling. In a minute or two it went out. The midnight town was silent except for the private lives of the cats. . . . The first mosquito sailed with a whine through the stifling dark, a shrill herald of what the night held.

★　　★　　★　　★

There is a morose delectation in recording, when it is all over, squalor and tribulation; Gissing's Calabrian mantle settles momentarily on one's shoulders. The temptation to luxuriate on our sojourn in Astakos is hard to resist: the fly-blown streets, the sluggish sea, the sirocco, the blighting heat, the stricken and the tormented nights. There are towns in transition which have lost touch with the difference between nice and nasty.

I wish we had known, at the time, that Byron had stayed here. Too late! I shall probably never return. Astakos, then, was still called by its mediaeval name of Dragomestri; it only reverted to the name of a nearby classical Astakos in recent times. (These changes make old maps and charts a deceptive guide.) It was his last stepping stone before Missolonghi. In flight from a Turkish frigate, the barque which was bringing him from Cephalonia took refuge behind a palisade of islets in the gulf, and Byron stayed in Astakos for three days. When the danger was over, the emissaries of Mavrocordato conducted him along the coast for his triumphal entry into the last town he was ever to see. I wonder where he slept? I might have struck luckier than in my search for the hypothetical lobster-prince: any link with Byron is a matter for pride in Greece. Only a week before, our guide at Zitza monastery had entertained us with tales of the poet's two halts there which had been handed down from his own great-grandfather.

*　　*　　*　　*

The only face in Astakos whose memory evokes a spark of pleasure is that of the old woman in the taverna. Later, I searched through many books to identify the prince she mentioned: a son of Poseidon and the nymph Olbia founded a town called Astakas in Bithynia; and a scholiast of the Iliad speaks of a Boeotian Astakos who sired a brood of heroes in the War of the Seven against Thebes. No mention of Acarnania. Where had that nice old woman heard of the untraceable prince? She couldn't remember; none of her fellow-Astakiots had heard of him, and the mystery stands. But far out in the gulf and enthroned many fathoms deep in an apse of anemones, I think I see him. Lord of a blue-green realm, his young eyes are vigilantly a-swivel for injustice or danger. Antennae plume him.

The right claw grasps a coral sceptre, the left a sea-egg orb and his greaved and vambraced limbs are flung wide like the arms of Krishna. He is a youthful and kindly despot in the dappled armour of a Samurai, the immortal tyrant of shell and tentacle and fin. Scaly counsellors, plated captains and sinuous aulic dignitaries attend his throne; shoals of citizens gleam in the peaceful arcades; they glide beneath triumphal arches of rococo and loiter among the columns and the obelisks and the slanting sunlight of the piazzas. None challenges his mild reign. No biped foes on shore, they know, can harm them while it lasts.

* * * *

On the third morning the rescue ship sailed down the inlet. We set off east and our spirits lightened. Loaded with goats, the caïque trailed its wake through the alluvial islets of the Echinades and past the shoals that the Acheloös river, gathering silt on its long serpentine journey from the Pindus, has jettisoned before its wide and wandering mouths. Levkas, Ithaca, Cephalonia, Zante and the north-west cape of the Morea wheeled slowly astern to starboard. Many leagues beyond our bows, nearly invisible in the shaking heat, the great masses escaladed down from north and south and reached towards each other across the Gulf. The Straits of Lepanto turn the Gulf of Corinth into Greece's own inland sea, a Mediterranean within a Mediterranean.

We hugged the northern shore. Acarnania ended at the mouth of the Acheloös, and the steeps of Aetolia rose from the tufted shoals and sandbanks. Late afternoon unfolded shade in the dips of these mountains and we sailed past a long lagoon in the mouth of which, on an islet tethered to either shore by fine stone bridges, the little town of Aitolikon clustered round the dome of its church. It hovered in the haze with some of the enchantment of S Giorgio Maggiore seen from the piazzetta in Venice. Missolonghi too, which soon floated towards us as

though raft-borne on its rank lagoons, has a faint air of the
Venetian approaches. The same amphibious feeling reigns. A
spit of land appeared, and a lighthouse and we shouted back
greetings to a russet Zakynthian caïque with her bowsprit
springing from a figurehead of Poseidon. To port lay salt-pans
and wicker labyrinths for fish breeding. A channel meandered
between two miniature lighthouses, a fisherman mended his
nets on a stinking dune. There were rush huts on the mud banks
and flimsy pens of reed and bamboo; the breeze had a miasmal
whiff. Half-naked men in enormous hats, up to their thighs in
the hot and stagnant water, toiled at fishy tasks. The momentary
air of Venice evaporated as the faded town grew bigger. A
dome, a line of trees, a warehouse and a factory cohered in a
medium-sized town of no particular character. On the left was
the shabby site of the house where Byron died. Beyond it
stretched the city wall through which the Greek population
made their heroic sortie through the ranks of the beleaguering
Turks. The thought of those four strange winter months of
Byron's sojourn here, his illness and death, only underlined the
presiding atmosphere of melancholy. It is a sad place to die.

* * * *

I had a special reason for halting in Missolonghi; a reason
which must carry us back a few months; back to a rainy day in
Sussex where I was staying with an old friend, Antony Holland;
to a morning when we were driving to luncheon with a neighbour through a downpour of rain.

The prospect was captivating. Lady Wentworth, whose
house we were heading for, was Byron's great-granddaughter
and, I knew, the owner of a hoard of Byroniana.* Her father

---

* Byron's daughter Ada married Lord Lovelace and he begat Lady
Anne King, who married Wilfred Scawen Blunt, who begat Judith (of
whom we treat), who married Neville Lytton, the painter, and he begat
the present Lord Lytton and his sisters. Through her mother, Judith Blunt
was the fourteenth holder of the old barony of Wentworth.

was Wilfred Scawen Blunt, the poet. I knew his legend well: how he lived as an Arab Sheikh and a rebel against British rule in the desert near Cairo and founded the Arabian stud there which was now his daughter's; his association with 'Skittles' was a literary link with Meredith's *Ordeal of Richard Feveral*, and perhaps with Lucy Glitters in *Mr Sponge's Sporting Tour*. In my youthful ears, rumours of his literary and sporting regime at Crabbet and Newbuildings had always held, probably wrongly, something of the legendary and lurid glamour of Medmenham and the Hellfire Club. His daughter's marriage was a fragile join with the *Last Days of Pompeii*.

Above all, there was Lady Wentworth's own myth. The portrait of her—a beautiful, smouldering-eyed, pre-Raphaelite girl in elaborate Arab costume—had long been familiar. Her early virtuosity and recklessness on horseback were as famous as her monumental book on the Arab horse was later to become. I knew she lived by a system of private conventions: a melancholy daemon of discord had set her at odds with her family and most of the outside world; rifts which even now, when she was over eighty, had lost none of their acerbity. Isolation surrounded her with a dark halo of fable. By a miracle of exemption, Antony Holland's father and his family were almost the only old friends or neighbours with whom Lady Wentworth was not in some degree at feud.

Rain was pouring down as we approached the park gates. The number and the fierceness of the warnings to trespassers suggested mantraps and spring-guns and filled the undergrowth with imaginary bloodhounds. Arab horses grazed under the chestnut clumps. We had to stop while a score of beautiful animals galloped across the drive with flying tails and manes and sailed in a long loop towards a tree-reflecting lake. The house appeared and a few moments later we plunged indoors through the deluge.

Nothing had changed since Regency and Victorian times. The sad charm pervading large houses in which only the owner and the servants live was paramount here. Lady Wentworth displayed the same disregard for fashion and change as the house: an indifference discernible in a skirt to the ground like the ones women wore for badminton at the turn of the century; many chains and lockets and a ribboned lace cap, obsolete for many decades, showed the same independence. Her abundant russet coiffure looked as strong in texture as though it were plaited from the strands of her stallions' manes gathered from the briars and the teazles in the park. Going in to luncheon, she said: 'I'm sorry appearin' in these,' and pointed to her blancoed gym-shoes. 'Just been playin' squash.' By far the most remark-able thing in her appearance was the beauty and distinction of her features: an exquisite high-bridged delicacy of bone-structure and texture that time had spared intact: Byron and Wilfred Blunt leapt to the mind. Her eyes were as clear and smouldering as those in the famous Arabian picture on the wall above the table; they were capable still, it was easy to see, of turning into emblems of her bent for strife. An old-fashioned elimination of final g's and sometimes of initial h's distinguished the chiselled clarity of her speech and her vowels were so patricianly thin that they almost came full cycle. The tone was sad, sometimes almost sepulchral, as though weighed down by distress. The words '*Have some more spotted dog?*' rang like a knell.

Antony Holland was a great favourite; she seemed really pleased that we had come to see her. Her talk ranged with dark humour over life in the desert and the breaking and training of Arab horses; famous figures long dead were stood up and bowled over like ninepins. Answering a question about a tremendous Edwardian statesman and grandee, she said, 'Oh, charmin', charmin', but such a milksop. . . .' She liked the idea of her great-grandfather: 'But Lady Byron had rotten bad luck with him,' she said. 'You just read my uncle Lovelace's book about it!' The row might have taken place only a few years ago. Afterwards we hunted through a huge, disused and heavily cumbered room for a full-face portrait of Byron as a young man, but we could not find it.* 'It's all a bit topsy-turvey,' she murmured, hopping nimbly over corded trunks and japanned tin cases. I saw, with excitement, that these were labelled on the side, in chalk or in white paint, 'Ld Byron's letters' and 'Ly Byron's letters'.† 'Yes, they're all in there,' Lady Wentworth said sombrely, 'and it's the best place for them.' We looked at a case with Byron's Greek-Albanian velvet jacket with its gold lace and hanging sleeves. There were his velvet-scabbarded scimitar and his heavily embroidered velvet greaves—the same accoutrements, I think, that he wears in the famous Phillips portrait. We explored the amassed relics for an hour. Struck by a sudden idea, she led us to her study. It was crammed with portraits, miniatures, framed eighteenth-century silhouettes; books, keepsakes and trophies were gathered in a jungle: rummaging in her desk, she turned over a chaos of farm accounts, horse-breeding literature, lawyers' letters, a battered missal, seedsmen's catalogues, a rosary, farriers' bills and circulars for cattle cake, until at last she found what she was after.

They were some letters, dated a few years back, from an Australian sergeant in Missolonghi. The Greek he was billeted on, he wrote, owned a pair of shoes belonging to Lord Byron; he said the owner would like to return them to one of Byron's descendants. 'But, of course, knowin' no Greek, I couldn't do anythin' about it,' Lady Wentworth said. 'I'd like to have them, if they were really my great-grandfather's.' She turned the letter over. 'He must be a nice kind of a chap, to take all that trouble. I hope I wrote to thank him. . . .' So she lent me the sergeant's letters and I promised to write to the owner of the shoes. She also gave me a copy of Lord Lovelace's *Astarte* and a sheaf of her own poems, printed, I think, in Horsham.

* I saw it next year.
† They were the famous Lovelace papers, which only saw the light of day in 1957, and were put to such brilliant use by Mrs Doris Langley Moore in *The Late Lord Byron* (John Murray, 1961).

They were violent, very colloquial rhyming diatribes against the Germans, written during the war after a stray bomb had destroyed the royal tennis court. (Crabbet was on the direct *Luftwaffe* route to London.) Her polemic gifts had at last discovered a universal rather than a private target. 'You're smilin',' she said. 'They're no great shakes, I fear. It doesn't always run in families. . . .' There was a pause. Then Lady Wentworth said: 'You're not in a hurry, are you? Let's have a hundred up.'

She led us along a passage and up three steps into the dim and glaucous vista of a billiard room. A log fire was blazing; brandy and whisky and soda water flashed their welcome. Lady Wentworth gazed out at the dark afternoon. Through the lashing rain we contemplated the sodden park, the weeping trees and a sudden cavalcade of Arab ponies. 'What a shockin' afternoon,' she said. 'Let's draw the curtains.' We sent the tall curtains clashing along their rods and blotted out the diluvial scene and the daylight and switched on the shaded prism of lamps above the enormous table. She slipped off her many rings and lay them by the grog tray in a twinkling heap; then, after interlocking and flexing her fingers for a few moments like a concert pianist, she chose a cue, sighing 'spot or plain?'

We played in rapt silence. A feeling of timeless and remote seclusion hung all about us, a half-delightful, half-mournful spell which the house and our companion conspired to cast. She had taken on both of us and it was soon clear she was a brilliant player: our turns were spaced out between longer and longer breaks. All was quiet, except for the occasional squeak of French chalk, the fall of a log, a splutter of raindrops down the chimney, the occasional hiss of the siphon. Sudden gusts made the trunks of the huge trees creak ominously outside. 'I shouldn't be surprised if it doesn't fetch one of them down,' Lady Wentworth said, pausing before a difficult shot. 'It's been a rotten winter.' She played the shot facing away from the table and behind her back, which she arched as pliantly as a

girl's. The balls sped unerringly to their destination and the
soft clicks and the thuds on the cushion were followed by two
plops. 'Put red back, would you, Antony?' She crossed to the
other side on silent plimsoled feet. . . . The huge scores mounted
up in game after lost game. The whole world seemed reduced
to this shadowy room with its glowing green quadrilateral; the
slow eddies of our cigar smoke under the lamps and the flickering firelight and the trundling balls. The light caught a brooch
here and a locket there as our hostess moved mercilessly to and
fro at her effortless, demolishing task. Tea, brought in by a
housekeeper and two Irishwomen (identical twins, quite
plainly), was no interruption. Lady Wentworth lifted a silver
lid. 'Oh, good,' she murmured sadly. 'Muffins.' We ate them
cue in hand, and the massacre went on. She looked disap-
pointed when, night having long ago invisibly fallen, the time
came to go. Why didn't we stay and take pot luck . . .? Her
slim silhouette and the anachronistic headdress were dark in
the doorway and she still held a cue in her hand as she waved us
goodbye. We drove away through stormy folds of woodland.
The 1950's waited outside the park gates. Meanwhile, shadowy
cohorts from Arabia shifted about among the soaking timber.
The whites of a score of eyes flashed hysterically or gaze for a
moment in the headlamps. Then with a wheel and a flounder
they vanished into the dark like rainy ghosts.

*　　*　　*　　*

The looming prospect of Missolonghi, as we mooned
about Astakos and brooded on our wrongs, had brought all
this rushing back.

I had written to the owner from England and he had sent a
friendly answer. Indeed, he said, he longed to send the shoes
of the illustrious Lord Byron to his descendant, but he was
anxious lest the precious relics should go astray in the post;
better wait till some reliable emissary could be found. Since
then all had been silence. Well, I had thought in Astakos, I'll

be able to clear everything up in a day or two, when the boat comes. I'll simply ask the way to the house of Kyrios——

That was the trouble! Mr Who? I had forgotten the name. It shouldn't be hard to find in a little town like Missolonghi. But, to leave nothing to chance, I went to the post office and sent a telegram to Lady Wentworth.

Her answer was waiting in the Missolonghi *poste restante*; *Sorry very provoking*, it read, *correspondence mislaid good luck Wentworth*. I asked the man behind the counter if he knew anything about a fellow-citizen who owned a pair of Lord Byron's shoes. No, he had never heard of them, nor had his colleagues, not even the postmaster himself. They and the other people in the post office were full of concern. The words '*Tà papoútsia toù Lórdou Vyrónou*' began to hum through the building. 'Ask at the town hall. They've got some Byron things there. The mayor might know. . . .' The mayor, a distinguished, spectacled figure, knew nothing either. We contented ourselves by peering at the sparse Byron relics in the glass cases. There was a cross-section of the last surviving branch of the elm tree under which the poet had reclined at Harrow; an envelope, addressed in the familiar writing, sere with age, to 'the Honble Mrs Leigh, Six Mile Bottom, Newmarket'; a letter beginning, 'My dearest Caroline'; the document declaring Byron an honorary citizen of the town; a picture of his daughter, Augusta Ada, as a girl; Solomos's commemorative hymn and the broadsheets announcing his death; an aquatint of Newstead Abbey and another of 'the Shade of Byron contemplating the ruins of Missolonghi'. A third print, published in 1827, depicted Archbishop Germanos, who had raised the standard of revolt at Kalavryta. The beard and the canonicals vaguely approximated to the attributes of an orthodox prelate; but the background was a soaring, Beckfordian complex of lancets, triforia, clerestories and crocketed finials: a telling proof of how dimly western Europe apprehended what Greece, during the eclipse of Ottoman power, was like.

But no trace of the shoes.

We drew blank everywhere; with the clergy, the police, the various banks. There was scarcely a bar in which we did not order a swig as a prelude to enquiry. In desperation, we even accosted likely strangers in the street.

Maddened by frustration, at a restaurant table near a statue of President Tricoupis under a clump of palm trees, we scarcely touched our luncheon octopus, swallowing glass after glass of cold Fix beer to replace the salt cataract which the heat summoned from every pore. We fretted through fitful siestas and surged into the streets long before the town had woken up, and soon found ourselves at the *Kypos tôn Eroôn*. I had begun to wonder whether the conversations at Crabbet and the exchange of letters had all been hallucinations.

This Garden of Heroes is a stirring place. There, among the drooping and dusty trees of midsummer, stood the marble busts and the monuments of the heroes of Missolonghi. It is a mark of the importance of Lord Byron in Greek eyes that his statue, the only full-length figure there, has been accorded the central position in this Valhalla. Dotted about, too, are monuments to the other philhellenes who fought or died for the liberation of Greece: the numerous Germans, the French, the Americans, the English, and, symbolized by a huge granite totem surrounded by boulders, the Swedes; on every side, mingling with these guest-warriors, are the great Greek paladins of the Siege.

We were sitting rather dejectedly on the low wall outside, and meditating on how to resume our quest, when a flutter of coloured flounces and a plaintive murmur heralded the onslaught of a gypsy woman. But we were in no mood for fortune-telling, and when, driven away at last by the persistence of her litany, which alms had failed to stem, we rose wearily to return to the town, she gazed balefully in our faces and said she saw unhappiness and failure written there. Further dejected by these tidings, we returned to our quarters.

But she was wrong. A nice-looking young woman was waiting for us. Her face brightened as we appeared: were we looking for Lord Byron's shoes? She had heard we had been asking about them. They belonged to her uncle: she told us his name; I recognized it in a flash as that of my correspondent. Could we call at his house in an hour's time?

Can a duck swim?

*   *   *   *

We climbed the stairs to the guest room of a substantial house built of yellow stone not far from the site of the house where Byron died. The shutters were still closed against the afternoon heat. Solid Victorian furniture fitted with anti-macassars materialized in the shadows round the welcoming figure of our host. He was a large and robust man, between sixty and seventy, with jutting black eyebrows and a tufted crop of grey hair and the simple and friendly manner of an old sea captain, which indeed he was. His niece was there with an artillery subaltern, her fiancé. The punctilio of their dress put our tired travelling outfits to shame. The niece busied herself with the ceremonial of a visit, administering spoonfuls of cherry jam, then a glass of water, a thimbleful of coffee and a scruple of *mastika*. Less forgetful than me, our host had politely greeted me by name at once and fished out my letters; he also placed on the table, among other treasures, a neatly-stitched canvas parcel about a foot long, from which we couldn't take our eyes; in laborious indelible-ink lettering of someone unused to Latin characters were traced the words: *The Baroness Wentworth, Crabbet Park, Three Bridges, Sussex. . . .*

I congratulated him on ferreting out Byron's descendant and asked, rather tentatively, how Byron's shoes had come his way. Had he inherited them?

'No,' he said. 'Though my grandparents, who were both Missolonghiots, must have seen Lord Byron often. Why, my grandpa was forty-two at the time of the siege, and my granny was thirty. He was born in 1784 and he died at the age of a hundred and four, when I was three years old! A hundred and four! He had pre-war bones! *Propolémika kókkala!* Not like our thin modern ones. . . . I can't remember him, of course, I'm only seventy-eight, but they all said he was a fine old man. He and my granny took part in the great exodus, fighting their way through the besieging Turks, and God be praised,' he paused to cross himself, 'they got away safely. This is his yataghan.' He handed me the curving weapon with its bossed silver sheath and branching bone hilt, I drew it and ran my finger along the notched blade, and wondered whether the edge was dented as he hacked his way out on that terrible day. 'There are his barkers'—we toyed with a heavy brace of pistols, almost straight ones encrusted with filigree, the butts ending in pearshaped knobs of Yanina silverwork—'and this is his *balaska*, the metal pouch they kept their bullets in, and here's his powder flask. And this is his pen-case and its little inkwell; the lid clicks open—all silver!—though he wasn't much of a scribe. But everybody wore them, even the ones without any letters at all, stuck into their belts,' he said with a smile, making a jutting gesture towards his middle, 'for the dash of it, *dia leventeiá*. The more they had in their belts, the better. Well, my absolved* grandparents got away all right, and came back after the battle of Navarino, when the storm had blown over, and went into shipping. In a small way, at first; then he built more and more caïques, carrying cargoes and trading up and down the Gulf and in the Ionian Islands to start with, and especially to Zante—our town has always had a strong link with that place—and then into the Aegean, and, finally, all over the archipelago and the Mediterranean. They were good times. My father carried on and so did I. You see this house? It was built in my father's day, and every block of it, *every block of it*, was brought in our own bottoms from—

* This word—*synchoriménos*—together with *makarítes*, blessed, is a slightly more pious way of saying 'the late'.

guess where? From Savona in Italy, near Genoa! Every block of it.' He tapped the wall behind his chair with a bent knuckle. 'There! As sound and as solid as when it was built!'

As he spoke we tried to keep our eyes from staring too pointedly at the canvas parcel. It grew darker; his daughter opened the shutters. The grape-green evening light flowed in through the mosquito wire. 'Things have changed now,' he went on. 'We're not what we used to be, though we've still got a roof over our head. But those were the days. They had everything! They could tie up their dogs with strings of sausages.'

He fell silent as though all had been said. The inrush of evening light revealed that his right eyelid had suffered some mishap on the high seas which gave the illusion of a wink. After a long silence, I ran a forefinger absent-mindedly along the top of the canvas parcel.

'Ah, yes,' our host said with a sigh. 'Lord Byron's shoes. . . . This is how they came my way. When O *Vyron* was in Missolonghi, he used to go duck-shooting in the lagoon in a *monóxylo* —one of those dug-out canoes they still use—belonging to a young boatman called Yanni Kazis. Kazis had three daughters. Two of them married and left our town and the third went away to Jerusalem,' he pointed out of the window, 'and became a nun in an Orthodox convent. Many years later she came back. She was a frail old woman, all skin and bones, in a nun's habit. Her family had been scattered to the winds and she had nowhere to go, so I gave the poor old woman a room in my house. That was in 1920—or was it 1921? Anyway, she lived with us for the last few years of her life. Just before she died she gave me this box'—he pulled a battered casket from under the table—'and in it were these papers and books, and the shoes of the Lordos. Also an icon of St Spiridion, which I hung up in the Cathedral.' The yellowed and flyblown papers turned out to be the black edged broadsheets published by the Provisional Government of Western Greece and signed by

Mavrocordato, announcing Lord Byron's death and decreeing a salute of thirty-seven cannon—a salvo for each year of the poet's life—and three days of deep mourning, in spite of the impending Easter celebration. The books were a dog-eared Orthodox missal and two devotional works, all deep in mould.

'The shoes,' he continued, 'were given to her father by Lord Byron. Byron used to wear them about the house, when her father had rowed him back from the lagoon. Kazis never wore them, but kept them as sacred relics and when he died, he gave them to his daughter; and when *she* had no more days left, she gave them to me as a thanks-offering for her bed and board. We buried her, and here they are. She was a good old woman and may the ground rest light on her.'

He seemed rather loth to undo the neat parcel, but at last snipped through the stitches in the canvas with the tip of his grandfather's yataghan and began to unwrap the tissue paper. We all craned forward.

Perhaps with Byron's Greek costume at Crabbet in mind, I had been expecting a pair of *tsarouchia*, those heavy Greek mountain footwear, beaked and clouted, sometimes with velvet tufts across the toe, that are the traditional accompaniment of the *fustanella*. But when the innermost cocoon of tissue paper had been shed, the two faded things that my host gently deposited in my hands were light, slender, faded slippers, with their morocco leather soles and the uppers embroidered with a delicate criss-cross of yellow silk and their toes turning up at the tip in the Eastern mode. They suggested Morocco or Algiers and a carpeted and latticed penumbra, rather than the rocky Aetolian foothills; or, even more, slippers in the oriental taste that a regency dandy might have bought in the Burlington Arcade or at some fashionable shoemakers' or haberdashers' in the galleries of Genoa or Venice. . . . The two flimsy trophies passed in silence from hand to hand. Something about them carried instant conviction. When we turned them upside down and examined the thin soles this conviction deepened: the worn parts of the soles were different on each. Those of the left were normal; the right showed a different imprint, particularly in the instep. We pointed this out to their owner, but, as he had never heard that there was anything out of the ordinary about Byron's feet, it evoked no more than polite interest. For us, perhaps because we were so near the scene of the harrowing last moments of the poet's life, perhaps because of our frustrating search and the sudden simplicity of its solution, these humble relics were poignant and moving to an extreme degree. It was as though that strange young man, as Hobhouse called him, had limped into the twilit room. . . .

The lamps were turned on, and when we had photographed and measured and sketched them, our host wrapped them up once more with a look of slight embarrassment. At last he confessed that, now that it had come to the point, he could not bear to let them leave the family: his niece was about to be married—'She's taking this young *pallikari* here,' he said, waving the shoes in the direction of the subaltern, 'and I want to make them part of her dowry. They could hand them on to their descendants, and they to theirs, and so on for ever. . . .' He felt guilty about changing his mind. We assured him no one would dream of blaming him, least of all Byron's great-granddaughter. She would wish the young couple luck and prosperity and a dozen offspring, as we did. His embarrassment vanished in a moment. We drank a final glass of *mastíka*, standing up, to toast the coming marriage. Then after a last look at the shoes and vicelike valedictory handshakes, we left our host still holding the shoes in his hand and wishing us godspeed. The town was wide-awake with evening doings and we felt as elated as though we were taking those elusive trophies with us.

*   *   *   *

The success of our search had sent our spirits soaring. Missolonghi, as we settled by the weary palm trees, acquired an unwonted aspect of hope and charm; it was a twinkling world of lights under a fading Tiepolo sky. I settled down at once to write an account of our find to my publisher John Murray (namesake and great-grandson of Byron's friend and publisher). I enclosed the sketches and tracings, and promised to send the photographs as soon as they were developed. I also asked him to compare them with the Byron footwear in his possession—his building is an Aladdin's cave of relics of the poet—and to consult other friends and experts, especially Sir Harold Nicolson and Peter Quennell. Then I wrote the bad and the good news to Crabbet.*

I wish that I had just re-read, as I did before beginning these pages, Harold Nicolson's *Byron: The Last Journey*.† I would have discovered much to my purpose. For the author, preparing his book in the early twenties by a scholarly visit to Missolonghi, had made friends with a Mr Aramandios Soustas, the headmaster of the municipal school in Missolonghi and a living repository of information about the poet's last days. How had I neglected asking the local schoolmasters—even if they were no longer the same? They are usually my first resort in such cases, and seldom vain ones: 'Mr Soustas', writes Sir Harold, 'was a friend of Costa Ghazis, the nonagenarian boatman, who, when a lad, had almost daily ferried Byron across the lagoon to where the horses waited by the olive grove; and Ghazis, before his death, had carefully and repeatedly recounted to Mr Soustas . . . how Byron would always sing strange Western songs‡ as they punted back together in the evening, and how on the

---

* The answers, when they reached me in the fullness of time, were all I could have hoped for. There was nothing whatever, as far as size went, against the authenticity of the shoes, and the lameness had indeed been, as I thought I remembered, in the poet's right foot. Lady Wentworth was all understanding and good wishes.

† Published by Constable & Co. Ltd (1924).

‡ *The Meeting of the Waters?; Those Endearing Young Charms?; Oft in the Stilly Night?*

last day that he had thus conveyed the general, the latter had
sat silent and shivering in the stern. . . .' I would have read that
Byron and Count Gamba, on their last ride, were overtaken by
a storm; when they joined Ghazis and his canoe, they were
soaked with rain and sweat; as they slowly punted home across
the lagoon in the downpour the ominous shivering fit set in
. . . the rest we know. The appendix would have told me that
Costa Ghazis died in 1890.

Now our late host had said that the recipient of the shoes
was called Yanni Kazis, and that it was duck-shooting that had
drawn Lord Byron into the lagoon in his boat, whereas riding
and swimming and shooting at bottles were, by then, Byron's
only sporting recreations; an easy mistake. Ioannis and Constantine are the commonest Christian names in Greece; short-
ened to Yanni and Costa, they are the equivalent to Tom and
Dick, and as easily confused. Finally, Kazis and Ghazis: in certain Greek mouths, K and G can be almost indistinguishable.
Costa Ghazis and Yanni Kazis are plainly the same man. Our
host's boatman and his far-wandering daughter stand forth
from the shadows and the shoes themselves step lightly into
authenticity.

*   *   *   *

Why, we wondered, over our mullets under the seedy palm
trees, should the tracing of these unimportant mementoes fill
us with such keen pleasure and excitement? The answer is that
nothing to do with Byron, even a pair of shoes, is wholly
without interest.

He monopolized our thoughts and our conversation all
through the second can of retsina that a neighbouring tableful
of Missolonghiots had sent us. On the fringe of this archipelago
of tables, three old men from the hills had for some time been
singing a klephtic song that I have always loved in honour of
Marko Botsaris, the great leader of Western Greece in the
War of Independence. Byron just failed to meet him: he was

shot through the head in an attack on the Turks at Karpenisi a few hours after writing to the poet. (Byron took many of his kilted Souliots into his service and a difficult handful they proved.) It was exactly the kind of long-drawn-out and wailing song in a minor key, whose waverings, in the mouths of his Souliot retinue, bewildered and irritated Byron's western acquaintances. To those fastidious ears, but not to Byron's, they sounded the extremity of barbarism. . . . No wonder we should be speaking of him; Byronic landmarks had scattered our journey through north-western Greece like the clues in a treasure hunt: Yanina, Dodona, the defiles of the Pindus, Zitza monastery, the Acheron, Souli, Parga, the Acherousian Plain, Cephalonia, Preveza, the Ambracian Gulf, Acarnania and at last, Aetolia, where, a bare fifteen years after his first wanderings, his travels stopped for good. The place-names of *Childe Harold's Pilgrimage* were the stages of that carefree journey through Greece with Hobhouse at the age of twenty-one: travels as remote, then, from the conventional Grand Tour and as adventurous and rare (so wide an ocean seemed the Adriatic, and so daunting a barrier the Acrocerau- nian mountains) as a journey today from Athens to the Hindu Kush. Their little cavalcade wound its way through regions of legendary beauty and great savagery; tall ranges, plunging cataracts and tufted gorges beset their track. Epirus, at the time and all north-western Greece, was in the grip of Ali Pasha: the Vizir's terrible Albanians tyrannized the lowlands, the Klephts and the Armatoles haunted the crags; the fastnesses of Souli were in perpetual revolt. It was a world of strife, ambush, revenge, burning villages, massacre, impaling and severed heads. This part of Greece was the scene of some of the most dramatic events in history and myth; names and reminders of the great days of ancient Greece were everywhere; above all, the Greeks still lived here. He was able to discern, among the ruins, in the seeming docility of the plainsmen and in the fierceness of the mountaineers, compelling messages of magnificence and servitude and the hint of future resurrection; a resurrection which was to happen sooner and affect him more closely than he can ever have thought. Plenty of raw material here for solitary brooding, soaring description, taunting apostrophe and incendiary peroration; and when *Childe Harold* came out three years later, all this, majestically thundering in those Spenserian cantos (the last foot of each stanza sounding, according to the mood, like a double thump or a distant echo), this irruption into an unknown world, the controlled fury with which it was conducted, the attack and argument and evocation and the impression of dangerous power contained, struck London, and later the world, like an explosion. Nobody had seen or heard anything like it, and his myth shot up in a night. Still, today, when we know it so well, its rhythms and its images strike with the force of a metrically transposed fusion of Delacroix and Berlioz and give us more than a hint of what its first impact must have been.

How surprised, how very surprised and mortified would Byron's detractors in England have been, could they have looked into the future! Ever since the Greek War of Independence, England has enjoyed a singular pre-eminence in Greek affections; a feeling unique in the flinty world of international relations. Solid reasons support this flattering image.* The enormous voluntary loan, privately subscribed to back the Greek struggle against the Turks; the participation of English phil-hellenes—though, to the credit of the rest of Europe and America, they were not alone—in the actual fighting; the destruction at the command of Codrington of the Turkish and Egyptian fleets at Navarino, which put an end to the long war;

---

* An image, alas, which recent conflict in Cyprus has battered. The bitterness of Greek feelings during this disastrous interlude were made still more acute by the extremity of the favourable sentiments which had prevailed before. Premature to say whether things will revert in time to their previous happy state. There are hopeful signs. But lilies that fester smell far worse than weeds.

the policies of Canning and Gladstone; the handing back of
the Ionian Islands and a consistent pro-Greek policy ever
since. Recent reinforcements of these bonds, and manifestations of them, were Greece's alliance with Great Britain in
two world wars. The record is impressive and honouring to
both.

But if, during the last hundred years, anyone were to have
asked any Greek at random why this feeling existed, the answer,
in tones of surprise at the naïveté of the question, would have
been, and still would be: Lord Byron. His reputation in
England has gone through many avatars. Things have been
different here: the news of his death, as it spread through the
dismal lanes of Missolonghi in that rainy and thundery dusk,
scattered consternation; his name, famous already, soared
like a skyrocket into the Greek firmament and lodged there
as a fixed star whose radiance grows brighter as the years pass.
'O Vyron', 'Lordos Vyronos', or, more sophisticatedly, 'O
Mpaïron', is Greek property now. Thousands of children are
baptized by his name, and his face is as familiar as any hero's
in ancient or modern Greece. Every English traveller, however
humble or unimpressive, and whether he knows or deserves
or wants it or not, is the beneficiary of some reflected fragment
of this glory. I wonder if any other figure in history has
achieved such a place in a country not his own?

Knowing voices sometimes question Byron's feelings towards Greece. He was a scorching critic of every country of
which he wrote, with England at the head of his list, and he
was no blinder to Greece's faults than were the Greeks themselves. But his resentment of shallow criticisms of the country
was the reaction of a man whose affections and loyalties were
deeply engaged. His life had reached a stage when death, perhaps, seemed its only logical solution. Even had this not been so,
the Greek cause would have claimed him. They were the only
people among whom he had been really happy. He meant to
die for Greece; but he was determined to help her to the utmo

of his powers. The instinctive Greek interpretation of his actions
is a just verdict.

His last poem, written on this thirty-seventh birthday and
shortly before he died, is surely a sincere picture of his feelings.

> The sword, the banner and the field
>   Glory and Greece, around me see!
> The Spartan, borne upon his shield
>   Was not more free.
>
> Awake! (Not Greece—she *is* awake!)
>   Awake my spirit. Think through *whom*
> Thy life-blood tracks its parent lake,
>   And then strike home!
>
> Tread those reviving passions down,
>   Unworthy manhood!—unto thee
> Indifferent should the smile or frown
>   Of beauty be.
>
> If thou regrett'st thy youth, *why live?*
>   The land of honourable death
> Is here:—Up to the field and give
>   Away thy breath!
>
> Seek out—less often sought than found—
>   A soldier's grave, for thee the best;
> Then look around, and choose thy ground
>   And take thy rest.

*　*　*　*

The tables by the statue of Tricoupis were emptying, and
our cigarette smoke, as we talked, rose unwavering into a wind-
less night. The neighbours who had sent us the wine and the
three shaggy singers from the mountains were the only others
left. One of the first group caught our eye.

'Did you find them?' he asked.

We were nonplussed for a moment. Our thoughts, lingering on Byron, had strayed from our search.

'The shoes? Did you get them in the end?'

We told them the whole story. The mountain men listened with interest.

'Eh!' said one of the wine donors. 'He was a wonderful man. A true hero.'

'*O Vyronos?*' one of the mountaineers said. '*Dikòs mas einai.* He's ours.'

'Of course he's ours,' said another, and lifted his glass of retsina solemnly. 'May his memory rest eternal. *Aionia i mnémi tou.*'

'Amen,' the others assented. 'Amen, amen.'

Postscript

Poets have strange posthumous careers. My old friend Tanty Rodocanaki (alas, now dead) told me the following. When Rupert Brooke died in Mudros in 1915 his body was buried in the west of Skyros, an island where he had never set foot during his life. The Skyriots are proud of his presence and though little is known about him, his name is second in honour only to that of the island's patron, St George. He is even mentioned in island songs. On a visit a few years ago, Rodocanaki was admiring the secluded olive-grove that shelters the poet's grave. As he read the inscription on the tomb, an old shepherd who was pasturing his flocks in the surrounding woods addressed him. 'I see you are admiring the grave of *O Broukis*,' he said. 'He was a great poet. We are glad to have him with us. He was a good man.'

Intrigued by the conviction of his tone and curious to discover how much he knew, Rodocanaki asked him what he thought of his poetry.

'I've never read any of it, I'm sorry to say,' the shepherd

answered. 'I'm not strong on letters and foreign languages. But you could tell he was a great man. You see that old olive over there? That was his tree.'

'How do you mean?'

'He used to sit under it every day and write poetry.'

Reluctant to contradict, Rodocanaki asked him if he was sure they were talking about the same person.

'Of course I am! *O Broukis* used to wander about the woods in silence, the very picture of an old-fashioned English gentleman.'

'What did he look like?'

'Magnificent, sir,' the shepherd answered. 'Tall, dignified, flowing hair, burning eyes and a long white beard.'

CHAPTER 5

The Kingdom of Autolycus

'*Do not blaspheme against God!*' The words, in bold calligraphy, was pasted on the windscreen above the driver's seat; '*Blasphemy is disrespectful and uncharitable. It is a stigma against civilization. Even the Barbarians and the demons themselves do not blaspheme.*'

Who were these non-blaspheming barbarians—let alone the demons? I was sitting beside the driver, so I asked him. He was a tall clean-shaven man in a cloth cap and horn-rimmed spectacles with a long, thoughtful and scholarly face. He turned with a smile and his hands left the wheel with a dismissive sweep. '*As ta daimónia!*' he said. 'Don't worry about demons!' His hands regained the controls just in time to pull up. Wild as a descent of Afghan tribesmen, a herd of goats came tumbling down the mountainside and across the road and down the canyon the other side in a cataract of derision and clanking. A small avalanche followed them. 'They don't exist. Not today. Unless they mean *those* hornwearers.' He pointed at the disappearing rumps, and, spreading all five fingers of his left hand, shoved it energetically palm outwards after the goats in the pan-Hellenic gesture of commination. '*Na!* They block the roads, they eat the trees, they strip the land—just look all round!—and they stink. I deflower their All-Holy-One.' We twisted up the stony ravine.

'What about the Barbarians? Anyone who isn't Greek? Me, perhaps?'

I didn't say this seriously, but a look of concern crossed his face; his right hand sailed perilously from the wheel once more and alighted on my shoulder in a reassuring pat.

'The very idea! I don't know who they mean. The priests have been sticking these notices up all over the place. Perhaps the Bulgarians (bad year to them!) or the Turks.'

I told him I'd been to Bulgaria, ages ago, and that their oaths were frequent and profane; English ones, too, though they were less explicitly so than the Greek. (Greek insults invariably take the form which he had just used: 'I sexually outrage your . . .!', and a sacred being or object is appended. The language is brief and blunt. The victim of the outrage is very often the All-Holy-One—the Panayía, that is—or the Holy Name or the Cross, or, more abstractly, Easter.)

The driver was relieved to hear that the Greeks were not alone in blasphemy. 'We're terrible,' he said. 'You ought to hear them in Cephalonia!' He whistled in censure or admiration. 'God protect us! And yet, you know, I have my private theory about our blasphemies. When we blaspheme, it isn't God and the saints we are insulting, only the man we are talking to.'

How did he mean?

'Listen,' he said, 'I get cross with someone—those goats, for instance—and I shout "I . . . your All-Holy-One, your Christ, your Cross, your faith." I don't say "I outrage *the* Cross," or whatever it is, but *yours*. *Why?* Because I mean that the people I am cursing don't know what's what; that the *osioi kai agioi*— the blessed and the sacred ones—of such people can't be real. Not *their* ones! You see? No profanity or blasphemy at all; the reverse really.' He smiled and touched his temple triumphantly with his forefinger to underline the point. '*Bíkis?*' (short for *bíkis sto théma?*, have you entered the theme?).

'*Bíka.*'

'All right! It's only my theory, mind you, and here's something that might disprove it. You've heard of people called *mángas?*'

I outlined all I knew about the *mángas*. They are a kind of proletarian freemasonry in the towns, especially in Athens and the Piraeus. ('And in Patras!' Andreas said, naming his own home town: 'we're famous for them.') They are independent and moody and they talk, in guarded and slightly jeering tones, a private jargon. *Bouzouki* music, and the geometric dances that accompany them, are their passion. A code of their own dictates their conduct and often leads them into trouble. Bohemianism and distrust of authority make them prone to lawless doings—smuggling, hashish smoking and so on; nothing very terrible. There is a studied melancholy in their manner and posture, a rarified plebeian dandyism in their dress. Was that right?

'That's it,' Andreas said. He dropped his voice to a drawling rasp in imitation of *mánga* speech. '*Ekonomizeís mavro, ré aderphaki?*' ('Do you economize any black stuff, little brother?', i.e. Have you got any hashish?) We both laughed. 'You should have seen them when I was young. Peg-top trousers they wore, and long, pointed boots with elastic sides; red sashes, narrow brimmed black *republikas'*—trilbies—'or caps, pushed back; oiled quiffs over their foreheads and heavy moustaches; and their jackets were slung across their shoulders with the sleeves loose. They walked with a roll, one hand behind the back flicking a string of amber beads with a tassel, *very small ones*, not like mine.' Andreas pointed to his own *komboloi*, swinging from the choke plug on the dashboard. 'They also carried knives in their sashes, "noses" as they called them, and they weren't slow to use them. Talk about touchiness! Pride ate them hollow. At the slightest insult—even if somebody trod on the end of their sash or in their spit on the pavement—out came the noses! Their main hang-out in Athens was the *plateia Psirí*, beyond Monastiraki. Respectable citizens used to avoid it, even the police only went in couples. They had something! It was a sight to see two or three of them swaggering down the streets with their sleeves and beads swinging and roses stuck between their teeth if they were in the mood.

'But their great days were over before I was born. The really

tough ones were known as *koutzavákides*.* They carried nobbly
sticks that they twirled in their hands. Bad politicians hired
them at election times—you know, to vote several times over
and stop the other side getting to the polls; breaking up meet-
ings, smashing the urns, and so on. Chaos! Then a new chief
of police was appointed, a really hard-boiled man called Baïraktáris. Guess what he did? After a bad outbreak he called out the
whole police force, surrounded the Psirí quarter and rounded
up every single *koutsavákis* he could find and marched them off
to police headquarters. Hundreds of them. He made them hand
in their boots and a policeman with a chopper cut off the
long toes and handed them back. Another sliced off the hanging sleeves. Then he set them free—I don't think he even disarmed them. Ever since then the favourite oath of the *koutzavákides* has been: *Gamó to Mpaïraktári sou!*—"I . . . your
Baïraktáris!" And they meant it this time! They only stuck to
the *sou* (the 'your') out of habit. Some old boys still mumble
it when they pass a policeman. Under their breath, of course.'

He was an enchanting companion. His lank frame, long
hands and the large eyes behind their spectacles gave him a look
of Aldous Huxley. Was I frightened, he asked, when he took his
hands off the wheel? I had been at first, but no longer. A sweeping skein of gestures beat time to the flow of his discourse.

'Don't worry,' he said, 'I've driven this road a thousand
times. You know what the Greeks are like; we can't talk without using our hands. When I was a gunner in the Asia Minor
campaign in 1920, we captured a Turkish *bimbashi* in the hills
outside Eskishehir. Our lance-bombardier came from a village
near Serres in Macedonia. "It's Galip bey!" he shouted.
"Petro!" the Turk shouted back. They nearly embraced! The
Turk was the son of the owner of a *tchiflik*—a farm—near
Petro's village!" ' (Macedonia was under the Turks till the

* *Mángas, Koutzavákis, Tramboúkos, Rebétis, Mortis, Dervísis*—a dervish!—
and *Daís*, though this is more an out-and-out tough—there are many words
with roughly the same general meaning, each supplying a different nuance.

First Balkan War in 1912.) 'They'd known each other as boys. The Turk was very smart: astrakhan fez, khaki tunic, leggings, sword, pistol, binoculars—we soon had those off him—and a little lacquered moustache.' Andreas's forefingers planted two inverted commas in mid-air. 'He and Petro sat up all night smoking cigarettes and drinking coffee as if they were back in Macedonia. The *bimbashi's* job was interrogating prisoners. Sometimes they were marched in with their hands tied. He questioned them for hours. Dead silence! They were dumb! Then he saw what was wrong and told the guards to untie their hands and out streamed a flood of words! All lies, of course.' Andreas laughed. 'The first time he found this out the Greeks knocked over the guards and ran for it.' The fingers of Andreas's left hand rippled over the valley outside the nearside window. 'They vanished like the dew! So you see! But it was a terrible war. Appalling things happened. Nobody fought with kid gloves on, believe me.'

On the windscreen under the anti-blasphemy notice was pasted a half-naked platinum-blonde on roller skates cut out of a magazine. Beside her, on a blue ribbon, swung a small icon of St Andrew the Apostle holding the saltire cross on which the Romans martyred him in Patras. Andreas indicated the saint and the girl. 'Sacred,' he said, 'and profane: perhaps they cancel each other out. . . . They used to have his head in the cathedral in Patras, but when the Turks captured the Peloponnese, a Byzantine prince ran off with it to Rome and sold it to the Pope. One of the Palaeologues, I think. It was a sort of a passport.'* The icon's ribbon also suspended a little chaplet of

* The head of St Andrew, smitten from the apostle's crucified trunk in the reign of Claudius, has just returned to Patras, after five centuries' sojourn in his brother's famous cathedral in Rome; sent as a token of goodwill to the Greek Orthodox Church by Pope Paul V. In 1461, eight years after the fall of Byzantium, Thomas Palaeologue, Despot of the Peloponnese and brother of the last emperor, translated the famous relic to Rome to save it from the advancing army of Mehmet II; there he presented it to Pius II

those blue beads that repel the Evil Eye from cattle; the corollas of purple plastic convolvulus nodded from the green-wrapped wire spiralling round the windscreen and a cone of tin screwed to the dashboard held three paper roses; yellow, magenta and pink. A celluloid cockatoo sprung to a rubber sucker on the pane bobbed to and fro with the jolting and the dozen cut-out bluebirds glued at random about the glass completed a decor that trembled and winked like a jungle between our eyes and the stark crags into which we were climbing. Rich in modulations and orchestrated by gestures, the voice of Andreas moved from theme to theme with a smoothness surpassing any change the hoarse gears of his vehicle could attempt.

We had set off from Navpaktos soon after dawn and headed deep into the hinterland of Aetolia. The road followed the eastern flank of a high ravine at the bottom of which, seldom visible owing to the steepness of the slope, a torrent twisted. But, looking back, I could catch the gleam of the Evinos river as it strayed out of the mountains towards Missolonghi in a litter of boulders to join the Gulf of Corinth, whose shores we had just left. As we gained height the Gulf expanded to an inland sea, contracting as it moved westwards to the straits where the castles of the Morea and of Roumeli, advancing from either shore on the tips of peninsulas, almost joined: Rion and Antirion, dimly discerned through the early haze. Beyond the Straits the Gulf widened again to form an ante-chamber to the Ionian where the liquid battlefield of Lepanto shone. South, dominated by the white giant of Mount Pana-chaïkon, range after range revealed itself, rising in step with our own ascent until the whole Peloponnese seemed on the point of levitating into the sky. Slowly the accumulation of our own mountains effaced the lower world and the Gulf as the

---

Piccolomini; Aeneas Silvius himself. The description of the renaissance splendour of the ceremony in the fields between Rome and Tivoli is one of the most striking passages in the memoirs of the great humanist pope.

ravine lengthened and narrowed and interposed buttresses of rock between us and all but the topmost of the Morean spikes. At last a turn in the track clenched the canyon behind and shuttered them away. We were locked in the heart of grey cordilleras and smoky shadows that slanted into the chasm.

We had passed a couple of meagre hamlets and the bus had emptied of all but Andreas and me and, in the seat behind us, a pretty mountain girl whose face was alight with candour and happiness. A voluminous black kerchief swathed her head, thick chestnut plaits fell down her back, and she was encased in one of those coats of homespun goats' hair, flaring from the waist and gallooned round the hem and along the perpendicular pockets with dark red braid, that they call a *segouni*. Round silver plaques as big as saucers fastened her woven belt. A swaddled baby in a hewn cradle like a little trough rested across her lap; it had been slung across her back like a papoose when she got in. She looked about fifteen. As she listened to Andreas her eyes grew wider still and laughter covered her face with the spread fingers of one brown hand.

There was plenty to marvel at. Andreas was telling the story of a friend who had worked as guide and companion to an English botanist. They explored the mountains of Aetolia and Acarnania and worked their way north to the Pindus, scrambling from sierra to sierra until one day they found themselves at the top of a gorge whose sides dropped sheer to a rushing river. (It sounded rather like the Aoös ravine in the Zagori.) One rare plant grew only on the side of this cliff and the Englishman insisted on making a rope fast to a tree and lowering himself down. His guide, prone on the cliff's rim, watched anxiously. All of a sudden there was a flurry and a shout and a loud noise! '*Kraa-Kraa!*' There below ('Come, Christ and the Holy Virgin!') was the botanist swinging on the end of his rope and beating with his vasculum at a golden eagle which was flapping round and pecking at him! She had been sitting on her nest on a ledge hidden by an overhang. Worse still, suddenly,

with a noise like an aeroplane, there was the husband! The
guide had a rifle with him, on the off-chance of shooting a
wolf or a wild boar—or perhaps a bear. But how was he to
avoid hitting the man? He was swinging like a pendulum,
twisting and flailing and keeping himself on the move by
kicking each side of the cave's mouth in turn. Saying a prayer,
Yanni fired ('N'tang!') and mortally wounded the hen-bird;
she sank fluttering down the cliff face. The cock flew up into
the air and floated there for a moment, about to plunge on the
intruder. (Andreas's arms, held wide across the interior of the
bus, indicated the enormous wing-spread.) He aimed, pulled
and ('N'tang!') killed it stone dead! With an explosion of
feathers, the bird dropped like a stone, moulting and spiralling
faster every second till it bounced off the mountain-side and
into the torrent, which whirled it out of sight. 'When the
botanist reached the cliff top—untouched—he said quietly,
"I've got it." "Got what?" said Yanni, mopping his brow.
"The plant." He showed it, a small green thing. Then he said:
"Well, Yanni, what about lunch?" *Psychraimos anthropos!* He
was a cool one!' (I always foster the myth of English *psychrai-
mia*. There are lots of comic stories about it in Greece, not all
flattering.) 'After lunch, he went down again to get the eggs.
"We can't leave the orphans," he said. Months later, from
Scotland, he sent Yanni a photograph of the only bird to
hatch out. It had wicked eyes! The botanist used to feed it
on. . . .' Here the girl let out a cry of alarm; rapt in the story,
she had been carried past her destination. We helped her out
with a small sack of corn, which, after re-slinging the papoose,
she balanced on her head; then she stuck a distaff into her belt.
Teasing a wisp out of the grey cloud of wool in the distaff's
fork, she pulled and twisted it into thread and notched it in
the spindle, which was soon rotating on its own at the end of
the lengthening twine. She set off up the mountain with her
back hollowed like a caryatid's to steady the load on her head.
'Thank God she's got shoes,' Andreas said. 'They are bad

mountains: all up and down, hilltop and valley, stones and thorns all the way. It's a five-hour climb to her village. A miserable place, poor devils.' As we paused in the road to light cigarettes, we could hear her singing, already some distance above.

* * * *

Andreas put me down at a group of huts where the road came to an end and shrank to a mule track, not far from the saddle which led into the Kravara. I had told him that was my destination and he burst out laughing. . . .

I heard about the Kravara years ago. Then George Katsimbalis lent me Karkavitza's book, *O Zitiános* (The Beggar); it is the adventures of an itinerant Kravarite just before the Balkan Wars; and during the following years a score of cross-references had converged and at last impelled me, as I was in Aetolia, to catch that battered blue bus. The *kapheneion*-grocery was the terminus and assembly point for all the mule traffic of the roadless region ahead. The *kaphedzi* echoed Andreas's laughter when he learnt where I was going; they were both grinning as I set out. I had only gone a few paces when Andreas shouted after me: 'Take care they don't *boliarize* you!' Boliarize? It was a word I had never heard. He repeated the phrase, grinning still more widely: '*Prosoché na mi se boliarépsoun!*'*

'What does *boliarépsoun* mean?'

'You'll soon learn! *Kalo taxidi!*'† My brow, as I went on my way, was puckered with conjecture.

* * * *

Villages, towns, regions and islands all over the country have cornered professions. The dwellers along the banks of the

* This odd word, logically, is the third person plural of the subjunctive of an unknown verb of which the first person present indicative would be *boliarévo*. ('Boliarize' is an attempt to turn it into an English verb.)

† 'Happy journey!'

Hebrus cut the reeds and strip and bind them into brooms. The closeness of vineyards to pines in Attica and Southern Euroea singles the inhabitants out as the best retsina-vintners. The olive-groves of Amphissa and Kalamata have made their oils famous. Sultanas and currants come from Cretan Malevizi and Corinth. The hardness and workability of the local rock makes Leros in the Dodecanese the source of most of the mill-stones in Greece. The clay at Coroni provides an endless supply of enormous oil-jars and Siphnos equips most of Greece with water pitchers that have changed little since ancient times. (Yes, but why does Siphnos also abound in cooks? Tselemendé, the Greek Mrs Beaton, was from Siphnos. And in janitors? This humble office is the goal of many unambitious Siphniots. The remainder of the population are poets.) As of old, Paros quarries marble. Athenian houses are full of maids from Tinos and the smaller Cyclades: the Catholic communities surviving from Frankish times maintain convent schools where the girls learn household skills. The village of Ambellákia on Mt Ossa soared to prosperity on the strength of a local root providing a colour in which the uniforms of the whole Austro-Hungarian army were dyed: ships set sail from Trieste and Fiume and unloaded their white bales at Ragusa; strings of camels crossed Dalmatia, Albania and northern Greece, and came back a month later with their burdens all sky-blue. (The discovery of aniline dyes sent the hamlet into a decline.) There are interesting reasons why Chios became so prominent in international banking; good reasons, too, for the old allegiance of Crete, Epirus and the Mani to the blood-feud. But why were the great cotton fortunes of the Nile amassed by villagers from Mt Pelion and Vlach emigrants from Thessaly? Why are the distillers of Constantinople mostly from Tsakonia, a Dorian-speaking mountain-pocket in the eastern Peloponnese? Abundance of timber accounts for the skill of the Zagorochória, near the Albanian border, in carpentry and lathmaking. The intricate wood-work and the florid altar-screens of the Pindus belong to a wider geographical phenomenon: at a certain height all over Europe the convergence of long winters, early nightfall, soft wood and sharp knives surrounds the mountaineers with shavings and chips. History accounts for Hydra and Spetsai being almost entirely populated by admirals; but why was Hydra, and why is Kalymnos today, the home of most of the sponge-fishers on the Lybian reefs and in Florida? Was it local toughness that made Roumeli the traditional recruiting ground for the Evzone regiments? Why were the Lydian inhabitants of Ai-Vali such famous smugglers? When did Salonika first become known for *koulouri*-baking and why are boys from Yanina their nimblest vendors?* Yanina is also famous for silverwork and filigree, and Paramythia, in the Souli mountains farther south, is deafening with coppersmiths. Thessalian Tyrnavos is the Mecca of ouzo; but what is the origin of the ribald wielding of earthernware phalluses, with which, on Clean Monday, the young men of Tyrnavos mark the end of Shrovetide? When, and why, did Pharsala first become the metropolis of *halva*, that delicious flaky sweetmeat of sesame and honey; or Levádeia, of those small sugar-dusted puffs of pastry called *kourabiédes*? What prompted Syra to concentrate on nougat and loukoum? A generation ago, all the boot-blacks of Athens came from Megalopolis in Arcadia; (this humble and amusing community is still the élite of this calling, but their old supremacy is challenged by interlopers from all over Greece). Volo is taxed with tight-fistedness and the islanders of Mykonos with their proneness to exaggeration and their belief in ghosts.

---

* *Koulouria* are hard-crusted circular rolls with a hole in the middle, sprinkled with sesame seeds. The inhabitants of Yanina and Epirotes in general are nicknamed *plakoképhaloi*, flat-heads; their mothers are said to smack their babies on the crown to make it more convenient, later on, for balancing a *koulouri*-tray. Traditionally, this smack is accompanied by the words 'Kai tzimitzís stin Póli!' 'May you become a roll-seller in the City!' The City—Constantinople—drew young Yaniniots like a magnet for centuries.

The aptness at procuring with which the Corfiots are teased
is a joke rooted in the long Venetian occupation of the Hepta-
nese. (Italians are slanderously thought to be pimps to a man.
Why Kalamata, with equally little truth, should share this fame,
is more mysterious. There is no steadier population.) The juxtaposition of Patras and pederasty is no more than comic alli-
teration; the vulgar as well as the classical word begins with
a P. The islanders of Naxos, when neighbours banteringly call
them thieves, smile tolerantly: this reputation springs from the
feat of a Naxian who is supposed to have stolen the silver
bridle, the gold-embroidered saddle and the ceremonial pistols
of King Otho the moment he dismounted after a state entry.
Now the Zantiots . . .

This could go on for pages; but my real concern is the
Kravara. Its fame springs from the prevalence, real or supposed,
of professional mendicancy.

The odd part is that there are scarcely any beggars in Greece.
Sellers of jasmine, violets, combs and pistachio nuts are constantly breaking into café conversations and sellers of lottery
tickets wend from table to table with their many-pennoned
lances; fiddlers scrape tunelessly for a few minutes then take
the saucer round; but all these are legitimate. Still more so are
the wandering boot-blacks with their brass-bound tabernacles
slung on baldricks and the sea-food peddlers with baskets of
oysters and clams. (For some reason, many of them are pock-
marked as though in sympathy with the rugous shells of their
stock.) Sponge sellers are the grandest of all. Ringed like Saturn
by their merchandise and sometimes invisible under a cumulus
of perforated globes, they float about the city crying '*Sphoun-
garia!*' When rival clouds appear in the sky, they hover near
the arcades and a single raindrop sends them scuttling for
shelter: they know that a brief shower turns their bouyant
wares to lead. A nocturnal and terrible old Cappadocian drifts

from tavern to tavern selling toys and practical jokes made of celluloid, cardboard, twisted rubber-bands and gunpowder and a device he invented himself, which, released by an unsuspecting victim, mimics the protracted report of flatulence.

Perhaps begging was not always so rare; but it jars with Greek ways and the pride that makes tipping difficult. Doors are opened and tables spread for any stranger arriving in a village; this surely spikes the guns of mendicancy as a skilled profession. The few beggars one does meet are pathetically amateur and innocuous; an old woman out of luck, a down-and-out whose modest demands are made with little conviction; sometimes a jovial old card with breath like a blow-lamp, a bloodshot wink as he points thirstily down his throat and a mock salute as he dives, clutching his winnings, into the nearest drinking-hell for his fifteenth ouzo of the morning; each dawn finds him, to the despair of his dear ones, snoring in a different doorway: the sort of figure, in fact, that we could all become. There is nothing to set against the rest of the Mediterranean, no competition with the infernos of Naples and Palermo. The only real professionals are the gypsies. Their single-mindedness overrides flight and rebuff with a patient erosion of whispers and plucked sleeves that exalts their takings from alms to danegeld. Where and how did the Kravarites deploy their skill?

A pathway to the eastern skyline of the canyon led to a notch that the *kaphedzi* had pointed out: the gates of the Kravara. When I reached it, the treeless hills sank northwards, a cauldron enclosed by the limestone summits of Aetolia and blurred by landslides of shale and scree. A triangle of mountain barred its nether extremity and the Eurytanian ranges rippled away beyond in a dim and scarcely discernible overlap: a gaunt, stricken, rather beautiful region where the shade was already shrinking under the mid-morning sunlight. A few small clouds loose in the pale air towed their bending shadows over the salients and ravines.

The Kravara covers, I think, about fifty square miles, but the figure has no meaning in such a terrain. A score of villages lurk there; not one was visible and there was no hint of the presence of man or beast, not a leaf or a grass blade. Under a sharp sky where late winter was turning into early spring, the sphinx-like region was replete with enigmas.

The first village came so abruptly that I had dropped into the middle of it only a minute later than my first plunging glimpse of its roofs. It slanted up and down the ravine's edge from an untidy quadrangle of dust and stone. Under a couple of acacias outside the *magazi*—the bar, café and grocer's shop where the heart of a Greek community beats—a handful of villagers were languidly conversing over a tin mug of wine and its brood of thick, squat tumblers. Further elongated by the soaring of his black cylindrical hat sat an amazingly tall priest with his hands folded over the crook of a bulky umbrella. Silence fell except for the growl of a dog worrying some shameful trove nearby. Greetings were guardedly exchanged; the stranger must speak first; then, 'you are welcome' evoked its response of 'you are well found'. Back came 'be seated' as a rush-bottomed chair was brusquely freed from its dreaming tabby and the priest filled a new glass of wine. I had been so intrigued by the *kaphedzi's* recent injunction that the question leaped prematurely from my lips: 'What does *boliarévo* mean?' The silence thickened; ambiguous glances were exchanged. An old man at last said: 'Are you an Athenian?' When my distant habitat was explained, their brows began to clear. A stranger from Europe! They were congenitally on their guard against compatriots, as though wary of ritual teasing. Suspect on Greek lips, the word *boliarévo* became guileless curiosity on a stranger's. A long time ago, the old man said—*palaia! palaia!*, corroborated the priest with a wave—the villagers of the Kravara were great travellers. . . . They used to wander all over Greece, and abroad too. They invented a secret language—all nonsense, the old man declared—in order to be able to talk without other

Greeks understanding. These wanderers used to call themselves *boliárides*, and the language they spoke was *ta boliárika*, and *boliarévo* meant—the old man paused here. ' Was it,' I asked, 'anything to do with the old tradition of begging—ages and ages ago?'

Everybody looked happier. 'Yes, that's right!' they all said. 'You've heard of it?' Relief spread through the company. The old man went on. 'That's exactly it! They used to earn their living by wandering about and begging. Can you blame them? Look at these mountains! Nothing grows here, you couldn't graze a mouse! So off they went. Some of the old ones were not very scrupulous; they didn't mind what they said or did. A few used to pretend to be lame or mad or holy men—anything to extort alms. This was what *boliarizing* meant: outwitting the mugs.' Everybody laughed. 'But it all died out long ago.'

I began to conjugate the verb: *boliarévo, boliaréveis, boliarévei*. 'We boliarize, ye boliarize,' the others chimed in to complete the present indicative, 'they boliarize.' The priest went off for more wine. His robes were a jigsaw of patches. The silver hair and beard, the wide blue eyes and the delicate moulding of nose and temples combined in a saintlike distinction. His quiet conviviality was more manifest as the glasses succeeded each other; it robbed his gait of its sureness but left his dignity unimpaired.

But where did the word *boliárides—boliáris* in the singular—come from? Nobody knew. It is inexistent in Greek. The only similar word I could think of was *bolyar*. The bolyars, linguistically akin to the boyars of Russia and Rumania—were the warlike noblemen of the mediaeval Bulgarian Empire. What had this obsolete Slav word to do with this community so close to the gulf of Corinth? The early Slav invasions of Greece left many place-names but only a handful of words and this is not one of them; and the Bulgarian-speaking 'Slavophone' villages of Macedonia, as they are discreetly called, were hundreds of miles away. As we talked, a possibility dawned. Many Kravarites set off for Europe through Albania, Serbia or Bulgaria, mainly the last. They picked up a smattering of these tongues; perhaps this was how *boliaris* found its way to the Kravara. But in what circles in Bulgaria would a foreign beggar learn the word for a mediaeval noble? Doubt returned. (There are one or two ordinary Slav words in *boliárika—tzerkva*, for instance, is 'church'—and perhaps people with more than my stale and swiftly diminishing supply of Slav words will recognize more. Another—*gaïna*—sounded familiar: it is Rumanian and Koutzovlach for a 'chicken', descending from the Latin *gallina*.*) But most of the words were fabricated. Everyone knew the small mysterious vocabulary by heart. It is like the thieves' cant of Alsatia in old London or Villon's in Paris, the Shelta of Irish tinkers and the jargon of highwaymen, in which a pistol was a barker, a lantern a glim and a baby a lullaby-cheat.

* The Vlach and Rumanian languages are so close that some authorities think that they are the same and the differences merely the result of a few centuries separation. Vlach (or Aroman) communities, some static and some semi-nomadic, are sprinkled across the southern Balkans. Others maintain they are similar but unrelated developments of low Latin springing up in the Roman garrisoned colonies of Dacia—modern Rumania—and Macedonia. The Vlach language in Greece has two slightly differing dialects, spread over the Pindus round Metsovo and Samarina respectively. They could, it is argued, be the remains of the Roman legion garrisoned in the passes of the Pindus, recruited among Italiots or locally among Greeks, all of them speaking camp-Latin. When Honorius recalled the legions to Rome, this order, which emptied Britain of its Roman soldiery, may have failed to reach these remote folds of the Pindus; and here the benighted legionaries have remained ever since, rock-pools of corrupt Latin-speakers waiting for orders and pasturing their huge flocks all over Thessaly and the Pindus; or so they say. This is dangerous ground: nationalism, irridentism and opportunism have blurred the purely scholarly approach which this odd survival deserves. Unless he is ready to plunge deep, a writer can only mention the phenomenon and pass on. I choose the latter prudent course. One bold theory—where did I read it?—upholds that the Vlachs are the remains of Pompey's army, defeated by Caesar at Pharsalus in the Thessalian plain, in 48 B.C. Enviable precision.

The table burst into a hubbub; strange words came showering out. The laughter and the gobbledygook made me wonder for a second whether the odd sounds were being improvised as a joke. Apart from one or two Slav, Vlach (or Rumanian) words, a sound here and there had a Turkish ring; others might almost have been Romany, but I don't think they were. The reader may spot and trace more words than I have; most of them, I think, are pure invention. I pointed to objects in turn, or said the words in everyday Greek and out leaped an emulous chorus of boliaric equivalents.

Q. (pointing to my eyes) 'What are these? *Ta matia?*'

A. '*Tziphlia!*' '*Otsia!*'—the last plainly Slav, from *otchi*.

Q. 'And this?' (pointing to my head) '*To kephali?*'

A. '*Koka! Karoni!*'

Q. 'And these?' (waving my hands) '*ta khéria?*'

A. '*Tchogránia!*' they managed the 'tch' sound, inexistent in Greek, with ease.

Q. 'And that? *I yénia?*'—pointing to Father Andrew's beard.

A. '*Máratho!*' Fennel . . .

Q. 'A foot? *To pódi?*'

A. '*Vatso!*'

Q. '*Moustaki*, a moustache?'

A. '*Douki!*'

Q. 'Door? *Porta?*'

A. '*Tchapráka!*'

Outlandish words! Back they boomed in unfaltering unison, only halted by an occasional brief bicker about the pronunciation. We were off.*

At this point food—*liópi*—appeared on the table. It unleashed a fresh swarm of syllables: *bouzouróno*, 'I eat'; *boudjour*, 'bread';

* Reluctantly, dreading lest the reader, daunted by pages of italics, should skip them, I have lifted most of the Boliaric glossary to the end of the book. It would be a shame if this curious secret language should vanish unrecorded. So there it is, in Appendix II. I long for the reader to turn to it at once but I am in no position to insist.

hasko (Slav?), 'fresh bread'; *sarlagaïn*, 'oil'; *bourliotes* and *solínes* (literally 'tubes', Why?) for 'olives'; *prasino*, 'flour' ('green'— again why?); *lópia*, 'vegetables'; *yanitza*, 'an egg'; *gnoshi*, 'salt': *beligrídia,* * 'grapes'; *ripo*, 'fish'; *mazarak*, 'meat'; *koukouroúzo*, 'sweet-corn' (pan-Balkan, outside Greece, for 'maize'); *patlísia*, 'cherries'; and *benir*, 'cheese'. *Mleko* and *voda* for 'milk' and 'water', are plain Slav; but water is also *kaoúri*. . . . The catalogue closed with *karaméto* and *daró*; coffee, that is, and a cigarette. . . .

* * * *

Gnóshi . . . *sarlagaïn* . . . *tchapráka* . . . *dervó* . . . *tchogránia* . . . *havalóu* . . . *tcharmalídi* . . . *lióka* . . . *hálpou* . . . the alien and the un-Greek ring of these wild syllables filled me with wonder. It was as though each villager, as a word was uttered and corroborated by the rest, were throwing a strange object on the table in a mysterious and insoluble Kim's game. A few were remotely familiar, the linguistic equivalents of rusty penknives, bus tickets of vanished lines, flints from a blunderbuss, snuffers, glove stretchers, a broken churchwarden, the cat's whiskers from a crystal set, a deflated million-mark note, the beer label of a brewery long bankrupt, a watchman's rattle. Others were familiar objects misapplied, latches used as bottle openers, ping-pong balls riddled with airgun slugs, cartridge-case ferrules, newsprint twisted into bottle stoppers; then foreign objects—a kukri, the stub of a Toscana, a medal from Lourdes, a Samoan blowpipe, a voodoo charm from Haiti. . . .

Others resembled scraps from newspapers in unknown tongues, nuggets of freak mineral and coins with the legend all but effaced which a trained linguist, geologist or numismatist perhaps, but not I, would identify in a flash. But most were puzzles of twisted metal gleaming enigmatically in the Aetolian noon.

Unearthing this stuff, abetted by the wine which had lulled Father Andrew asleep, had sent all our spirits soaring. (A wine

* Again, Slav?

splash still blurs the pencilled page in front of me and may have misplaced an accent or two.) I read the list out loud and amended it. Then my companions began to glue the words together in sentences. '*Phóta pou spartáei to houmouráki mou!*', one cried, pointing to his daughter trotting down the road. '*Kitta pou phevgei to koristaki mou*', I would laboriously work out. 'Look at my daughter running away.'

Another, spotting the gendarme strolling our way, whispered in mock concern: '*Stíliane! Mas photáei o bánikos pátellos!*'

'*Prosochí!*' I construed. '*Mas kittázei o megálos chorophýlax!*' (Beware, the important policeman is watching us!) The gendarme was bewildered by the laughter as he sat down.

'Don't tell him!' everyone cried, pouring him some wine. 'It's a secret!' The gendarme, a nice man from Amorgos, accepted this mild chaff with a tolerant Cycladic smile. I had the agreeable feeling of being in league with outlaws.

The session turned into an exam. Darting about my notes, I slowly put together the following: '*Tchekmekiazei o verdílis sto koutióu*'—but it will shorten matters to put the actual *Greek* into English: 'The virdil tchmekizes in his box while the matzoukas, stílian-wise, manes the houmouraki's klítzino. The maláto pulls his fennel and anyrizes, but all the maletchkos, including the gotopoules, are gaskinning in the dair and mandaring the skarlaimdjis. The banic patello koupons the boliar to the gavin where he eats dervo and calls on his Markantonies. The phlambouri sinks and it starts to kranize as halpou comes . . .!' 'The father sleeps in his house', that is, 'while the beggar furtively steals his daughter's ring. The priest pulls his beard and grows angry but all the children, including the young gents, are laughing in the street, and making fun of the peddlers. The great policeman takes the rascal to the prison where he gets the stick and calls on his saints. The sun sinks, it starts to rain and night comes on.'* Impossible, without seeming to boast, to

* *Harman's Caveat, or Warning for Common Cursetors, vulgarly called vaga-bonds* (1567) gives the following example of 'peddelars Frenche or canting':

describe the success of this gloomy little story! Best to set off
for the inner Kravara on this note of triumph. I stood up, exchanged farewells and reached for my stick. My elderly
instructor grabbed it first and held it out of reach: 'What's it
called in Boliaric?'

'*Stravi*.'

'And?'

'*Kaníki*.'

'Another?'

'*Dervó*?'

'And another?'

'*Grígoro*.'

'One more?'

'*Matsoúka*.'

'One last one?'

I was stumped. 'You can't have it till you remember,' the
old man said. At last it came.

'*Láoussa!*'

He handed it over amid applause and laughter. I set off,
followed by cries of well-wishing and invitations to return;
followed also by the injunction to *stílianize* in the next *sielo* as
it was stuffed with *boliars* and *shoreftis*.

*   *   *   *

The village of Platanos had turned up trumps. How vain the
kaphedzi's warning had proved! No boliarization there. In fact,
I might almost be said to have boliarized them, as I hadn't been
allowed to pay a single lepta. 'It's paid fór,' they said. 'Your
turn when we come to England,' or 'Put that cash away,
Mihali. It has no currency here. . . .'.

'Bene Lightman's to thy quarromes, in what tipken hast thou lypped in this
darkemans, whether in a lybbage or a strummel? (Good morrow to thy
body, in what house hast thou lain all night, whether in a bed or in
the straw?)'

One of them accompanied me out of the village to put me on my way. The poverty-stricken ranges soared reproachfully all round. ... Something my companion said deflected our talk from secret languages. We had been speaking of Father Andrew.

'Yes,' he said, 'he's even taller than his brother—and he was enormous. Did you never see him? Archbishop Damaskinos?'

I halted, amazed. How could one relate our tattered and delightful drinking companion to the gigantic figure of the famous Archbishop? A vision of that beetling titan, robed in the canonicals of the Archbishopric of Athens and the Primacy of all Greece, shot through my brain; his breast was ablaze with pectoral ornaments, his huge hand grasped a pastoral staff, and the veils which, on state occasions, are draped from an orthodox dignitary's headgear, fluttered about his enormous trunk like black plasma. He was vested in the temporal as well as the spiritual leadership of the country; Regent of Greece until the return of King George II, it was as a Head of State that he negotiated with Churchill, Eden and Macmillan. Once, on a rainy morning in London, when the Regent was there on a state visit, I went to see him celebrate High Mass in the Greek Cathedral in Moscow Road. Under a globular gold tiara a foot high and armed with a crosier glittering with gems and twisting serpents, the majestic colossus intoned the liturgy in a voice of modulated thunder: the thurible, as he censed the iconostasis and the congregation, was reduced by his tremendous size to a toy. At the end of the service, he emerged into the drizzle and the crash of presented arms and an escort of motor-cyclists and a Rolls Royce a-glitter with gold-fringed pennants wafted him back to Grosvenor Square. . . .

The slight coarseness of feature of the huge and controversial Archbishop—the 'wily mediaeval prelate' of Churchill's famous phrase—was no match, I thought, for the mandarin looks of his humbler brother. Haloed by the spun silver of his hair and beard, those noble and transparent features were, plainly, proof against any Dionysiac onslaught and safe from the stigmata of power.

*   *   *   *

My companion left me on the brow of the gorge. A canyon yawned and the downhill path between the boulders and black-berry clumps and the occasional tufts of bracken must have been a foaming torrent when the snow melted. Now it was only to be picked out from the havoc all round by a hardly-discernible pallor which the hoofs of goats and pack animals had chipped on the rocks' surface and by the precious scattered clues of their droppings. Paths like this, even with half a gallon of midday wine raging in the blood-stream, are best descended at speed: leaping helter-skelter from rock to rock and bouncing on one foot to land with the other on the next boulder in a breakneck concatenation of parabolas. The rate of such descents and the fixity of one's gaze, blinded to all but the random stair-case underfoot, lands one at the end of them—panting, with temples pounding, salty-throated and glittering with sweat—in a world that the violent interval has utterly transformed. I slowed up in the nethermost depths among bleached stones by a clump of trees. Deep-probing sunbeams revealed a thread of water snaking from a cranny of rock and expanding for a foot or two among fine pebbles and cress, then trickling away under the trees. Here, sheltered by an oleander, with his head on a haversack, his beret over his eyes and the red and blue ribbon of the Greek Military Cross on the breast of his battledress, a second-lieutenant reclined with his combat-booted ankles crossed, the image of young martial repose. But he wasn't asleep: one eyelid and an eyebrow like a rook's feather were lifted to take in the newcomer.

'I saw you coming down,' he said with a smile. 'You look thirsty. It's remarkable water.'

I swallowed long draughts of this wonderful liquid, chewing it as a horse does then letting it sink to its goal like an icicle.

'Didn't I tell you?' he said, looking pleased as I extolled it. 'From Crete?' he added, pointing to my old knapsack: those faded yellow and scarlet stripes, woven years ago in Anoyeia on the slope at Mt Ida, betrayed its origin. I explained myself and we exchanged names and formal handshakes. I took one of his offered cigarettes and lay under the next oleander, propping my feet on a stone to tip the blood into a more level irrigation and watched the smoke climb to the lanceolate green criss-cross that a month or two would deck with pink flowers. I fell asleep half-way through the delicious Papastratos No. 1; but only an inch below the surface, subliminally floating and still aware of the afternoon, the leaves, the lattice of their shade and the trickling water.

*　　*　　*　　*

The springs and wells parsimoniously scattered about the mountains leave memories of their blessings for years. Occasional waterfalls, plunging down the rocks and opening private rainbows across a soaking jungle of leaves, seem almost immoral in their spendthrift opulence. Sometimes they drop to a forgotten mill that laces the freshness with a whiff of weeds and toadstools and the waterlogged timber of mute wheels. The hollow dens of Cyclopes yawn among the rocks under ilex-shade, the gape of their lower jaws barred by stones and thorns to form a goat-fold; the water spills from the limestone through a funnel of twisted leaf and the hollowed tree trunk that catches it is tressed inside with dark green weeds. The rocks are mattressed by a thousand years' accumulation of pellets riddled by the slots of cloven feet; a spiralling goat's horn lies there, moulted from a skull stuck on a branch to ward off the Eye: the roving bane that can fascinate the ewes and rob them of their milk and their kids and the rams of their vigour. Some of these springs emerge in the darkness of the caves themselves at the end of long climbs into the heart of a mountain range. Others drip in high clefts dedicated to the

Assumption, St Antony of the Desert or the Prophet Elijah to quench the thirst of an extinct line of hermits.

Giant plane trees often mark their issue; without them, neither the trees nor the surrounding houses would have sprung up, and the villagers sitting in the shade and the drinking mules would never have assembled. How miraculous, on the way down from baking watersheds, seems the green froth nourished by rock-borne springs! The water is husbanded in conduits, bean tendrils steal up flimsy obelisks of cane, medlar, lemon and orange trees form cool undercrofts. Pumpkins scatter the channelled soil, gourd stems climb the trunks and the branches to hang dappled green globes in the penumbra, goitrous with the damp. The wells that dive through the floors of lonely houses fill the cisterns with acoustics that capture the clank and splash of the bucket and send the rumour of the upper world booming about the vaulted dark. Sometimes thirst turns mediocre water into good: a gulp of cloudy liquid in the wilderness of the Deep Mani, for instance, or brackish draughts on a gasping Cretan shore. Round the mouths of some old wells, castles and monasteries fall to bits. Rope-grooves fret the coping and the roots of fig trees prise the steyning askew. After the lizards and kestrels and the Herculean mountains all round, it is hard, looking down, to focus the gloom of those cylinders. Small as a coin at the end of a tufted descending mile of cobwebs and as though seen through a telescope the wrong way, a disc of reflected sky looks back stamped with one's own craning torso. After seconds of waiting a dropped pebble fractures this medallion with the report of a cork drawn in the Antipodes and the splashing echoes mount as faintly as the voices of the hamadryads calling to Hylas. Into these dark and plunging tunnels, in a score of fairy stories, are dropped the goblets and rings and swords whose recovery, after years of trouble, settles a princely identity, a claim to a kingdom or reconciles lovers long estranged or spell-bound.

Of so polar a chill is one blue dragon's eye of water half-way up Mt Olympus that a stranger tempted to swim across it climbs back into the heat of August frozen to the bone. Running springs are the surest talismans against the noonday. Nereids are said to make some of them perilous for shepherds and many are heavy with fable. There is a spring between Mt Ida and the White Mountains that has the attribute, like many fountains in myths, of bestowing immortality. During the war we would halt here and, leaning our guns against the trunk of an arbutus, lie flat, lower our turbanned heads and drink deep and long. Moments of tranquillity and benediction! But better than all of them today seemed this legendless Aetolian trickle. I could hear each drop falling like the note of a celesta the other side of a brittle wall of sleep.

*　*　*　*

I watched the second-lieutenant peeling an apple fast and deftly so that the skin fell off in an unbroken coil. He cut it up and offered a neat slice on the tip of a silver pen-knife.

'It's from Naoussa,' he said, 'in Macedonia. The best in Greece.' He was stationed in Perista, the village for which I, too, was heading. 'You must stay with me,' he said, looking pleased at the prospect of company. 'I'm all alone there, just back from leave in Athens. There's a marvellous leg of lamb in here.' He patted his haversack. 'A present from a friend in Navpaktos. The woman where I'm billeted will roast it, all wrapped up in grease-paper so that none of the goodness gets out! She's an ace; she pokes whole garlic cloves *right down* between the meat and the bone! You'll see. . . .'

Marko, the second-lieutenant, a lithe, good-looking Athenian with shining black hair, gave off sparks of enjoyment and energy even in repose. He was an epicure and a hedonist and, as I soon saw, nimble as a lynx on the ascent, which was long and steep. Too young for the war and the occupation, he had grown up in time to get the civil war as a coming-of-age present. Much of it he had spent in precisely the region where his present assignment lay. This valley had been the theatre of dogged and merciless conflict. Marko paused to describe the advance of his company up the slope we were climbing in pursuit of a force of communist guerrillas. His rapid discourse seemed to fill the empty chasm once more with machine- and sub-machine-gun fire and the explosion of grenades and mortar bombs; it peopled the slopes with running and crouching figures and splintered the air with fragments. At a bend in the track where a group of boulders slanted higgledy-piggledy—I think he had been waiting for them—he stopped again.

'It was afternoon, just about now. I was working my way uphill *there*,' he said, 'dodging behind those boulders to avoid bursts of fire coming from that rock by the bracken. It turned into a duel: we were both determined to get each other. I managed to creep within about five yards, with fire coming down in bursts all the way. While the enemy was changing his magazine, I tossed a hand grenade behind his rock, ducked, slipped in a new magazine and waited for him to break cover. Out leaped a khaki figure with his tommy-gun blazing and shouting "*Na!* Scullion of the Glückbergs"* in a peculiar high voice. I dropped just in time and fired a whole burst from the ground. The guerrilla let go his gun, stumbled downhill a few paces and lay still—just over there. And do you know'— Marko's voice after a pause had dropped to a lower pitch—'it was a woman! I had thought there was something odd about the voice. And a very good-looking one too, with her hair cut short. She'd stopped the whole burst. *Phoveró itan! Phríki!!* It was horrible, terrible.'

After another pause he went on, 'They used to be trained along with the other communist irregulars in enormous camps the other side of the Yugoslav border. That was before Tito broke with Stalin. Some of them fought like dogs. Poor Greece. . . .'

He was amused by my eagerness about the Kravara. 'They

* An insulting term for the Royal Family.

are a queer lot,' he said, 'as bright as they make them. The old ones could tell you a lot.' He gave me a few names.

We came to the top at last and a fresh landscape slid downhill into a further rolling and mountain-girt gulf of country into which I had caught a far-away glimpse from the slopes above Platanos: a bare, mountain-locked, magnificent region. Much of its asperity was tamed and softened by the gold afternoon light. Marko had to call at a house in the outskirts of the village. As he flew up the steps he told me not to be late for the leg of lamb; anyone would tell me where he lived.

*　*　*　*

There was no comparison between Platanos and Perista; the ragged and dusty look was quite absent. Trellises from opposite eaves reached out to join hands over the slanting pebbles. Shade abounded. A ball came bouncing down a steep wynd and a troop of pretty children flew squealing after it into the lane until the sight of a stranger froze them into a battery of eyes agog with wonder while the ball continued its orphaned career downhill. A small girl was pasturing a goat overhead—on what? It seemed to be grazing on shale—and singing a desperate song to herself about ambushes and bloodshed.

The priest was also a cobbler. He sat crosslegged among the lasts on his doorstep, his mouth full of wooden tacks. His hammer halted in mid-air as he mumbled through the tacks. 'What news?—*Tí néa?*—where are you from? *Anglia? Po! Po! Po!—makrya!* A long way.'

He smiled to himself as he resumed work, selecting the tacks and banging them neatly home in an upturned sole. The absurdity of such a distance tickled him: *Anglia*, indeed. . . . A charming man with a hunchback took me under his wing and we headed for the *magazi*. He admitted that it was a pretty village; yes, pretty but wretched: they had to bring earth up here by donkey from the Kotsalos, which flowed along the ravine between Perista and Dorvitza, the next village north. A hopeless region. Nobody wanted these barren hills, so people, long, long ago—*palaiá! palaiá!*—took refuge here from the Turks. Soil erosion and fire had stripped it bare and reduced the villagers to poverty, emigration, living from hand to mouth, peddling, even beggary. . . . There was a rumour that the place had been prosperous once: look at those mulberry trees! People said they might have been planted long, long ago by Jews who grew rich on silkworms and then vanished, or most of them anyway. There might be a few of their descendants left: what about names like Rorós, Kagánis and Solomos?* Otherwise there was nothing to pasture flocks on, not a square inch of soil to grow grain, no heather, even, for bees. A little water there was, thank God; enough for a few potatoes and chick peas, not much else. The tops of some plane trees showed where the path coiled into the valley; and the pale green of young poplars intercepted the slanting light. A few cornel cherry trees flourished and a sprinkling of wild pears and crab-apples. One of the planes and a raft of vine shaded the little space outside the *magazi*. Inside it was wide and cool, sparsely stocked with bales of cloth, wool, horse nails, saws, tinned stuff, coils of rope (always, rather oddly to a Western eye, sold by weight), baskets, open tubs of salted sardines and anchovy, or

---

* Every now and then one is surprised by this rumour of evaporated Jewish communities. As we know, there were plenty in the time of the Acts of the Apostles and there are frequent mentions of them by Jewish travellers and Byzantine writers in mediaeval and early renaissance times. (I have touched on the question at some length at the beginning of *Mani*.) Greeks connect the silk industry with Jews and the resemblance of the name Solomos (which means 'salmon' and is also the name of Greece's greatest nineteenth-century poet, a Venetian count from the Ionian Isles) to Solomon seems, to villagers, to clinch things. But they are not accurate in these matters: sometimes '*Evraioi*' or '*Ovraioi*' means little more than 'foreign' and sometimes it merely designates a Greek speaking a different dialect, such as Tzakonian. The last village to which I have heard Jewish origins ascribed, on the strength of the name Solomos, is Koutíphari, in the outer Mani, the ancient Thalamai of Pausanias.

ouzo 'loose' in big jars (as opposed to the smart 'sealed' kind),
slabs of salt cod, and, looped on strings and painted black to
keep off rust, except for the edges still bright from the forge,
were looped the haftless heads of *skeparnia*, those biblical, all-
purpose adze-like tools with a curved blade for cutting or hack-
ing on one side and a flat surface on the other, which Greeks
use as a spade, a hoe, an axe, a hammer, a rough plane, a pruning
knife or, in masons' hands, a trowel for slicing and trimming
bricks. There were mule bridles and lengths of webbing for
girths and a wooden saddle or two.

A sloe-eyed boy, writing in an exercise book, shouted to his
mother that a stranger had come—*Mammá! Ena xéno!*—and
went on with his work. She brought me a coffee. I looked
through my midday scribbling. After a time the boy said,
'What are you reading?'

'You'll never guess.'

'Go on.'

'All right, then.' I read out the boliaric sentence about 'looking out for the important policeman'. He laughed.

'*Sovará?*' he asked—'Seriously?'—and came over to have a
look: then, after reading a few words, he told two men who
were just coming in that I was a foreigner and reading
bóliarika.

The words acted like Open Sesame on the two newcomers
and on the others, including my hunchback mentor, who soon
followed them in. Why had I ever thought there would be any
difficulty in learning about the old days in the Kravara? *Of
course* there had been beggars here, hundreds of them, the best
in Greece—not so much here in Perista, one of them said
deprecatingly; Dorvitza was the place, the next village along
the valley, and Platanos, the one I had just left. Loose, cupping
gestures suggested multitude and the long whistles on all sides
could be interpreted as admiration or implied rebuke. It was
exactly what I had heard in Platanos, except that there, Perista
and Dorvitza were the two villages cited: and in Dorvitza,

when I went there, Platanos and Perista. . . . And what about Vonorta, Simi, Palaiópyrgi, Aráchova—yet another Aráchova out of the many in Greece—Pevkos, Diasyláki? As they spoke they pointed at the barren ranges all round where, invisible from where we sat, these hamlets were dispersed. And Kastaniá, Houmouri, Perdikóvis, Neochori, Ayia Triada, Elevtheriani, Kositza, Terpitza, Artótiva, Ternos, Lobótina, Stránoma, Klépa, Pokistá? These were the nests from which the Kravarites had set out on their travels 'in the old days'. There was something in their voices of the affectionate homesickness with which people in England speak of lamplighters, muffin-men, horse buses and German bands, and a shade of the rue that accompanies the remembrance of past heroes. They had been *tou diavólou i kaltza*, the Devil's sock: all the epithets suggesting quick wits were lavished on them—ownership of four eyes, the ability to fly and to sleep with open lids, the dexterity to horseshoe flies and lice. And the gift of the gab! (Perista, I learnt afterwards, was the most famous of them all for eloquence and, as it were, the knack of talking the hind leg off a donkey and replacing it with a wooden one without either the animal or its owner realizing that anything was wrong.)

Villages specialized in different devices. Vagrants from Ternos were adept at herbalism—not really adept, they quickly explained—but at pretending to be: quacks in fact. 'I wouldn't like to try their remedies,' one of the company said. 'Nor would I,' added another, 'but I'd rather swallow their muck than consult the eye specialists from Dermati! If you're blind, your eyes drop out and if you can see, they blind you.' Ternos, Kambia and Karva lived entirely by rascality, it seemed: when someone from these places came to a village, it was no good locking the doors and the windows: they'd be down the chimneys in the night; and next day, where are your trousers? There were dealers in trinkets and counterfeit gold who spirited rings off people's fingers to examine them and then replaced them with gilt brass. Others, in the early days of photography, wandered about with empty boxes on tripods; after making passes with voluminous black cloths and resounding clicks, they left their customers with squares of black celluloid which had to be kept in a dark cupboard for a week before the picture appeared; by which time . . .

Others dealt in sacred books 'blessed by the Oecumenical Patriarch', holy relics, bits of the true cross from Jerusalem, incense from Mt Ararat. . . . But all of these, as far as I could gather, were elaborations of the basic local calling. The true Kravarite vocation was straight mendicancy; but mendicancy elaborated by many ruses: feigned blindness, madness and epileptic fits, and, above all, the semblance of lameness, loss of limb, and malformation. Some would be hunchbacks. ('Not real ones, like me!' my earlier mentor said.) Others contorted their arms, turning them, as it were, inside out with a tangle of suppliant fingers at the end. Some even pretended to have lost both legs, or, at least, the use of them. They strode cheerfully whistling along the road until a village came in sight; then out of their bags came little trolleys on which they settled and then punted themselves along the main street with their hands to take up their stations at the likeliest points. Rolling back their eyes till only the whites showed and contorting themselves into postures that made them quite unrecognizable from the swagmen of the highways which they had been a few moments before, they waited with their brass bowls for the first musical tinkle of a coin. Their trollies were miniature wooden horses for the conquest of Troy after Troy.

These disguises, the old ones said, achieved a perfection which was not learnt overnight. A few villages were the headquarters of specialists who trained promising boys in all the arts they needed for their careers. They were mountain academies of begging in which the classes, *mutatis mutandis*, must have resembled Fagin's school for young gentlemen. When they had no more to learn, they set out on their travels, paying the fees retrospectively from the takings of their maiden journeys.

I knew about these real or fictitious classes: it is one of the fragments of rumour which anybody who knows anything about the Kravara has heard; and I had been waiting to ask if there was anything in it. There is an associated rumour, widely bandied about and mentioned in Karkavitza's novel, about which I longed, but did not dare, to ask. I managed it in the end: Was there any foundation for the report that, in the bad old days, parents—or others—would sometimes distort the limbs of children when they were very young, in order to help them in their foredestined careers? There was a pause. They had all heard of it, they said, but there was, as far as they knew, no foundation for the rumour. Perhaps, one old man said, some wicked parents long, long ago might have done such a deed—after all, there were bad folk everywhere!—but if it had ever happened it must have been a single case. Nothing of the kind had ever been heard of in his day and he was a very old man: nor in his parents' or grandparents' time, which took one back to the days of *Turkokratía*, long before the War of Independence. Everyone agreed, and their tone and their openness about every other detail of old Kravarite life carried conviction.

The old man asked where I had heard such tales. I said, in the Great Greek Encyclopaedia. 'Under what?' the boy asked; he had been listening to the conversation and occasionally joining in. I said, 'Under Kravara.' He went to a cupboard behind the counter and there, to my astonishment, lying on their sides, pile on pile, were the huge quarto volumes of the *Megáli Elleniki Enkyklopaídia*.* He lifted out the appropriate volume —*Kosmologia–Leptokaryon*—and lugged it to his table. 'Here

---

* I was as surprised to see this tremendous and expensive set of books in this poverty-stricken village as I would be to find the *Encyclopaedia Britannica* in an English farm labourer's cottage: more so; the poverty in the Kravara defeats all comparison. Greece is full of surprises like this. I bought these wonderful volumes, all thirty-three of them, for £50 secondhand some years ago, brought them back to England in a crate and nearly lost them all in Belgrade. A terrible moment.

we are,' he said, 'Kravara' and read the paragraph out loud, dealing with the fairly elaborate *katharevousa* of the dictionary —he went to school at the Gynmasium in Navpaktos—with impressive ease. 'Some of the inhabitants,' he read 'in accordance with old custom, twisted their arms and legs at a youthful age or feigned blindness with intent to deceive as they wandered about the towns of Greece and, frequently, of foreign countries. . . . *Kravarite*: derogatory name for an untruthful person, a feigner, charlatan, tramp, deceiver or beggar.'

He shut the book with the word '*Keratádes!* The Horn-wearers! They oughtn't to have written that! Especially as it's not true!' I wished now I hadn't brought the subject up. 'Eh!' somebody said, 'the chap who wrote it was probably jaundiced. Perhaps he'd been boliarized by someone from the Kravara and wanted to get his own back!' The awkward moment dissolved in laughter.

They were surprised and incredulous when I told them that though tramps and beggars may have dwindled to a small number in Greece, there were still plenty in Europe. They found it hard to credit that they were a common sight in a bourgeois and orderly place like England, and even in the heart of London. It was emigration to America which had changed the Kravara, they said. Inhabitants sailed away by the thousand. The villages remained nearly as poor, but an artificial economy kept them going: all the Kravarites in the United States sent money back to their families. Cash for the first journey was often collected by the old means. The brief expedient of begging had led now and then to substantial fortunes. Look at . . ., an old ex-boliar from Vonorta, who now owned three blocks in Larissa! Kravarites in Rumania grew rich as agents and rent-collectors for landowners; a calling in which they earned a reputation for ruthlessness. . . . Many of the churches towering like cathedrals above the humble villages were founded on alms given twice over.

'That was the extraordinary thing,' an old man said. 'They

would be up to a thousand and one dodges on the road. God knows what!' He laughed. 'Never ask! But at home these old scoundrels, our ancestors, were pillars of rectitude, dutiful sons, faithful husbands, stern fathers, pious and Godfearing men, fierce patriots and model citizens.'

The Kravara abounds in talent. Roumeli has always furnished some of Greece's best soldiers, and the Kravara has not lagged behind. 'We've turned out countless generals,' the old man continued urgently, 'and at this very moment there are four on the general staff. Archbishops, too, as you know; professors, teachers, lawyers—that's where the gift of the gab comes in!—judges, administrators, governors. . . .'

I suddenly remembered that a friend of mine, a Nomarch—a regional prefect with enormous powers—came from exactly here. When I first knew him his little kingdom included part of the Aegean archipelago. He was a small, dark dynamo, a dashing administrator, and a quick and cogent speaker. Compelling language streamed out of him, all obstacles dissolved at his approach. The glint in the eyes round the table suddenly became familiar by association.

Were there still any practising boliars? There was a laugh. 'Not officially. Only a few itinerant peddlers and photographers; if a Kravarite peddler ever tries to sell you anything, don't buy! it's bound to be trash! And beware of their watches: they tick for a day and then stop forever. The photographers are all right. They have to be, nowadays. . . .'*

Shadows heaped up in the gorge below the window. Mt Ardini towered at the end of it. Is it the same—for so many villages and rivers and mountains have two names or more—as

---

* The last statement was corroborated later. There are two in the heart of Kolonaki, the fashionable quarter of Athens, who are both from Kravara villages. Impressively clad in the shiny peaked caps and white dustcoats that photographers have turned into a uniform, they woo passers-by to their tripods. Since this visit, whenever our paths cross now, it is a race to see which of the three of us will say first: 'Stíliane! Mas photae o banikos patellos!'

Mt Oxya? Tall triangles ascended and the evening sun struck their western edges; the rest was invaded by an icy blue that faded to grey as it grew darker. Through the grim chaos beyond lay the route along which the old ones had set out: two days' march through the pathless Eurytanian wilderness to Karpenisi. At Mt Tymphrestos they turned east to Lamia where they took the old road north to the Balkans and Central Europe. . . .

A tinkle from the mountains told of a small flock homing and the glimmer of a fire, unsuspected by day, indicated a fold. We seemed lost in a hinterland of unbelievable remoteness. The vanishing of the daylight sent a tremor of misgiving through the ravines and touched us briefly with something akin to a child's fear of the dark. Conversation languished under the spell, reviving as the petrol lamp was lit. It was time to set off to the second-lieutenant's.

'Come back later,' they said. 'We'll get hold of Uncle Elias for you.'

'Who's he?'

'He knows a lot. *Pollá xérei!*'

My hunchback friend guided me along the lanes. Our hobnails struck sparks from the cobbles. Another *phlambouri* was finished: *halpou* was here. . . .

*   *   *   *

'It's nearly ready!' Marko exulted. He sprang to his feet and advanced to the middle of the firelit room rubbing his hands and almost dancing with contagious delight. 'Just listen to that wonderful smell!'*

The fragrant noose had ensnared me several yards up the lane. The whole house trembled with marvellous fumes.

He seized a bottle of ouzo and tapped it on the flank, exclaiming, '*Sans Rival* from Tyrnavos!' and poured out two

---

* By an odd demotic usage, smells are acoustically perceived: *Akou tin miroudiá!*: 'Listen to the smell!'

glasses. Then he started slicing sausage and cheese and spring onions and *avgotaracho*, delicious grey mullet's roes from Missolonghi densely compressed and enclosed in an oblong carapace of yellow wax. He put a handful of giant olives and white and blood-red radishes in a saucer and showered them with salt: a magnificent *mézé*, in fact, to accompany the ouzo.

'And we've got some retsina you'll like,' he went on as he poured a second glass of ouzo. 'A whole demijohn from Spata in Attica.' He pointed to the great osier-cradled vessel in the corner. 'I've put a couple of bottles in the well to get cold.' He went out to fetch one.

I envied his quarters. They were whitewashed and spotless with low divans along two walls and a red and black rug on the floor: across it Marko had flung the skin of a large wolf shot in the Grammos mountains, where he had won his decoration: I knew because I had asked him. 'But it wasn't for that,' he smiled: the noise of the fighting in the mountain-tops had driven the wolves down to the foothills and even into villages; bears too. A fireplace arched with an ogee made a wide niche in a jutting semi-cylinder of white plaster and the bisected cone of the chimney tapered to a low wooden ceiling which wove a faint fragrance into the other drifting smells. An old woman in black squatted on the hob. Peering from her task, she quavered a greeting. Kyria Diamánti looked light enough to lift in the palm of one hand. Marko sometimes called her *theia* or 'auntie'.

Drinking our ouzo we settled on either side of the *sofra*: a low circular wooden table still common in some parts of Roumeli, Epirus and Macedonia; one eats cross-legged on the floor, or slightly levitated, as we were now, on little rush-bottomed stools. The blue and white check cloth was laden with the implements of our impending feast. At a warning cry from the fireside, the remains of the *mézé* and the ouzo were thrust aside and the great metal pan was lifted sizzling from the flames to the table's centre. Marko begged our cook to join us.

No, no, she had supped; and anyway, no meat for her! She grasped her upper gum between a finger and a thumb to display utter toothlessness, like a horse-coper refusing a deal, and went off into a cracked and engaging laugh. '*Na phate, na phate, paidia!*' she squeaked: 'Eat, eat, boys!'

Marko caught the shrouding grease-paper by the corner and carefully unwrapped the joint. A golden brown leg of lamb emerged, blistering and bubbling with juice and surrounded by a brood of spitting potatoes. The full redolence exploded on us, not of garlic only but of thyme and rosemary too. His knife flashed in the light of the fire as he drove it down alongside the bone: the promised cloves were there! We put a handful of cress, picked at the spring, in both plates.

'What did I tell you!' he said with kindling eyes. 'It's a three months' old lamb, born about Christmas.'

Our eagerness now was touched with frenzy. He made the sign of the cross thrice, we clinked our glasses together.

'*I tan i epi tas!*' he said, like the Spartans before Thermopylae. 'Behind our shields or on them!'; and we fell to. A passion of destruction held us in thrall. Not a word was uttered as we guzzled our way deep into the joint. Holding the joint upright in the pan, Marko sliced away helping after helping and heaped our plates in turn. We halted an instant now and then to grasp our glasses, touch them rim to rim and, after a murmured toast, swallow the delicious wine in unison. Only these brief liquid caesurae—brief but frequent enough soon to summon a second bottle dripping from the well—scanned the breakneck tempo of the meal.

Instead of slackening, the rhythm accelerated with every mouthful. We might have been vying with each other or eating against time or for a bet. The zest and the scope of ogres had descended on us. The only utterances were an occasional ringside murmur of encouragement from the frail crone on the settle. Her arms were clasped about her knees. Goshawk eyes lit with pleasure at the demolition of her handiwork and her features radiated with the total smile that accompanied tooth-lessness at either end of a lifetime. Now and then she stressed her murmur with a pat of her knotted fingers on our knees or our shoulders. When it passed before the fire, her hand was as transparent as a leaf.

My forehead was damp with sweat and I noticed an answer-ing lustre on Marko's brow. I suddenly thought of Theseus and—was it the wicked Kerkyon?—in *The Heroes*, devouring whole oxen face to face and glowering at each other in silence before their fatal wrestling match. But there was no enmity in my host's eyes: only charmed collusion and benevolence. Our work was too wild for speech. With a sulphurous, inaudible thunderclap the deadly sin of Gluttony had risen flaming through the floor.

At last we halted, our knives and forks idle, our mandibles at rest and falling hair glued to our streaming foreheads. Laughter broke the awed hush of this sudden truce, for the whole leg of lamb had vanished. Bare and polished, only a bone gleamed in the firelight in the middle of the dish.

Marko was soon dropping slices of his Macedonian apples into the retsina. When they had soaked up the wine, he offered them on a fork. Kyria Diamánti poked the coffee-saucepan into the embers.

We talked of the war, of Athenian taverns, of girls and books and poetry. I had noticed a couple of Kazanzakis' novels on a shelf, also *The Three Musketeers* in translation and some poems of Valaoritis and Palamas, notably *The Decalogue of the Gipsy*; no Cavafy or Seferis, which he had heard of and wanted to read; and we talked about the Kravarites. I told him that my evening was not yet over. He had to rise at four, so while I filled in some notes about the day's doings, he went to bed on the divan on one side of the fire. Before retiring Kyria Diamánti had laid out sheets, a quilt and a pillow on the other side for me. I had scarcely written a line before Marko was sound asleep.

✴   ✴   ✴   ✴

'Uncle Elias is the man,' they told me in the lamp-lit tavern. 'He'll tell you all about the old Kravarites in the epoch'—this vague term, '*stin ipochí*' always refers to an indeterminate yore, a vague period of old days long sped. 'He's ninety.'

His long, clean-shaven face was a network of wrinkles but his dark eyes darted eagerly. When he took off his cloth cap of mock-leopard's skin—headgear which has long enjoyed an intermittent proletarian vogue in Greece—a snowy shock fell thick and straight over his corrugated brow. A handsome, humorous and slightly actorish mobility stamped his features. He looked much younger than ninety and I said so. The compliment called two new fans of wrinkles into play and his smile revealed long palisades of teeth from which not one was missing.

'Those teeth are all his own, too,' the hunchback said.

'The teeth are all right,' Uncle Elias observed, flashing them once more, 'but they're out of work.'

Everyone laughed. He came from a different village and the locals treated him with a mixture of affectionate teasing and respect. Laying his thick stick across the lamp-lit table he slowly crushed tobacco leaves in the palm of his hand and stuffed them into a home-made pipe. 'Contraband from Agrinion,' someone murmured. 'Don't tell the *patellos*. . . .'

As we talked, he fished a little bar of steel out of his pocket and then, holding it between finger and thumb with a disc of dried fungus held tight against it, he struck it repeatedly with a chip of flint. A faint whiff as of singeing cloth told us that the sparks had ignited it. Blowing until the glow had spread, he laid the smouldering fungus on his pipe-bowl and puffed until a cloud of illegal and aromatic smoke embowered him.

'*Barba Elia*,' someone said, pointing to his disintegrating footgear, 'you ought to get a new pair of boots. Those have seen their day.' 'Don't you worry about them,' Uncle Elias answered from his cloud. 'They are laughing.' It is true that the gaps between the uppers and the soles curled in the semblance of dark smiles.

The old days in the Kravara. . . . The utterances of this fluent old man revived them with great vividness. A mass of circumstantial detail suggested that he had played a considerable part in those ancient doings; but it was never explicit. I expected in vain that his narrative would slip at some point from *oratio obliqua* to *oratio recta*; the collusion of his glance, however, was something more than a hint.

The first impediment a young beggar had to discard, Uncle Elias instructed us, was an attribute called the *tseberi*, or the *tsipa*, of shame. The *tseberi* is the headkerchief that village women wear and the symbol of their modesty; the *tsipa* is a thin layer or membrane, and in some regions a foreskin; its loss was a kind of psychological circumcision. Those handicapped by the stigma of its presence, which was detectable to initiates at once by the expression on their foreheads, could never come to much; they must be armed by a brazen front that no insult could shake. Old Kravarites dismissed their daughters' suitors with the words: 'Go away, boy! You've still got your *tsipa tis dropis*. Get rid of that shame-brow and then we'll see.' The emblem of success was the heavy staff, or *matsoúka*, which accompanied each new journey. An array of these, hanging on the wall, proved the owner a man of substance. They were polished with handling and scarred by the fangs of a hundred dogs; these gnashing and hysterical foes invested the approach to a village with the hazards of an invasion. The trophies accumulated like quarterings of nobility and dynastic alliances were contracted between the children of households boasting an equal display. These sticks, it was said, were sometimes hollowed for the concealment of the gold coins: the weight of small change was intolerable until it was converted. British sovereigns were highly treasured.* Normally

* Throughout the Orient and the Levant, from patriarchal bias, these coins were worth a fraction more if they were stamped with a king's head instead of Queen Victoria's. Conversely, in Albania and Montenegro, Maria Theresa thalers formed the backbone of the currency, as they did in Ethiopia.

the gold coins were dispersed and sewn about the owner's rags.
The *tagari*, a roomy woven bag, slung on a cord, was essential.
This they filled with *paximadia*, bread twice-baked and hard as
a stone, once the diet of the hermits of the Thebaid and now
the sustenance of shepherds. Accoutred with staves and sacks
and this almost unfissile food, they set out; usually alone,
occasionally in couples. Sometimes their professional devices
were a handicap. Uncle Elias cited a duumvirate in which one
member pretended to be one-legged and the other one-armed:
but the one-legged partner could eat at twice the speed of his
mate, so they split up. 'Dumbness', too, had drawbacks: 'mute'
beggars had been bitten to the bone by dogs rather than give
themselves away. . . . Did they always manage to keep up their
disguises? Not always. Uncle Elias told us of a champion beggar,
a tall and burly man, who had perfected the knack of extreme
malformation: his legs and arms became a tangle, his head
lolled, his eyes rolled and his tongue hung out: 'like this!'.
With these words, Uncle Elias shifted on his chair, and with a
click, as it were, became a scarecrow. His face switched to a
burlesque mask of tragedy; a maimed arm shot out, a suppliant
litany streamed from his lips: 'Kind people, spare a mouthful
of bread or a copper for a fellow-Christian who has lost the use
of his limbs from birth and has eaten neither crust nor crumb
for a week. God and Christ and the All-Holy-One and all the
Saints and prophets and martyrs shower their blessings on you!'
The metamorphosis, total and astonishing, had taken place in a
flash. Just as suddenly, he relaxed into his normal self. 'He used
to almost overdo it,' he said with an engaging laugh. 'But he
made plenty of money. A very bright fellow.'

'Well,' he went on, 'one day he arrived in a Bulgarian
village inhabited by Pomaks, terrible men. But instead of
alms, he got sneers, insults, shoves, pinches, kicks. He stood it
as long as he could, but his blood was beginning to boil, and
suddenly——' Here the old narrator uncoiled from his chair,
jumped to his feet and soared above the lamp-lit circle. Under

those hoary brows his eyes fired glances like harpoons from face to face. '... suddenly he straightened up and set about them!' Uncle Elias' clenched fists mowed through the air in a whirlwind of scything sweeps and jabs and upper cuts. *Dang! Ding! Boom! Bim! Bam!* Down they went like the dead! *Pam! Poom!* There must have been ten of the hornwearers flat on the ground! And the others! You should have seen their faces! Their eyes were starting out of their sockets as though the Devil had sprung from Hell! They took to their heels; the village square was empty.' He sat down again grinning. What happened to the beggar? 'Why,' he said, mopping his brow from the exertion, 'he ran for it too, far, far, far away over the hills! When they came round he was kilometres off! *Paraxena pragmata!* Strange doings!'

It was vital to get out of Greece as early as possible. The Bulgarians, although they were fellow-Orthodox, were stingy and xenophobe and hated the Greeks. The Serbs were not bad. Things began to look up the moment the Danube was crossed: Rumanians were more prosperous and more open-handed; the place teemed with cattle and fowl and livestock of every kind, even buffaloes, that the Rumanians used for ploughing. The Hungarians were good but of course they were Catholic; lots of livestock, specially horses. It was the same in Poland. Someone interrupted here and asked, with that curly back-handed scoop that always accompanies the mention of theft, whether the old ones ever lifted things. Not often, no, Uncle Elias said. The point was to use one's wits. But a few of them used to 'vanish' things. . . . One pinched the laundry off the line at one end of a village and sold it back at the other. Poultry was hard to resist. Experts would peer into hen-coops with a two-legged fox's glance then spit and roast their takings in the woods. Hens, ducks, geese, guinea fowl and turkeys flew into their embrace. Sheep and lambs sometimes met the same fate. One gifted Kravarite had the mysterious knack of silencing pigs, nobody knew how: once he removed a farrow of six without a note being heard from either the sow or the piglets; he got away with four in his bag and one under each arm. There were several specialists in this line. Property dwindled at their passage, movables moved, barnyards depleted, orchards lightened, eggs melted away by the clutch the moment they were laid from under the sitting fowl; whole landscapes yielded a sporadic toll. Some professionals were irresistibly seductive in their patter; if the coast were clear, alms and a square meal were sometimes followed by the flattening (as the rather short-sighted phrase goes in vulgar Greek) of the hostess. Used as they were to the fierce morality of Greek village life, the ease and frequency of these favours filled young beggars with surprise. Their itineraries were starred with brisk hurly-burlies in barns and ricks and sometimes by snug nights indoors. Eastern Europe, Uncle Elias thought, must have been full of small Kravarites; Russia, especially. . . .

For Russia was the place! Uncle Elias's eyes blazed at the memory. The Russia of the Tsars beckoned them like the promised land. The inhabitants were moody, drunk, rough, a bit mad; but they were Orthodox like the Greeks and very pious; also superstitious, kind-hearted, reckless, gullible and generous. It was no good since the Revolution; you couldn't get into it. In their early heyday, the Kravarites irrupted into the Empire from Poland, after doing the rounds of the Balkans and Eastern Europe; or, striking across the Danube at Rustchuk, they followed the dotted line of Bucarest and Yassy to Czernovits, the easternmost wing-tip of the Hapsburg monarchy (before it was Rumanian and then Russian), at the end of the Carpathians: (that peculiar multi-lingual town that has enriched so many theatres and circuses with comic turns, and, they say, with lifelong child-performers carefully stunted from the cradle with spirits). From here they advanced into Podolia, a Babel world full of great estates and of the huddling beards and elflocks of the Hasidim. Many took a shorter cut, heading straight for Bessarabia and crossing the Prut and the Dniestr

into the Ukraine; no passports then! Here the Black Sea coast-
line beckoned. They haunted Krim Tartary and the Sea of
Azov, and thrust on to the Caucasus, pausing on the way
among the Greek communities of the ports: Odessa, Taganrog,
Mariupol, Rostov-on-the-Don. Farther south, scattered across
the Caucasus between the shores of the Black Sea and the
Caspian, were whole villages of Lazi; others proliferated near
Trebizond in Asia Minor, all speaking Greek. 'You couldn't
understand much,' Uncle Elias said, 'but it was Greek all right.
They'd been there since the time of *Megaléxandros*—what do I
know? Perhaps even earlier than Alexander. . . .' Sometimes
they would swerve north to Kiev, Smolensk, Moscow, St
Petersburg and the shores of the Baltic. Great cities loomed
and churches, castles, palaces, avenues and bridges with many
spans. . . . Carriages with six horses . . .! Cavalry all in white
with breastplates and helmets . . .! Many struck east to Kazan,
Perm and Omsk. . . . What rivers! the Dniepr, the Don, the
Volga! Uncle Elias conjured up oceans of wheat, forests, mountains, horses—hundreds galloping together—huge herds of
sheep and cattle, wide extents of snow; Cossacks, barges, nomads, turbans, caravans of gypsies and slant-eyed men in giant
fur hats dressed all in sheepskin: 'you could smell them a mile
off'. Some wanderers stayed away for years. A few left their
interim-hoards with Greek traders in Taganrog or Rostov
while they plunged farther east, recovered them on their way
home and worked their passages to Constantinople and Piraeus
on steamers and sailing ships. Back at last in the Aetolian thorpes
that hovered round us in the dark, their deceptive tatters, and
perhaps their hollow staves, yielded their lucre: a chinking
shower of northern and transpontine gold from a dozen
vanished mints: dinars, levas, sovereigns, piastres, lei, pengös,
thalers, zlotys and roubles stamped with the heads of Haps-
burgs, Obrenovitches, Karageorgevitches, Saxe-Coburg-Go-
thas, Hohenzollerns and Romanoffs: the crown of St Stephen,
St George's charger, rampant lions, and a whole metallic flight

of single- and double-headed eagles emblematic of a world as remote as the Heptarchy.

'Barba Elia,' I asked. 'What is the farthest that any of them got?'

'A few,' he said, 'used to push on to Siberia. It was all right in summer, but the snow in winter! *Po! Po!* . . . Early snow was a blessing, mind you.'

'Why?'

'They could track hares and bang them on the head.' A tap with his pipe stem between fingers upheld in a V demonstrated a stick striking a snowbound hare between the ears. 'But later it was their enemy. You see, it didn't look right for them to wrap up too warm. Bad for trade. And there were wolves; not small packs like ours, but whole troops. One of our people from the village of Klepa over there,' he pointed through the window at the dark, 'perished in the snow a few miles outside Vladivostok. Frozen stiff as a plank, the ill-fated one, all that was left of him.'

This journey, farther-flung than Marco Polo's mission to Kubla Khan, was almost too much to take in. When did it happen? 'Oh, a long time ago. It was during the war.' Which war? The Great War? Or *ta Valkánika*? 'No. Earlier. When the Russians were fighting the Japanese. . . .'

The old man smoked in silence as though he were scrutinizing these remote events; and we marvelled by proxy. The chill of Manchuria had broken in to our southern lamplight. Oddly venerable all of a sudden, he towered over the rest of us: the last survivor of a race of lonely skirmishers that for generations had invaded kingdoms and looted empires under the flag of General Cuckoo.

More cheerful thoughts soon routed the pensive moment. The gullibility of the Russians woke fond memories: you could steal a bone off a dog and sell it to its master as the shank of St Barnabas, pick up a bit of firewood and auction it as the True Cross. A long beard and hair down the back, worn with some religious emblem, would turn the wearer into a minor prophet and loosen a tinkling cataract of charity. Love potions made of flour and pepper, remedies for barrenness, charms against bad crops or the Eye, all fetched good prices, especially if they were administered with an incantation. They had a deep trust in magic. (I privately wondered how they compared to similar beliefs in remote parts of Greece.)

'A fellow-villager of mine called Luke was very good at this. He knocked on the door of a lonely farmhouse in the Ukraine where he had heard that the farmer's wife wanted children. He declared that he was *Grtzki* and *Pravoslavnik*—Greek and Orthodox—and knew how to make the barren fertile. "This is a holy house," he said. "a silver cross is buried here." The farmer's wife asked what he meant. "Yes," he said, "a silver cross. I can feel it." Luke began to wander about the room with his eyes shut and his hands held out like a sleep-walker. "It's here!" he cried, pointing to the floor. The wife fetched a knife and dug into the earthen floor at the spot he was pointing to, and there was a little tin cross; Luke had slipped in and buried it early that morning while she was feeding the farm animals. After this she believed everything Luke said. She looked on him as a saint. He sold her a charm made of some rubbish, then asked her if she would like twin boys, which doubled the price. Overcome with gratitude, she kissed his hand: she would give him anything he asked for. Well! . . . She had big blue eyes, plump as a partridge. The scoundrel stayed there all the afternoon, and at the end of it she pulled the eiderdown off the bed and gave it to him. He set off with it over his shoulder. He'd only gone a couple of miles when he saw a horseman galloping after him; the husband! Luke sat down on a tree stump and waited. "What's this heap of lies you've been telling my wife?" the husband thundered. "Give me back that eiderdown!" "If I've been telling lies," Luke said with dignity, "may that eiderdown burst into flames!" The husband seized it in silence and set off home at a gallop. It was beginning to get dark. All of a sudden the horseman stopped dead and Luke saw a great flame and smoke coming out of the eiderdown! The farmer threw it away in terror and, galloping back, dismounted quaking all over and fell on his knees begging forgiveness. He made Luke mount behind him and took him back to the farm and loaded him with gold. He asked him to stay for a month, a year, forever. But off he set next morning, a much richer man.' Uncle Elias was shaking with silent laughter at the recollection. Everyone asked how it had all come about.

'When he saw the husband riding towards him,' Uncle Elias said, 'he lit one of these,' he held up a bit of the fungus he used as tinder for his flint and steel, 'and slipped it inside the quilting. The wind soon saw to the rest.

'But that wasn't the end of it. A twelvemonth later, on his way back westward after many travels, Luke lost his way on a plain one night. It was pitch dark; no moon. He found a barn, went in and slept on the straw. When day came, there, in the yard, was the farmer! Luke had come back to the same place by mistake! "I'll catch it," he thought. "If he sees me I'll have to eat wood! *Aieel!*" He tried to slink off; but the farmer caught sight of him. "Holy Virgin, now I'm for it!" thought Luke. But the farmer ran up and clasped him in his arms and covered him with kisses. "My benefactor!" he kept shouting. He led Luke indoors. There was the farmer's wife weeping tears of joy and there, in the cradle, were two splendid boys! They loaded him up with money all over again; slaughtered a sucking pig, opened the best wine. In a couple of hours, the farmer was dead drunk and snoring on the floor. The twins were fast asleep in their cradle, only Luke and the farmer's wife were awake. So . . .' Uncle Elias broke off. His shoulders and his hands lifted and widened palm upwards; then his hands, as though he were ill-resigned to the thought of these ancient backslidings, fell limp between his knees. His snowy head shook and his tongue clicked slowly and sorrowfully in a mock disapprobation which, as he looked up, also embraced the hilarity he had unleashed in the taverna. He turned up the wick and peered round at the heightening chiaroscuro of our joyful masks.

'No danger,' someone said, 'of the farmer, when he got older, going shorthanded at haymaking'.

'Shocking doings,' the old man resumed, as his own expanding smile brought an infinity of sharpened wrinkles into play once more. 'Charis and Panos from Pokista were even worse. *Mí rotáte, paidiá!* Don't ask me, children!' When we did, he settled back comfortably.

'It was the custom of Charis,' he said, 'to arrive in a Russian village carrying Panos on his back—Panos was the lighter of the two—then he set him down under a tree and knelt beside him wringing his hands and weeping bitterly. A crowd would gather and ask what was wrong. Then Charis said: "My poor brother is dying!"—and Panos really looked like it, all grey in the face, with hollow cheeks and glazed eyes—like this.' Uncle Elias's own features for a second mimicked a moribund rictus of alarming verisimilitude and then sprang as abruptly back to normal—' "Here we are," he would moan—*"Grtzki! Pravoslavnik!*—thousands of miles from home!" All their hearts melted. They would be taken into someone's house and that night, Panos would die.'

'Die?'

'Die. Some of the old ones had the secret. He could stop his breathing, turn white and cold: everyone would have said a corpse. They laid him out, put a clean suit of clothes on him, covered him with flowers, dug the grave and, as the custom is, all the village would contribute to a collection for the family; that is to say, for Charis; they filled his hat with roubles as he wept and mourned beside the bier. Charis explained that, in Greece, only the family must attend the vigil. So, the night before the funeral, they left him alone there lamenting. When the village was asleep, he gave the dead man a shake, and

Panos sat up scattering the flowers and stepped from the candles. Then, hop! they were out of the window and away over the steppe with a new suit and a hat full of cash to the good! After a hundred versts or so, on the outskirts of a new village, Panos climbed on Charis's back again and they headed for the market place. . . . They were very fond of Russia.'

Our response was noisy. When it had died down, the tavern keeper said 'Travel broadens the mind.'

'That's true,' Uncle Elias agreed. 'You see strange places and strange men. But,' he said, standing up with a sigh and picking up his stick and standing with hands joined over the handle, 'it's a young man's game. Rain . . . wind . . . snow . . . dogs . . . wolves . . . wicked men . . . Lent was a bad time. . . .'

The rigours of fasting at certain periods in the Eastern Calendar whittle the intake down to a drastic minimum. The piety of the Russians must have reduced free meals to almost nothing.

I cheerfully suggested that there were always those hen-coops as a last resort. He looked at me with an expression of a genuine shock that was echoed by all the rest. 'The hen-coops? You don't imagine that our villagers would eat meat during the Great Fast? *Mnístite mou, Kyrie!*' He crossed himself as though to aroint the heathenish thought and then covered his white locks with his leopard-skin cap. 'Forgive me, Lord!' I had put my foot in it again. The eyes of the company, suddenly all aimed at me, held no trace of censure; merely the kind, sad smiles that an artless Hottentot might elicit among missionaries.

'I wonder what they thought about it when they found out.' The hunchback's question halted the general move to the door.

'Who?'

'Why, the Russians, when they saw the room was empty next day.'

Uncle Elias halted in the threshold; his face, lit from below, lengthened in thought. 'Who knows?' A possible solution struck him, and the long countenance dispersed in cheerful fragments. The end of his stick rose from the floor and twirled in a swift corkscrew till it touched the centre beam of the ceiling. 'They probably thought they had been plucked into paradise, like my patron saint, the great prophet Elias.' Elias is the Greek for Elijah, whose chapels, as successor to Helios Apollo, are always raised on hilltops on the way to Heaven. 'They would believe anything.'

There was another access of hilarity. Uncle Elias left us with a wide and fluttering wave of the hand—'Goodnight, boys'—and vanished into the dark.

CHAPTER 6

Sounds of the Greek World

The olive-groves of Amphissa, the terraces of corn and vine, are notes on the syrinx, the Pindus is a jangle of goat-bells and the single herdsman's pipe.

Arcadia is the double flute, Arachova the jingle of hammers on the strings of a dulcimer, Roumeli a klephtic song heckled by dogs and shrill whistles, Epirus the trample of elephants, the Pyrrhic stamp, the heel slapped in the Tsámiko dance, the sigh of Dodonian holm-oaks and Acroceraunian thunder and rain.

The Meteora soar twisting to the sky as a Byzantine litany ascends in quarter-tones to the Christ Pantocrator across a cupola's concavity.

Mystra is a swoop of kestrels among cypress trees, a neo-Platonic syllogism under provincial purple; Sinai, a fanfare of rams' horns, Daphni, a doxology, Athos the clatter from cape to cape of semantra, drowned by the waves, the millionth iteration of the Hesychastic prayer.

Constantinople is the Emperor's acclamation, the commination of Chrysostom, a lament for the Fall, the wail of amané, a grammarian's cough and the mewing of cats; Alexandria the valediction of the Gods deserting Antony, a creak of papyrus, the eleven-fold wake that follows a quinquireme, a Judaeo-Ptolemaic bargain.

The Propontis is the combustion of Greek fire from the bronze beaks of galleys, the Symplegades the breaking of ships' timbers, Anatolia the epic of Digenis Akritas, Iconium the shock of Byzantine lances on the shields of the Sultan of Rum,

Caesarea the echo of Arian-fulminating anathema, Bithynia a
prince's cheetah pursuing an antelope through flower-strewn
meadows, Cappadocia the wheeling of wood-pigeons between
cones of tufa hollowed into monasteries, Trebizond a black
Pontic gale from the Caucasus.

Crete is the rhyming of couplets to the three-stringed *lyra*,
the bang of gunfire, the roar along canyons of a landslide un-
loosed by the leap of an ibex, a maze-muted minotaur's bellow,
the brush of peacocks' feathers through blood-red columns.
Apokoronas is the treading of grapes, Malevisi the grumble of
must fermenting and Ida a shepherd's voice calling to the
White Mountains. The Hindu Kush, the Khyber and the Indus
are the footfalls of the Macedonian phalanx, Persia the homage
of satraps in broken *koinē*. Sicily and Magna Grecia are inaudible notes of underground music. The Aspromonte is the
sound of Ψ reversed, Poseidon's failing symbol in the rising
Calabrian tide. Apulia and Salento are the shrinking Byzantine
words of Otrantine speech, Stilo a covey of Kyrie eleisons on
the wing. Ravenna is a letter dictated by the Exarch to the
Catapan of Bari; Cargese, the Corsican erosion of Maniot
syllables.

Gavdos is a wind called Euroclydon.

Eastern Macedonia is the pibroch of a shaggy bagpiper moc-
casined and cross-gartered in goathide, Western Macedonia a
war-cry and the whisper of a snowfall. Oeta is the death agony
of Hercules.

Thrace is the beat of a drum.

The Asian coasts are the poems of Anacreon and the Lydian
mode; the Aegean, the songs of Alcaeus and Sappho, an Aeolian
harp hung in a mastic-tree, a storm-drowned Gorgon's voice
wailing for Alexander; the Cyclades, the lyre-strokes of dol-
phin-borne Arion and the prehistoric tap of Helladic hammers.

Aetolia is a scraping of cicadas, the Kravara a beggars' chorus,
Eurytania a drilling of crickets.

The Rhodope is the click of anemones opening, Acarnania the crackle of withering asphodels.

The Hellespont is the whips of Xerxes, the waves closing over the head of Leander; Lemnos, a carousing of Argonauts; Tenedos, a tall story on the way home from Troy.

Chios is a cakewalk on a cottage piano, Syria is Offenbach from a bandstand.

Hermoupolis is the *filioque*.

Athens is a canticle of columns and a music-hall song, a jangle of trams, a pneumatic drill, a political speech, the inaudible paean of the Panathenaic hymn and the little owl hooting.

Psychiko is *la Tonquinoise*, Kephissia a soirée musicale with a background of *Yes, sir, that's my baby*; Leophoros Syngrou, an exhaust-pipe, Patisia a gear-change, New Phaleron a metrical hard-luck story to the accompaniment of bouzoukia, Old Phaleron a tango heard through convolvulus horns.

The Plaka is a drunken polyphony at four in the morning in praise of retsina and the tune of a musical-box perched on a photograph album of faded plum velvet with filigree clasps at five in the afternoon.

Omonia is an equivocal whisper, a boast about Brooklyn; Kolonaki, the rattle of ice-cubes and a radiogramophone, Maroussi a monologue.

Piraeus is a hashish-smoking rubiyat to the geometry of the butcher's dance and a ship's siren.

Hymettus is the hum of bees, Attica a footfall on pine-needles.

Salonica is an argument over a bill of lading, a Ladino greeting outside a synagogue; Volo, the smack of backgammon counters, Patras, the grate of cranes unloading, Samos, the bubbling of a narghilé.

Kalamata is a piling of crates and a pattering of olives.

Yanina is the clash of scimitars, the clink of silversmiths, Trikkala a stork's beak-rattling from a broken minaret, Para- mythia a coppersmith's clank.

Navarino and Lepanto are the boom of cannon, Tripoli the crisscross of yataghans, Psara the smouldering of fire-ships, Hydra a shout in Albanian from the cross-trees of a brigantine, Arkadi the explosion of powder-kegs, Souli the reverberation of long-barrelled guns, Zalongo the sound of women singing that grows fainter by seconds.

Tyrnavos is the Priapic song of a phallophore, Mavrolevfi the ululation of icon-bearing firewalkers.

Olympus is the sky's echo, Parnassus the rush of an eagle's wing.

Delphi is a mantic muttering through marble under moun- tains, the dying-away of a murmuring spring, Olympia the music of the spheres, Sparta an anvil's ring. Thebes a riddle, Mycenae an axe falling, Ithaca an arrow's flight.

Karytaina is the echo of Frankish horns blowing, the distant baying of Burgundian hounds. St Hilarion is a tournament and the ghost of a *chanson de geste*, Navpaktos a virelai, and Monemvasia the crash of a mangonel.

The shores of Cyprus are the doves of Aphrodite, the voices of Achaeans landing, of Argives, Laconians, and Arcadians, the lutes of the Lusignan.

Nicosia is a slogan for Union, the sizzle of kebabs, the drip of HP sauce, the splutter of soda syphons, the hiss of a fuse; Kyrenia, a ten-year-old rumba, a sahib's guffaw, the limericks of remittance-men.

Bassae and Sunium are the noise of the wind like panpipes through fluted pillars, Nemea the rumble of a column's collapse. Naoussa is the thud of a falling apple, Edessa a waterfall, Kavalla the drop of an amber bead. Metzovo is a burning pine- cone, Samarina a voice in Vlach, Avdela a stag's belling,

Grammos, the breath of a hibernating bear, Tzoumerka a wolf's howl.

Delos is the birth-wail of Apollo, Paxos a voice crying for the death of Pan.

Andros is running water.

The Ionian scatters the sound of mandolines towards the sunset.

Corfu is the sirocco lifting a doge's gonfalon, Zante is a guitar, Cephalonia a curse, Cythera the dip of an oar, Levkas the splash of a trident.

Chalcis is the flurry of the tide, Naxos the boxwood click of a rosary muffled by a nun's skirt; Ossa is a giant's tread, Pelion the beat of centaurs' hoofs through glades of chestnut, Tempe a susurrus of plane trees, and Rhodes a flutter of moths.

Santorin zigzags to the sky at dawn like a lark singing but dies at sunset with the *Dies Irae*. Komotini is a muezzin's call, Patmos the faraway trumpets of the Apocalypse.

The Dodecanese is a sea-song by twelve sponge-fishers, Antikythera a mermaid forsaken; Skopelos, a lobster's and Poros, a mock-turtle's song, Aegina a tambourine.

The Sporades are the sea's whisper through olive trees.

The Ambracian gulf is a lowland lament with brekekekex! from Preveza, koax! from Amphilochia and an answering koax! across the mountains from Missolonghi.

Thessaly is a scythe's blade through cornstalks.

Leonidion is a dialogue in Doric, Lemonadassos a mill-wheel grinding, the swing of a lantern through lemon-woods.

The Hebrus river is a song floating seawards, the Struma a challenge, the Aliacmon a ravine's voice, Pamisos a lullaby, the Alphaeus a clatter of pebbles, the Ladon a midsummer gasp under oleanders; the Acheron, blue-green thunder falling through forests. The winding Acheloös is a reeds' conspiracy, the call of a heron, the bittern's answer; the Eurotas is an elegy, the Louros a trout's ripple, the Spercheios a flutter of flagleaves.

Larissa is a bray, Tinos a chime of bells, Avgo a seal's bark. Icaria a moan in a nightmare, Scyros an anchor's drop, Paros the sound of quarrying, Cnidus the chip of a chisel, Amorgos a stream under leaves, Thasos a nightingale, Seriphos the hiss of Medusa's head and the wind, Pholegandros a seagull's and and Anaphe a swallow's cry, Siphnos a lyric, Samothrace a snore, Ios a soliloquy, Gavdopoula a sigh, and the Strophades, silence.

Methone is a fugue of cormorants through broken demilunes, Corone an amphora that holds the waves' fall captive.

Cape Taenarus is the squeak of bats in a cave that leads to Hades, Cape Malea a wrangle of tempest-haunting birds, the cries of drowning men. The Mani ascends in a shout for vengeance and dies in a dirge turned to stone.

The seas of Greece are the Odyssey whose music we can never know: the limitless sweep and throb of prosody, the flux and reflux of hexameters scanned by winds and currents and accompanied, for its escort of accents,

> for the fall of its dactyls
> the calm of spondees
> the run of tribrachs
> the ambiguity of trochees
> and the lash of anapaests;
> for the flexibility of accidence,
> the congruence of syntax
> and the confluence of its crasis;
> for the fluctuating of enclitic and proclitic,
> for the halt of caesurae and the flight of the digamma,
> for the ruffle of hard and soft breathings,
> for its liquid syllables and the collusion of diphthongs,
> for the receding tide of proparoxytones
> and the hollowness of perispomena stalactitic with sub-
> scripts,

for the inconsequence of anacolouthon,
the economy of synecdoche,
the compression of hendiadys
and the extravagance of its epithets,
for the embrace of zeugma,
for the abruptness of asyndeton
for the swell of hyperbole
and the challenge of apostrophe,
for the splash and the boom and the clamour and the echo
and the murmur of onomatopoeia

by the

islands and harbours and causeways and soundings and crescents
of shingle, whirlpools and bays and lagoons and narrows and
chasms and roadsteads, seismic upheavals of crags in the haze of
meridian panic, sockets and smouldering circles of stone and
dying volcanoes; islets lying in pale archipelagos, gulfs, reefs
and headlands, warrened with cavities, that end in a litter of
rocks and spikes where the limestone goes dark at sunset;
thunderbolt sea-marks scattered on the water, light in the reign
of the Pleiades, slowly spinning the sea-sounds that sigh in the
caves of solitary islands.

ΤΕΛΟΣ

APPENDICES

Derivations of Sarakatsán

On the face of it—and, alas, as deep as one can dive—the word Sarakatsán means nothing at all. Nevertheless, there are several possibilities that beckon enticingly (one in particular shines with a seductive glitter) and this has proved a stimulating challenge to ethnographers, philologists and publicists, both Greek and foreign, for many decades. Conflicting derivations are always fascinating and the Sarakatsáns (who are also less correctly known in the Balkan countries outside Greece, as Karakatchans) have given rise to a rich and varied crop. Greeks are invariably fertile in this field. Aravantinos declares that they originated in an Akarnanian village called Saraketsi and later took to a wandering life. Another opinion maintains that they once lived near the Katsanó villages in Epirus, and are thus *para* Katsanoi, *para* meaning, in this instance, 'near'—near-Katsánians in fact, the P mysteriously and un-Grimmishly turning into S. I. Lampides thinks they were actually *from* the Katsáno villages but takes the alternative affix *kara*, which means 'black' in Turkish, and metaphorically, 'wretched', and makes them 'woebegone Katsánians'. As a second string to his bow, he derives them in vague and doubting terms (as Uncle Petro did himself) from the Vlach village of Syrako on the Acheloös river; in yet a third alternative he mates the Arabic words *kara*, 'on land' or *sara*, 'swift', to the Turkish verb *katchan*, 'to depart' or 'to flee'—in two hybrid matches, giving birth to 'land-wanderers', and 'swift wanderers', Yet others link *katchan* with the Turkish *kir*, 'desert', to arrive at 'desert departers'. Another links *kara* with the Albanian adjective *katsianon*, which is applied to dark or purplish-faced sheep, of which, indeed, Sarakatsán flocks contain large numbers; this gives us 'black dark faced ones'. The great Danish authority on these Nomads, Axel Hoeg, thinks the Vlacho-Rumanian word *sarac*, or 'poor', may have something to do with it. So does J. Ancel. A. Dimitriades couples the Turkish *saran*, 'a load', with *katchan*, to make 'burdened wanderers'. I. Sayiaxis brings *sarika*, a Slav word for the fustanella, the kilt which they once all wore, into play: 'the kilted ones'. B. Skaphiadis, on the other hand, would like to connect them with a hellenized Vlach word, also *sarika*, but meaning here, 'raw wool': 'the shaggy men'. D. Georgakas manages to bring in the Turkish word for 'yellow'—that is, *sari*—which strikes a new note: 'yellow wanderers'. G. Kotsi-oulas, sinisterly, links our old friend *katchan* with the Turkish *siari*, 'a thief', transforming them into fugitives from justice. With disarming simplicity and enviable boldness, I. Vlacho-yannis declares them to be Saracens. . . . A current derivation is the combination of the two Turkish words which crop up most frequently in this catalogue into 'The black ones who depart'. It has no better claim than any of the others—except the ones which are patently absurd or linguistically impossible —and I have called this chapter 'The Black Departers' merely because the term *does* happen to conjure them up, but the ini-tial K instead of the much more widespread S, casts doubt at once. To close this list, a writer whose name escapes me for the moment vies with Vlachoyannis' Saracens by coolly turning them all into Syracusans from Sicily. . . . There is something wrong with all of these solutions, and nothing to recom-mend one at the expense of its rivals. Nearly all the names I have cited are those of respectable writers. It is typical of the most serious student of them all, Dr Axel Hoeg, that his suggestion is the most diffident and tentative of the lot. His only peer in the field, Mrs Angelica Hadjimichalis, offers none at all. The name is as useless a guide to their origins as are historical records.

Glossary of Boliaric Vocabulary

Perhaps it's better to leave out the ordinary Greek words, with the proviso that they are never the same as the boliaric ones. A few bear the same link to the object described as fennel does to a beard—*velazoura*, for instance, means 'sheep' and 'goats', 'a flock'—*velazo* is the Greek for 'bleat'; similarly, *bokla*—'hair'— is probably the Greek *boukla*, 'a curl', a recent acquisition from French. A town is *kio*—surely the Turkish *kioi*, just as *sielo* is Russian—and boliaric—for a village, and *kaïn*—'dog'—the Vlach or Rumanian descendant of *canis*. *Gaïna* we have already met; with *neró*, the Greek for 'water', affixed, it becomes *nerogáina*, 'waterfowl', viz. 'ducks and geese'. But what have *koubouria* (the same, incidentally, as the *manga* slang for 'pistols'), or *tchillingária*, to do with 'a woman's breasts'? *Kouti*, in Greek, is 'a box'; but why is the boliaric for 'house' always its genitive —*koutiou*? Perhaps it has nothing to do with Greek at all. . . . *Tchmeki* is 'sleep' (also 'hotel'); *tchemkiazo* is 'I sleep', *tchmékiza*, 'I slept' and *tha tchimikiázo*, 'I will sleep'. Here is a boliaric zoo of domestic animals: cow, *marini*; pig, *birdzin*; hen, *gaïna*; waterfowl, *nerogáina*; hare, *daousénos*; mule, *mangatchko*; dog, *kaïn*; sheep, *bikiaïn*; flocks, *velazoúra*; horse, *pharí* (akin to the Greek for mare, *phorada*?); donkey, *mánganos* or *yipsíni*; lice, *maritzes*; and cat, *markantós*.

Markantós. . . . I wonder what 'a cat' has to do with 'the saints', for these, in Kravarese, are *Oi Markantonaioi*, the Markantonies (and what have they to do with Cleopatra's lover?). Some objects that play a great part in mendicant life had several synonyms, each slightly different. 'Money' is *alepoú-*

mata—something to do with *alepou*, a fox?—and *matzónia*;
kítrino, meaning 'a sovereign', is literally 'a yellow one'; perhaps *kolyva*, or *koulouva*, also meaning 'a gold coin', is related
to the big round funeral cake to which it sounds similar in
ordinary Greek. *Platanóphylla*, literally 'plane tree leaves', is
'paper money'; *photerí*—perhaps 'a shining one'—is 'a drachma',
a *diphóteri*, 'two drachmas'. (Confusingly, *photerà* is also 'letters',
'writing') and 'a thousand drachmas' is a *hína*, or 'goose'. . . .
The sticks that are so important in a beggar's life ('wood'—
xýlo in Greek—has the second meaning of 'the stick', 'a thrash-
ing', e.g. 'I ate wood' = 'I was beaten up') has many synonyms:
grigóro, *ldoussa*, *matsoúka*, *straví*, *kaníki* and *dervo*—all 'sticks'.
Lachanídi, for 'a knife', suggests 'cabbage-cutting'; but whence
comes *beldevéni*—also a knife? *Tcharmalídi* is 'a gun', *tchóki*, 'a
stone', *karvoúni* (coal), 'a train'; *armabíl*, which sounds just
like the Greek-American word for a motor, is exactly that and
usually a bus; *mákina*, 'a camera', suggests an Italian machine:
it takes *mouta*, or 'snapshots', related, perhaps, to the everyday
moutra ('face', 'mug', 'phiz'). *Sardinia* are 'shoes', *daïri*, 'a road',
klitzino, 'a ring', *batzoutou* or *koutzourou* (lame or stumbling?
rickety?), 'a table'; *kranídi* and *traganída* are 'time', while
traganídi is 'a watch', whose dial records the march of the
phlambouri. This word means, 'the sun' or 'day'* and the plural,
phlambouria, is days. When the *phlambouri* sets, *hálpou*, 'the
night', follows. *Hálpou* . . . an eerie word.

Bánikos, which, in Greek slang, means 'nubile' or 'ripe for
coition', denotes, in boliaric, 'big', 'good', or 'important'. The
only other adjective on my scribbled list (but there must be
lots more) is *stíliota*, 'furtive' or 'wary', akin to the key-word
stíliane! 'Look out!' 'Beware!' The recorded verbs are few.
Anisévo, 'I grow angry'; *tchmekidzo*, 'I sleep'; *glavízo*, 'I run';
photáo (related to 'light'?), 'I know', 'I see', or 'look out';
panteládo, 'I talk nonsense'; *karkévo*, 'I hit'; *manízo*, 'I steal';

---

* Unhelpfully, the sound in Greek suggests both a linden-tree and a
banner.

mandarono, 'I make a fool of'; *banízo* and *sarafízo*, 'I understand'; *siorévo*, 'I get drunk'; *stíliano*, 'I beware'; *spartáo*, 'I run away'; *tzoumízo*, 'I kill'; *gáskino*, 'I laugh' and *kranízei*, 'it rains'.

Several words suggest that this vocabulary is more up-to-date than it might at first appear: *grobaíoi*, for instance, meaning 'guerrillas', and *groúmpos*, a communist, irresistibly suggest E.L.A.S. But *matzoúkia* (literally 'stick bearers') for 'beggars' and *shoreftis* for 'a thief', sound older. 'A doctor' is *mantzóunas*, *patéllos* is 'a policeman', *maldtos* and *lépho* are 'a priest'; and *maletchko*—plainly from the Slav—is 'a child'; hence *maletchkás* for 'a teacher'; but what about *khakhás*, meaning the same thing? *Verdílis* and *verdílo*, are 'father' and 'mother', *ingótina* and *gotiméno* mean 'married', *got* and *gotina* (Slav again), are 'lady' and 'gentleman'—a bourgeois couple, parents to a *gotopoulo*, or young gent. But *litzko* and *liókia* also mean a bourgeois figure, 'a mug' perhaps, married to a *matzio*, or a *shveri*, 'a woman', who soon becomes a *houmoúrou*, 'a mother' to a *houmouráki*, or 'girl'.

Here also are a few of the mildly improper words in the vocabulary. *Perdikis*, the Greek for a young partridge, is 'the rump' or 'behind', *havalóu*, the female pudendum, *lióka* its convex masculine complement; *manganízo* is 'I fornicate'; *souravlízo*, which normally means 'playing a reed pipe', here means 'I urinate'; *kouphróno* and *tzarmízo*, identical in sense, are its solider companion verbs and *koúphrisma* and *tzármisma* their end products; *tramalízo* and *lazinízo* both mean to break wind and *tramálisma* is the same wind once broken. One or two nouns, proper in every way, seemed even more enigmatic than their fellows: *Gramki*, for instance, means 'an Albanian'; could it be some little-known tribe? surely the Ghegs, the Tosks, the Mirdites, the Liaps and the Tchams are enough . . .? And *Eskebez* for the Peloponnese: *eski*, Turkish for old, but *bez* . . .? *Kina*—'China'—meant 'safety'. Why? What Cathayan refuge? . . . Queerest of all is the word for Athens: *Ghiona*. This is the demotic name for Mt Oeta, a hundred miles from Athens or more, where Hercules, in the shirt of Nessus, died in torment. But the *ghioni* is the demotic word for the *Athene noctua*, the little owl of Pallas, the ancient emblem of the goddess and of her city and the theme of many popular legends. It sits askew on branches and roof trees with its round-eyed head twisted full face under its frown just as it appears on old Athenian silver coins. The note of its sad, intermittent and oddly moving little pipe still sounds in the lanes.* Could this cryptic name have some subconscious, underground link with the city's small companion and symbol? Going too far, perhaps.

* Less than formerly, alas! *Komizo glavkes stin Athena*, 'I am taking owls to Athens', is the Greek equivalent of coals to Newcastle. The *glavx* is generic; it is the *ghioni*, I think, which is meant. I have heard larger owls hooting in the city (or, off-hand, I think I have) but I have never seen one.

Index